P9-CQF-691

Witches of America

Witches of America

Alex Mar

Sarah Crichton Books
Farrar, Straus and Giroux New York

Sarah Crichton Books
Farrar, Straus and Giroux
18 West 18th Street, New York 10011

Copyright © 2015 by Alex Mar
All rights reserved
Printed in the United States of America
First edition, 2015

Library of Congress Cataloging-in-Publication Data
Mar, Alex.
    Witches of America / Alex Mar. — First edition.
        pages   cm
    ISBN 978-0-374-29137-2 (hardcover) — ISBN 978-0-374-70911-2 (e-book)
    1. Neopaganism—United States.   2. Wicca—United States.   I. Title.

BP605.N46 M325 2015
299'.940973—dc23

                                                    2015010897

Designed by Abby Kagan

Our books may be purchased in bulk for promotional, educational, or business use. Please
contact your local bookseller or the Macmillan Corporate and Premium Sales Department at
1-800-221-7945, extension 5442, or by e-mail at MacmillanSpecialMarkets@macmillan.com.

www.fsgbooks.com
www.twitter.com/fsgbooks • www.facebook.com/fsgbooks

1   3   5   7   9   10   8   6   4   2

The names and identifying details of some persons described
in this book have been changed.

To D.A., my first reader

Contents

Witches of America

1

Stone City

Witches are gathering.

Witches are gathering all across California, witches and their apprentices and little children and polyamorous collection of boyfriends and girlfriends. They are gathering for the season of death, the days leading up to the high holiday of Samhain. October is the time of year, they say, when the veil between the worlds becomes thin and the multitudes of the dead can reach across to touch you, brush your cheek, whisper in your ear, drink your whiskey. So the priestesses pull out their sporty West Coast vehicles, from gnarly pickups to gleaming, eco-friendly mini-mobiles, and they load up, with complicated tents and pillows and crockery and duffel bags full of ritual gear and brown paper bags crammed with discount groceries. They are leaving their cities for the mountains and the woodlands of this schizophrenic state: the rocks and the trees and the clearer skies will bring them closer, perhaps, to friends and family who have passed to the other side.

They spill out onto the highways, then fan out, leaving behind their tech ventures and professorships, their accounting firms and bio labs, their yoga studios and bookshops, heading toward covens in so many counties. Some go even farther, east into the hills, until their earth-worshipping caravan clears the electrical grid and finally comes to stop in a red clay clearing. Here, they start to unpack: all across the landscape, out come the coolers and sleeping bags, the exotic fabrics, the amulets, the baggies of herbs, the idols and carefully bundled wands. People are slipping into velvet, or black leather kilts. A priestess stands brushing out her long hair, uncut for twenty years. Another wraps a belt around her waist, heavy with stones and metalwork, then swings a cloak over her shoulders, so long it drags across the dirt.

This is Stone City, one hundred acres dedicated to witchcraft in Santa Clara County.

Beyond this property, back where everyone came from, the rest of the country celebrates Halloween, with their rubber masks, Blow Pops, and toilet paper. Here, far off the grid, at a recently installed stone henge the neighboring ranchers know nothing about, *these* citizens are preparing to summon their dead. Within a few hours, at dusk, they'll begin gathering in a circle, even the children, chanting the words to set things in motion.

I am not what you would call witchy. Raised in Manhattan, I confirm plenty of the stereotypes of a New Yorker: an overeducated liberal, a feminist, a skeptic long suspicious of organized religion, surrounded by friends—several of them artists, writers, and filmmakers—who consider agnosticism an uncomfortable level of devotion. I'm not prone to joining groups of any stripe, particularly the spiritual variety. I believe in something transcendent, but I've yet to meet someone with a convincing label for it.

At the same time, we each have a dimension hidden beneath our carefully cultivated surface, a piece of ourselves that we can't shake off or explain away. For me, it's this: I've always been drawn to the outer edges, the fringe—communities whose esoteric beliefs cut them off from the mainstream but also bind them closer together. As a writer, I took a stab at a novel about the life of David Koresh, in part because I envied the plain certainty of his followers; I cooked up thin excuses to report on a Billy Graham revival in Queens, visit a New Age commune in California, move into a convent in Houston. On one level, I've been driven by an easy curiosity, an attraction to the exotic and far-out—which the whole spectrum of belief has long seemed to me—but I've also been looking hard for those intangibles

I might have in common with even the most alien congregation. As a natural outgrowth of this impulse, I am setting out to make a documentary about American forms of mysticism. Finally, through the drawn-out, painstaking production of a feature-length film, I'll come to understand what I've been chasing, beat it into a tangible product, a neat conversation piece, and move on.

This is what takes me to Stone City.

In the early evening, I find myself heading down a perilous, zigzagging road into the Middle of Nowhere, Northern California, a cliff drop always on my right, watching as ranching country turns to meth country and then who-knows-where as the light begins to fall.

I'm at the start of my odyssey across occult America, in the last available rental car from the San Francisco International Airport—a twelve-passenger van better suited to taking a kindergarten class on a field trip. Instead, it is carrying a wary New Yorker thirty challenging miles into old mining territory. The boat-on-wheels winds around shocking curves every twenty seconds, each time threatening to toss me headlong into a valley dotted with vultures. I head out past nouveaux villas; then scrappy working ranches; then trailer homes set few and far apart; and, finally, past the first in a string of ghost mines where so much magnesite was pulled from the ground long ago. Back then, for the miners, this would have been a drive full of expectation. A century and a half later, it is for me, too, but with a difference: this trip—not horse-drawn, but more nauseating for it—is leading me to Craft sanctuary land, land that belongs to Morpheus, a priestess who has steadily been making her name known among witches out west for fifteen years.

As the sky darkens, I rumble up the dirt driveway, past a metal-scraps heap, a shed built out of glass bottles, and an improvised chicken coop, to stop in front of a double-wide trailer in the twilight. Just then my headlights flash on a Doberman who, with pitch-perfect timing, comes bounding toward the car, barking until its fist-sized heart seems ready to burst.

Slightly stoned on Dramamine, I sit and watch, stock-still, as Cerberus is followed by a thin rail of a man in fatigues, combat boots, and white-man's cornrows.

"Heel!" he shouts, rapping his knuckles on the dog's head. This would be Shannon, Morpheus's husband.

I dismount from the van, step lightly past the dog-monster, and follow Shannon inside—into a bargain-basement Paul Bowles fantasyland. Everywhere there are lanterns covered in lace metalwork, leather pincushion seats, Moroccan wall hangings, animal skulls, and images of the goddess of this, the goddess of that. A clay statuette of Pan sits atop a library of occult titles like *Transcendental Magic* and *Deciphering the Witches' Sabbath*. I am still getting my bearings when, across the threshold of bright purple carpeting, steps the priestess herself.

Morpheus: like me, in her thirties; in baggy jeans, tank top, and an asslength braid of red hair. She is pale and lean, with large blue eyes—not at all intimidating. (What did I expect?) She approaches, carrying a pan of premade enchiladas.

The three of us sit at the dining-room table, by the cabinet of loaded rifles and underneath the generator-powered chandelier, Cerberus curled up like a cat at Morpheus's feet. We drink the cheap wine I've brought and settle into talking the rest of the night, Morpheus now and again busting out a big, broad laugh—geeky, unguarded. We discuss their plans for the solstice, initiation rites ("Not telling!"), and the Stone Circle—the henge this place is named for. They'd spent a year and a half erecting it, marking out the positions of the sun from season to season—"never mind dragging those half-ton rocks into place," she says. "Now we have nearly all our rituals up there."

Exhausted, and with little more to learn tonight—we'll get to know each other carefully, in stages—I turn in. Armed with a tiny flashlight and a sleeping bag, I make my way up the brush-covered hill toward a makeshift cabin somewhere in the distance. Once I reach a plateau, I stop in my tracks, because there it is: the Stone Circle, visible in the moonlight. A gathering of enormous standing stones, huge slabs buried in the ground to rise six feet tall, a very specific fantasy imposed on the landscape.

Once it's daylight, I see that Stone City alternates between untamable, prickly undergrowth and gutted stretches of dry red dirt. Here and there, dotting the land, are guest trailers, broken boats, outdoor hot tubs, goats and Polish roosters, evidence of the pantheon—altars built from Home Depot gazebo parts and statues ordered off eBay—a Maypole covered in last year's ribbons, a "meditation" labyrinth of palm-sized stones, the Stone Circle itself. This assembly of structures has been the single-minded project of the last few years, the excavation (with tractor and borrowed earthmover), then erection (with bare hands and pulleys and the occasional blowtorch) of a peculiar architecture. All this for Morpheus, priestess. Stone City is her place to practice witchcraft safely, and to gather people together for ritual and to build fires and drink and sing and (when the spirit strikes) have sex somewhere in the wilderness, where the bones of wild pigs are scattered.

I may not know it now, but my relationship with Morpheus will go beyond the making of a film, deepen and grow more complicated (she'll prove a lot more formidable than the blithe, skinny redhead who served me dinner). And through our relationship I will realize that this hidden dimension of myself, this curiosity about the outer edges of belief, is not something from which I can recover. Because I *envy* them, the believers. They have guidance; they have clarity; their days have structure and meaning. And, quietly, for a long time, I've coveted these things—after all, they're what most of us want *badly,* regardless of whether we consider ourselves lapsed Catholics or born-agains or strident atheists. Morpheus has perfect conviction in a world that I do not understand, and I feel compelled to step inside her belief. When I put my work aside, I have to admit that I am searching—hopefully, and with great reservation—for proof of something larger, whatever its name.

I have a closer connection to the occult than I'd first recognized. Before my immersion, my ideas about witchcraft had come from obvious sources. Halloween brought witches flying on broomsticks. *The Wizard of Oz* taught me that there are "good" witches (pretty blondes) and "bad" witches (green-skinned brunettes). History class, and a school production of *The Crucible,* sparked a macabre fascination with the seventeenth-century witch trials. But as I began visiting with priestesses and covens around the country, memories rose to the surface, and I learned that my impressions are also rooted in my family.

Like many Americans, I'm of a mess of backgrounds. When he was ten years old, my father emigrated from Crete, the ancient seat of some of the very gods that Christianity sought to snuff out—from the Mycenaeans' Zeus and Hephaestus to the bare-breasted, snake-wielding Minoan goddess. For me, as an American-born child, the church of my father's parents, even after centuries of Greek Orthodox Christianity, was still evocative of another world: the long black overcassock, the wizard's beard, and the imposing *kamilavka* of the priests; the palpably foreign, musky scent of the clouds of incense the altar boys would shake from censers as they trailed down the aisle; the Byzantine angles of the saints' heads, not in round, fleshy tones but flat, gold, abstract.

As for my mother, her family had moved from northern Spain to Cuba generations ago, and her Latin brand of Catholicism took on a fantastic quality. We lit candles in memory of family members, trying to lure their presence into the house through photographs, votives, trinkets they used to own. I imagined the incredible quiet of cathedrals we'd visit, and the shadowy chapels contained within, to be full of hidden information. The symbolism in paintings of the saints remained bizarre and enigmatic, often with more than a hint of violence—the martyred St. Ursula bleeding from the neck, gripping the arrow that shot her dead; St. Agatha carrying her dismembered breasts on a plate—and my younger self was a little terrified that communion involved the chance to eat the body and drink the blood of Christ. Beyond that, the women in my mother's family were not immune to the notion of communications from the other side—true for quite a few Latin Catholic women. So my religious upbringing, though two flavors of Christian, was defined less by discipline and self-denial than by proximity to mystery.

My mother would tell me of how, in her town of Gibara, on the far eastern end of Cuba, a neighbor who'd given a dirty look to a *brujo* on the street awoke to find a dead rooster on her doorstep.

"All these sensitive cultural relativists—they don't understand that there *is* such a thing as a curse," she would say.

Years later, when I was in college and experimenting with visual art, I called my mother and told her that I had been making my own version of *vévés* (Vodou symbols that invoke spirits) on huge swaths of paper in my bedroom. She sighed, and in a practical, good-humored tone told me, "Look, you can do what you want, Alexa, but here's what you *should* do: you should stop playing with that stuff, go to a Catholic church, and get some holy water. You bless yourself and sprinkle it on those drawings. And then you *throw them out.*"

My mother wasn't condemning all of Vodou practice; she was simply unimpressed with my amateur-hour dabbling in potentially serious spiritual business. So what did I do, a young woman getting a degree at Harvard in a department rife with the very "cultural relativists" my mother had sneered at? I did what I was told: I got hold of some holy water at the nearest church and followed her instructions. Better to be safe than risk awakening something unfriendly.

This idea—that spirits, good and bad, linger nearby, ready to intervene—has been handed down by the women on my mother's side. Two stories, told and retold quietly over the years, illustrate this best.

I was about nine years old when my mother first shared with me the story of her best friend's murder. They'd grown up together in Cuba, she and Mireya, but separated when my mother was sent far north, to a Catholic boarding school in Maine. The pair stayed in touch by writing letters every few weeks, my mother sharing the shock of her first snow and the travesty of American foods like peanut butter and sweet New England beans. After about a year, the letters stopped, as happens with long-distance friendships. Then, one night, my mother had a dream: Mireya was walking toward her, slowly, as if to give her a message. Suddenly a young man appeared and stepped between them—and, just as suddenly, he plunged a knife into Mireya's chest (my mother felt as if *she* had been stabbed). Several months later, my mother returned home for a visit and saw an old friend at a party. Hadn't she heard? Mireya had been killed by a boyfriend. My mother did the math: the murder had taken place just days before her dream. The dream had served, in a way, as Mireya's final letter.

Fast-forward a generation, to right after I'd left home for college. My mother's aunt Norma, perhaps the most no-nonsense woman in the family line, rang her up.

"Your mother keeps wandering around my apartment," she said, referring to my *deceased* grandmother. "She's worried. There's something wrong in your house."

But there was nothing wrong. My parents, recently retired, were preparing for a long vacation, an entire month in the South of France, leaving in a week's time. Since she had a checkup scheduled, my mother went in for her doctor's appointment and, that image of my grandmother fresh in her mind, asked for her annual mammogram early. She was quickly diagnosed with cancer that, had it been detected two or three weeks later, could have turned deadly. It seemed possible that maybe, just maybe, a spirit had reached across on her behalf.

None of us would claim that there are hard, verifiable facts in these stories—I can't emphasize enough how little patience my mother has for what she calls the "hippie-dippie." This is the woman who taught me to question church authority and sidestep the Pope completely. ("He's just some man who claims he knows what God thinks," she likes to say.) So is this witchy stuff or mere coincidence? I'm not sure. The world is full of strange and inexplicable business. There are many Americans—not just out-there Americans, but high-functioning people with mainstream jobs and houses with backyards—who have stories like those of my family. Stories of mysticism, of communications from the other side, whether handed down, hearsay, or their own. All you need to do is press a little harder, and out they come: from supermarket cashiers, retired cops, psychologists, high school jocks—it doesn't matter where they live or what they look like. The overriding culture trains us to dismiss these stories as New Age babble, signs of wayward fanaticism, rather than greet them with a healthy dose of curiosity— but Americans are compelled by the mysterious more often than we feel permitted to admit.

Most people, when witchcraft is mentioned, think of horror films or the witch trials in Europe and colonial Massachusetts.* But today when people talk about witches—living, practicing witches—they're usually talking about *Pagans*. The word itself comes from the Latin *paganus,* which became a slur for non-Christian polytheists. Centuries later, academics adopted "paganism" as the catchall for religions that predate Judaism, Christianity, and Islam (the big Abrahamic trio). But by the sixties it began to refer mainly, in a positive way, to capital-*P* Paganism (or *Neo*paganism): contemporary practices pieced together from the salvaged scraps of pre-Christian European religions, Western occult and Masonic societies, and forms of witchcraft. Some Pagans subscribe to new religions, belief systems invented out of whole cloth; some practice traditions that claim "ancient" roots but can be traced back only a few decades; some found the Goddess through

---

* In spite of how literature and pop culture return again and again to the trials in Salem, there's still no real evidence that those tried and executed practiced any recognizable form of witchcraft.

second-wave feminism, eager to place a Creatrix at the center of the universe.

There may be hundreds of strains of Paganism, but these super-esoteric paths share a clear core. They are polytheistic and nature-worshipping, and believe that female and male forces have equal sway in the universe. They teach that the divine can be found within us and all around us, and that we can communicate regularly with the dead and the gods without a priestly go-between. Contrary to popular hysteria, a witch is unlikely to try to recruit your child—mainly because Pagans, who respect many paths to things holy, consider that rude. Similarly, there's no points-system afterlife, sifting through the dead and depositing them into either heaven or hell: maybe you're reincarnated, or maybe you end up floating in a zone called the Summerland. There is no concept of "shame," but an idea of karma: do whatever you want, as long as it doesn't harm others. ("An it harm none, do what thou wilt," reads the Wiccan Rede, or moral code.) There are structures of authority within specific groups or covens—someone to do the initiating, for instance—but then there are also "solitary" practitioners, who believe you can initiate yourself. Local consensus can hold sway, but there is no conclave, no pope.

Paganism evolved here over the last fifty years as an exotic religious movement imported from England, where a new witchcraft religion called Wicca had been introduced to the public in the early fifties. Wicca's major spokesperson was a retired civil servant named Gerald Gardner, and the first known Wiccan coven in America was founded by one of his initiates in New York State. In the sixties, Wicca rode the counterculture wave (particularly on the increasingly alien West Coast), attracting radicals ready to shrug off the Christian patriarchy and embrace confrontational words like "witch." The path was cleared for a slew of Pagan traditions to rise up, some direct offshoots of Wicca, many an "eclectic" mix of magical sources. By the eighties, thousands were attending Pagan festivals, many even in public; and the late nineties brought that great unifier, the Internet. Suddenly solitary practitioners or witches still "in the broom closet" could seek each other out, swap spells, arrange to meet way up on the hillside behind the local Walmart. Entire virtual networks of tens of thousands of witches multiplied, connected, and fused into covens in cities and suburbs across the country.

Today, allowing for those still practicing in secret, Pagans may make up as many as one million people in America.*

From this perspective, building Stone City starts to make a lot more sense.

Most weekdays, Morpheus drives to work in the early-morning half-light in her Toyota pickup. Her job—for a federal agency created in response to the Dust Bowl—has her meeting with the aging population of local ranchers, walking their land, and recommending changes to help conserve soil and water. (Staunch Christians, none of them are aware that she's Pagan, in spite of their requests for someone to "witch" their wells.) On these days, we—me, my cinematographer (a tall, deep-voiced guy from Philly), and our sound recordist (a Brooklyn kid who builds fixed-gear bicycles)—follow Shannon on treks across the enormous, barely habitable property as he maintains the guerrilla facilities.

Though his work can at times seem like a Sisyphean effort, this is the realization of a dream. Even in her earliest days of training in witchcraft, as young as eighteen, Morpheus had a notion that she would someday like to create land in California dedicated to Pagan practice—something her community, in the mecca of American Paganism, did not have. (Imagine Christians without churches, Jews without synagogues, Muslims without mosques.) When Morpheus, working at an occult shop in Mountain View, met Shannon, she found someone with whom she could share the fantasy.

Young American entrepreneurs first forced their way into the Diablo Range in the 1910s to mine for magnesite, then used to help smelt metal. A road was built, Mines Road, a two-day horse-drawn-carriage ride from the nearest town, Livermore; a string of bars and whorehouses were erected between there and what is now the Stone City site. But mining declined steadily after World War II, and by the early eighties, Shannon's grandfather was able to buy his parcel cheap. The area was still pretty wild then. A biker gang used to set up roadblocks and rob people, and his grandfather was once chased off the property by a group of armed partyers camped where the Stone Circle stands now. Today a lot of the guns and motorcycles in the

---

* Their numbers put them on a par with the Jehovah's Witnesses (1.2 million) and Seventh-day Adventists (1 million), and far ahead of, for example, the Church of Scientology (50,000).

area belong to wealthy retirees from Lawrence Livermore National Laboratory (a nuclear research facility)—or the occasional pot grower or meth cook.

It's California land, populated by oaks, junipers, and manzanita shrubs, with their red bark and waxy leaves—a landscape that's meant to burn out every few years. During the right season, tarantulas emerge into the moonlight from perfectly round, web-covered holes in the ground to find one another and mate. Hardly the lush, redwood-studded land Morpheus had envisioned, in keeping with her childhood home. But when Shannon's family offered them the chance to buy the hundred acres, Morpheus, a practical priestess of limited means, decided it was worth the gamble. And so, like a good-humored, decidedly uncelibate incarnation of the desert hermits of old, the Pagan couple trucked it out there, bracing themselves for a different life. They relinquished their material comforts, abandoned the electrical grid, and settled into a shed with no power or hot water, a few candles, a camp stove, and a hand-crank radio. Morpheus's term as the priestess of Stone City had begun.

The brush on the hilltop was impenetrable, so they rented a backhoe to clear out a campground. They were able to get an abandoned mobile home to use as "the guesthouse," eventually adding a whole array of custom "cabins," including The Dollhouse (a grounded treehouse) and Boat Land (a fleet of junked boats embedded in the dirt).

The jewel in the crown, of course, was the erection of their very own henge.

Morpheus had never actually visited a henge in the British Isles, but she'd always been drawn to the feeling of them, and dreamt of having a "natural temple" for rituals. They picked a hilltop and took alignments, throughout the year, for sunrise and sunset. Then came the grunt work, dragging in these massive rocks from all across the property. The largest, final stone, an eight-footer, required the help of seventeen volunteers and a wrought-iron gate jerry-rigged into a cantilever.

But once the circle was raised, the fledgling Stone City gained a powerful draw for the celebration of the witches' sabbats. "The stones have this property of moving power through them," Morpheus says, "and they draw it up out of the earth kind of like a candlewick. They form this really strong container"—a container for magical energy—"that acts like a gateway." Pagans began traveling from miles around for the experience.

. . .

The first time I witness a ritual in the Stone Circle, it's in honor of one of the sabbats: Mabon, the autumn equinox.

The sabbats mark the Wheel of the Year, the turning of the seasons. For Wiccans and Pagans of some other traditions, these are the spine of the Craft, and some fall on dates that are closely aligned with those of major Christian holidays: Yule, the winter festival from which we get the Twelve Days of Christmas; Ostara, the spring equinox and the source of Easter's fertility symbols (the rabbit, the egg); Samhain,* the time of communion with the dead, dressed up in mainstream culture as Halloween. Two of the stones in the Stone Circle are capped by a third, and they are perfectly positioned, on the high holiday of Samhain, to frame the full moon: a ritual gateway to the other world. Also on the grounds, a short hike down into a valley, is a Maypole for Beltane, the May Day sabbat: a fertility celebration that's decidedly bawdier in Pagan circles. What else would you expect from a holiday centered around a two-stories-high phallus? Here the Maypole is kept up year-round (they use a living tree), and when the sabbat comes, Pagans dance in circles, braiding long, silky ribbons around its trunk.

But this evening they're celebrating Mabon, given its name by American Pagans in the seventies, after a Welsh god. This is the time when the days and nights are once again of equal length, the land is transforming, the cold is settling in, and Samhain is on the horizon. It's a moment for giving thanks for the harvest and asking for blessings during the harsher winter months. Not that any of the Pagans I meet live completely off the land—but the sabbats are for remembering that connection, for conjuring up a time when we were more aware of what we took and what we gave back to our surroundings.

The circle was consecrated—as you can do anywhere, without these massive stones—and maybe fifteen men and women stand forming its inner periphery. I've never seen Morpheus in her priestess incarnation before, and now she stands at the center of the circle, in fitted black velvet that trails to the ground, all eyes on her. She has let loose her hair so that it falls, very red, down the length of her back. Her chin is tilted up, her gaze focused on some point in the distance. She stands before an altar, and atop the altar is a bread

* Pronounced *SAH-win*.

sculpture: a sun god. I'd watched her bake the bread, and once it had risen, she'd laid the god out on a dish and placed a dry ear of corn between his dough-legs: his penis. He was carried up the hill and placed in the Stone Circle, surrounded with pomegranates and apples, to create an image so British Isles–primitive I can't help thinking of *The Wicker Man*.

Morpheus raises her arms—and now her slight frame seems to expand and grow stronger, larger, imposing ("holding space," the witches call this). I understand immediately that this is her natural role. Her place. Following her lead, everyone chants as the sun sinks: *Lord of the wild things, lord of life! Lord of the shadows, lord of life! Lord of the wild hunt, lord of life!*

Morpheus is here to serve them, her witchy folk, but she also stands apart. Whereas they are visitors to this place, this occult no-man's-land, she *lives* in this alternate universe—it is her permanent residence, beaten into existence through the force of her imagination and a lot of uncomfortable living. She's taking steps to shake loose from the mundane world, to collapse her double life. *This* version of herself, she's decided, the more expansive person standing in the center of the circle, is the best part of her.

I belong to that *other* world. With the camera running, I keep myself apart, well outside the circle, still an observer. And the ceremony is a good primer: a ritual salute, a simple offering of bread and fruit and prayers—gentle stuff, basic, nothing that disturbs. No possession, no tranced-out frenzy. At the same time, this is so foreign—these people in shades of black standing inside a henge in American mining country, chanting around a bread-and-corn god—and I want to get closer. I wish I were standing with them.

I decide that sometime, somehow, when no one is filming, I'll find a way to do just that.

2

Little Witch

Through the making of the documentary, I spend more and more time with Morpheus. I learn a lot about the Craft simply by watching her, talking with her. I get to know her—and I give as good as I get, answering whatever questions she has for me in turn. While I still feel like some kind of anthropologist, an interloper, my connection to Morpheus becomes a way in. I want to know just how this person, an American woman my age—my peer, I guess—became not only a believer but a priest. A Pagan priestess. A witch.

Morpheus is a child of Northern California, raised with a name far more prosaic and all-American than the one she'd choose for herself years later.* Her first memories are of running down the hallways of a house built in the shadow of the redwoods in Forestville, in Sonoma County. A tomboy, she'd wander for hours through those trees, with their bark like rough and heavy strands of burnt-red hair, each a reminder of general human smallness, a

---

* Since plenty of magical power is attached to a name, I've agreed not to reveal the one on her birth certificate.

powerful finger pointing up, up, up, to vertiginous heights, with only the slantiest light allowed to slice through.

Her family soon relocated to Santa Rosa, then a small town, her father working as a contractor and her mother staying home to raise her and her older sister. Two girls, two opposites: brown-haired Mirabai studied French literature and schooled herself in European fashion; redheaded Morpheus was the tree climber, the frog catcher. Their mother explored a strain of perfectly Californian Hindu-inspired mysticism, but their father was a bit of a transcendentalist, fond of Emerson and Thoreau. He took Morpheus on hiking and camping trips in the woods. She thought of herself as the surrogate son.

As idyllic as her surroundings were, natural disasters tend to change the way we look at our environment, and that's just what happened with the Loma Prieta Earthquake. By the time Morpheus was in junior high, the family had moved deeper into the Santa Cruz Mountains, and in 1989 the deadly earthquake, a 6.9 on the Richter scale, forever altered her relationship to the woods. In their mountain home that day, she braced herself in a doorway as the furniture stuttered across the room and china came crashing out of the cupboards. The earth broke wide open in the front yard. Their house was declared "unsafe for human occupancy," and the family was forced to move into town for several months before things returned to normal. But a shift had already occurred: nature had revealed herself to be threatening, unpredictable, complex. Her father would later claim this was the moment Morpheus changed as well: at thirteen years old, she became "a darker person."

For high school, Morpheus had to commute to Los Gatos, a wealthy town at the foot of the mountains. Already shaken by the physical instability of her home life, she was further alienated by her new social setting. "I was angry. The students all seemed pretty shallow and entitled," she says. "My friends were generally the bad-kid outcast group." Following teen protocol, she began remaking her outside to match her inside: goth one day, all white makeup and lace; punk the next, in rags full of safety pins. She experimented with alter-ego monikers like "Monday," "Cobweb," and, eventually, "Morpheus"—after the Greek god of dreams.

She was experiencing "an awakening to being, you know, not your average person." Her outsiderness began to make her *special*. Morpheus was curious about the occult and was experimenting with her own private spirituality, more conscious of the cycles of the seasons. Hers was not a sudden, radical conversion, but a slow, natural slide into the Craft. She started communing with nature late at night. "My bedroom was on the second floor of the house, and I would go and sit out on the roof and listen to the owls and sing to the moon." She began to feel that something unhuman was out there—she could feel its power move through her. The redwoods transformed from a place for bonding with her father into a place that called to her alone, set her apart.

She soon discovered her first book on witchcraft, at the house of a friend who looked uncannily like Robert Smith of The Cure. This was before witchcraft became friendlier, New Age–ified, so most of the books available were less spiritual and self-helpy and more compendiums of have-a-blast, make-crazy-shit-happen spells. "It was 'how to do spells and promise yourself to the Horned One and deny Jesus,'" Morpheus says. "I *loved* that." She remembers a love spell that required using a mirror to capture the reflection of two dogs mating, inscribing it with the name of your love interest, and then burying it at a crossroads. What she read reinforced the instinctive spellwork she'd been doing on her own: chanting, playing with candles, improvising rituals when the moon was full.

And her experiments went further. At sixteen, she'd started cutting herself, for typical adolescent reasons—she was unhappy and numb, and the cuts made her *feel* something—and she became fascinated with blood as a kind of "concentrated power." She'd take out a razor knife and ask her boyfriends if they could taste each other's blood; or she'd use her own as ink, for writing out whatever she wanted to transpire. Teenage angst fed her magical technique.

Her earliest sexual feelings became a source of power as well. When Morpheus first discovered masturbation, touching herself became ritualized and, in her imagination, connected to larger forces. It was, basically, primitive sex magic—or magic that draws on sexual energy to achieve a goal. "I had these ideas that I built up in my head, like 'If I do this, and I'm thinking about a certain thing, when I reach a climax *something will happen*.'" At just ten years old, she'd worked out an elaborate scenario with her dolls. She had a blue-haired doll that was her "little witch," and the witch had a shop where she doled out spells; when Morpheus would orgasm, the doll's spell would be complete. In a household in which her parents were "shy and awkward" about sex, somehow their younger daughter had become convinced that the intensity of her first orgasms could create change in the universe. When Morpheus discovered sex magic nearly a decade later, the concept was already natural to her.

After her junior year, bored and frustrated, Morpheus dropped out of high school and threw herself into a series of random jobs. She laughs at the self-conscious teenager she was then, remembering how she was fired from a "nouveau-riche yuppie" travel shop for being "too grim." "I would be dragging my ass around there, dressed in black, trying not to talk to people. 'I don't care what wattage of adapter you need—it's all meaningless and void! You're all androids!'" But when she was hired to work at a Mountain View metaphysics shop, the Psychic Eye—a place that sold everything from talismans to cauldrons and crystal balls—her identity came into focus. As did many budding witches in the pre-Internet era, she found in the local occult shop her first real resource. Her self-taught, book-learned witchcraft, her private experiments, her angst-in-black and rooftop chants to the moon—it all made sense. At eighteen, she finally found herself among real priestesses.

Shannon and Morpheus first met when he strolled into the Psychic Eye, a lonely Pagan looking for community, and laid eyes on the beautiful women working there. He asked for a job application. Morpheus was quickly impressed by Shannon's dedication to his spiritual practice, heavily influenced by Native American shamanism. Soon the two began working magic together, one thing led to another, and they became a couple.

For a few years, Morpheus trained in the secretive Feri witchcraft tradition—through Linnea, an older woman she'd also met at the shop—and was finally initiated into her coven, known as Vanthe.* But her instincts told her it was already time for a change. Shannon had a plan: he wanted to go to college in Humboldt County—something he encouraged Morpheus, a high school dropout, to consider as well. She decided to move north with her guy. He enrolled in college; she started earning junior-college credits. She knew her relationship with Vanthe would suffer, but she was younger than her covenmates, by twenty to thirty years, and she felt she was des-

---

* A "tradition" (or "trad") can spawn several "lines," each of which may consist of a cluster of covens. In this case, the Feri tradition forked off into numerous lines, including one called Wings of Vanthi, which in turn gave rise to a coven called Vanthe (pronounced VAN-thee).

tined for bigger things. As young as she was, Morpheus had greater aspirations.

"I had a trajectory in life," she says. "I just thought, 'I have a *path.*'"

Witchcraft had given her an appetite.

For the whole spectrum the sanctuary attracts—mainly "eclectic Wiccans," which most Pagans are—Morpheus's practice is more specific. As trained by Linnea, she is a Feri priestess—which means nothing clear to me right now, but will come to mean a great deal.

In their wood-paneled bedroom, with a utility lighter, Morpheus lights a candle on top of a rolltop desk she's converted into a home altar, draped with satiny crimson fabrics and covered with statuettes of Pan (hooved and horned, pipes in hand) and a white goddess (after a Paleolithic cave painting) and bronze stags' heads and wax drippings and crystals and a carved wooden pentagram and a framed photograph of her wedding to Shannon, both smiling as they face each other, garlands around their heads, foreheads touching. Now Morpheus raises a chalice of water to her face carefully, as if it contains something too hot to drink, and breathes into it—breathes her *energy* into it. She arches her neck back, then takes a breath for herself. She places a pomegranate on the center of the pentagram, slips a boline (a small sickle) from her belt, and slices the fruit in half; its juice is very red. She picks out the seeds with her white, white fingers, places them in a glass bowl, and carries them across the room: an offering to lay on another altar, by the bedside. A close friend died only weeks earlier, at thirty-five, of brain cancer—Tara, known as a powerful priestess—and here are photos of her and white taper candles and, in pride of place, the goddess Morpheus works most closely with: a goddess she inherited from her coven, a Celtic goddess called the Morrigan. In this statuette, the Morrigan is redheaded, red-cloaked, and barefoot, carrying a spear and shield. A goddess of the battlefield, she's present at the moment someone crosses over, they say—and what is cancer, if not another kind of violent death? Morpheus grips the Morrigan with both hands.

What she is doing is praying—just as Christians and Jews and Muslims and Buddhists pray. And when she casts spells, whenever she finds one necessary—to heal a friend or protect herself or bind someone from doing harm—it's with the same prayerlike focus and intention.

Her dark goddess presides over Stone City: Morpheus is building a human-scale statue in her honor, using a male department-store mannequin as the armature, widening its arm span. She's dedicated a particular spot on the property to Morrigan devotionals. She walks heavily up the hillside in rugged boots and a long black skirt, black hoodie pulled up over her long red hair, a silver raven tied tightly around her neck with a black ribbon. She heads past the Stone Circle, past Boat Land, through the dry shrubbery, pushing aside thick tangles of branches to get to the spot: the Morrigan's perch. From up high, far from the campground, she can see the low, thick fog, as white as smoke, roll slowly across the valleys and up into the hills, as if there were a fire nearby. She climbs onto a cluster of boulders and speaks the names: "Morrigu! Badb Catha . . ." She crouches down and removes two jars from a leather bag and, one after the other (cream, dark ale), unscrews the cap and pours it out: again, offerings. As often as possible, offerings.

I cannot claim to understand Morpheus yet—she has a more private magical life that will take years for me to unravel. But I know that I *like* her. She is utterly unpretentious, doesn't care what you think of her. When she laughs, she laughs loud and hard, like an announcement—*"Ha!"*—her face bright and open. She laughs at the scrappiness of her lifestyle, at Pagan fashion, at the crunchiness of California. When I ask if she spells "magic" with a "k," in old-school occult style, she says absolutely not: that reminds her of people who use words like "womyn" and "herstory," "which makes me want to stab pencils through my eyes."

Plus she's able to talk straight about her witchcraft practice. Morpheus is super-articulate (it's uncanny how often she speaks in thoughtful, complete, transcribable sentences), but rarely mystical or "glowy" in her tone—even when describing, say, a chat she had with a particular god. When something witchy has her excited, she becomes like a kid, busting out with *"Awe-some!"* and *"Bad-ass!"* or (in our e-mail exchanges) an explosion of emoticons. All the while, she remains formidable, seemingly unshakable. She has a relaxed and total acceptance of my skepticism: she doesn't need to persuade me. After we've wrapped the film and my skeleton crew and I have returned to New York City, I'm surprised to find that my friendship with Morpheus remains intact—rarer than you might think, once a project comes to a close.

I discover something else after filming ends. My personal pattern is playing out—I cannot shake my curiosity. I want to understand the strange confidence necessary to climb onto the roof and sing to the moon, or to write out commands in your own blood; to train in a secret tradition and be initiated; to move out to the middle of nowhere and drag heavy stones to stand upright in your very own henge; to say, *I have a trajectory in life.* I want to grasp the moment when that confidence becomes conviction; to know what it's like to believe, without doubt, that you hold the key to the Mysteries, that you are capable of magic. I decide to press deeper, to try to discover just what that faith is built on.

3

Naked in the New Forest

To make sense of Stone City and this sprawl of American witches, I first had to go back in time about sixty-five years, to England and the beginnings of Wicca, the Craft religion that sparked the Pagan movement.

Picture a brisk night in the late forties, an hour north of central London, in the Bricket Wood. A group of about ten men and women, solidly middle-class, teachers and typists and anthropologists, enter the grounds of England's oldest nudist club, many of them members. They walk along carefully trimmed pathways and then off, between the beeches and oaks, to a "witch's cottage," acquired from a defunct folklore theme park, its exposed wooden crossbeams daubed in clay, the roof covered in tile. Inside the squat single-room building, maybe twelve feet by twelve feet, they remove their coats: nothing more than bare skin and necklaces. Equal and at ease without their social armor, they gather to form a circle. Now a woman kneels inside it, bound with rope. A man steps forward: the high priest. He is in his late sixties, his tan skin slightly puckered, his head capped with a shock of white, forearms tattooed in black Bornean ink—the black dragon that marks a man's status as an outsider. He raises a short whip in one hand and the coven's *Book of Shadows* in the other. Lightly, he strikes her: forty lashes.

Witchcraft has been practiced, in one form or another, for as long as there's been a moon to shout at and herbs to collect and a fire to dance around. But as a *movement*, it can be traced back to this one gnarled old Englishman: Gerald Gardner, godfather of Wicca.

A common agreement exists that the further back a religion can trace its roots, the more legitimate it must be. American nonbelievers like to bring up Mormonism's relatively recent founding as reason to dismiss its doctrines. As if the angel Moroni guiding Joseph Smith to a box of divine gold plates buried in the ground were so much stranger than Jesus' resurrection from his tomb. Or Muhammad's ascension to heaven to speak to Allah. Then again, Joseph Smith's revelation came in 1823, more than a thousand years later, making it easier for us to imagine the very human life of the prophet, to talk to his living descendants, only a few generations removed, and to judge them as we'd judge our contemporaries—to whom we don't attribute miracles freely. In this way, the origin story of any younger belief system is sketchier (in both senses of the word), that much easier to brush aside as just another story written down and passed around by humans.

For this reason, it's tempting—*I* was tempted—to focus on when Wicca was born. Is it actually the survival of an ancient (or at least medieval) witchcraft religion, as some of its first generation claimed? Or was it instead created as recently as the fifties, a movement built on the fabrications of a lone eccentric and a bit of a hustler? But this is the narrow view. A religion might best be measured not by its myths but by its impact. And whatever your opinion of Wicca, Gardner was able to construct the ultimate occult legacy—a quantifiable, practicable version of the "Old Religion."

From tales of Gerald's life as told by his disciples, the disciples of his disciples, the British tabloid media, and, more recently, a handful of serious academics, here is the story that shakes out.

Though he was born into a well-off family of merchants and magistrates near Liverpool, by the time Gerald was four, his asthma had already relegated him to a life on the fringe. To protect him from England's harsh winters—this was 1888—his parents enlisted his governess, "Com," to take the boy to the South of France. So young Gerald's wild, not-so-age-appropriate life abroad with the nanny began, the two of them wandering exotic lands as an improvised remedy.

They traveled for months at a time, eventually going even farther abroad, to Madeira and the Gold Coast (present-day Ghana). And the farther they went, the less the nanny seemed constrained by the upper-middle-class English sensibilities of her employers. She was working-class, single, and without any hang-ups about how much she enjoyed a good drink and the company of men; Gerald remembered her as "a flamboyant, deep-bosomed, blarneying Irish girl." So the life of this odd duo took on a rhythm over these years: arriving in a new port and settling into a hotel suite, Com would immediately hunt down and purchase a piano and a stock of whiskey and open their door to whatever rough European expats were around, sometimes enlisting young Gerald to lure in company. (In at least one port of call, the local missionaries tried to run Com out of town.) Left mostly to his own devices by his nanny's low-rent hostessing, Gerald passed the time consorting with the locals, starting an amateur's collection of tribal weapons, and teaching himself to read with the Sherlock Holmes stories serialized in a British magazine. This was a great distance from the life in the Liverpool suburbs for which the kid had previously been destined.

When Gerald was fifteen, Com got married and moved full-time to Ceylon (now Sri Lanka), taking him along with the promise of a job on her new husband's tea plantation. Over the next ten years—in Ceylon, Malaya, and Borneo—Gerald worked at a series of plantations (tea, then rubber), and as a government inspector of opium shops (the medical marijuana vendors of their day). He was self-taught on the most basic level, a jack of many trades, a horrible speller, and a reader of whatever caught his eye. True expertise was not important—he was swept up in a romance with Experience! (In photos of him much later, his love of life, the full scope of it, is still written in his face.) It was this spirit that led Gerald to assimilate more deeply with the natives: he lived in a thatched hut, tattooed his arms in tribal style, and coveted any insight into local ceremonies. Through native friends, he took part in the ritual folk magic of the Malays, the Senoi, and the Borneans, and learned about their shared belief in life after death, spirit possession, and a multitude of deities. In Malaya, Gerald studied the *keris*, a knife thought to have magical powers—he found that wearing one earned him instant street cred—and witnessed a "séance" in the hut of a shaman.

As unconventional as his lifestyle was for an Englishman, Gerald was not as much of an outlier as he seems. The climate in his own country had steadily been changing. His grandparents' generation had seen the rise of Romantic ideas in reaction to industry and science. The arts promoted an idea of the soulful individual (an original! a genius!) who stands apart from a cool society; the exotic, the sublime, the awesome, and the impractical were a dreamy, heroic alternative to the rationalism of the day. With this also came a new reverence for ancient myths. By the mid-nineteenth century, the "Goddess" became a recurring image in English literature, and Pan was transformed from the crass demigod of rural life to the original god of nature. Druidry experienced a revival, inspired by the nature-worshipping practices of that educated class of ancient Pagan Celts, with self-proclaimed Druids celebrating seasonal holidays at Stonehenge. A return to nature was seen as the cure to modern alienation, the way to reconnect with our true humanity.

So even before Gerald was born, a subculture of secret societies was gaining hold in London, setting the stage for the rise and spread of Wicca, and these overlapping occult systems formed an intricate web of associations. I found it, at first, mindbendingly hard to follow, but you can get by, for our purposes, with a string of exotic-sounding names: Spiritualism, the Theosophical Society, Rosicrucianism, Ordo Templi Orientis, and the Golden Dawn.

Two were exports from New York: Spiritualism, which claimed proof of an afterlife through communication with the dead, and Madame Blavatsky's Theosophical Society, which promoted her idea of a universal spiritual system inspired by Eastern religions.* And from Germany came Rosicrucianism, a kind of Protestant mysticism intertwined with science supposedly lifted from the Moors, and Ordo Templi Orientis (OTO), a new mystical society originally modeled on Freemasonry. Plus, by the time Gardner was four, London had seen the creation of its own magical society, the influential Hermetic Order of the Golden Dawn. The Golden Dawn—itself drawing

---

* Blavatsky claimed she'd channeled this wisdom through a psychic connection with immortal beings in the Himalayas.

on Rosicrucianism, Theosophy, and Freemasonry—spawned a number of prominent occultists, including William Butler Yeats and the notorious magician and mystic Aleister Crowley. (Crowley would go on to lead OTO—I'll return to him a few times.) These societies were generally seen as intellectually driven, sometimes connected to progressive science, and often still compatible with Christianity, if a more esoteric brand. The Golden Dawn and OTO in particular became associated with "ceremonial magic," a catchall term for schools of highly choreographed magic. "Witchcraft" continued to seem like dangerously visceral gut-level magic, less cerebral and more intuitive, ecstatic—and with a stronger streak of female power running through it. It was folksy, free-form; it didn't assimilate nicely into elite cultural circles. But magic, and its culture of hidden meaning, had become a glamorous thing.

This was the undercurrent that Gerald, now a retired civil servant, would tap into when he returned to London in 1936. He'd spent decades mostly abroad, and now, in his early fifties, having remade himself as an amateur archaeologist (with a handful of hollow titles to prove it), he imagined he would retire at home. Almost immediately, however, Gerald was reminded of the reason for his childhood exile: his asthma flared up. He went to see a doctor, who prescribed an unorthodox Romantic cure: a healthy dose of outdoor nudity—or *naturism*, as the Brits call it. Perhaps thinking back to his first days as a boy on the Gold Coast, jealous of the locals' ultra-minimal clothing, Gerald gave it a go.

This bohemian prescription seemed to do the trick, and soon Gerald joined the Fouracres Club, in Bricket Wood, just north of London.* In the buff, they discussed philosophy over cocktails on the lawn, and sometimes gathered in the clubhouse for dinners or folk dancing. The fifty members shared not only an acceptance of the human body, male or female, but a wide-open worldview. The carefully screened group included academics, nearly a dozen West End doctors, young professionals—but some of them might also have been labeled (apropos of the time) Rosicrucians, Freemasons, Theosophists, or Druids. Following his life in far-off Asia, where he traveled and dug up ancient relics and danced with the Malays and sampled their magic, Gerald's time with the naturists formalized his identity, even

---

* This place still exists: it's the oldest naturist club in England.

on English ground, as a freethinker in every way, an explorer on his native turf. In Bricket Wood, Gerald could talk openly with other English men and women who wished to explore what he called "the fourth dimension."

For his health, Gerald and his wife—they'd met on one of Gerald's stays in London—moved south to Highcliffe, near the New Forest, a forest on the Hampshire coast created for the royal hunting of deer. There, he quickly became a member of two unconventional groups: the naturist New Forest Club and a small Rosicrucian theater company. At the playhouse, Gerald had noticed one of their lead actors: Edith Woodford-Grimes, an elocution-and-drama teacher, also in her fifties, with a teenage daughter. They shared their memories of previous lives—his in ancient Cyprus, hers as a witch burned at the stake—and became constant companions, with Gerald regularly visiting her home. Decades later, she would be remembered in the Craft by his nickname for her, "Dafo."

In the story that Gerald would tell about his life, this is the moment when everything changed. Because in the following year (1939), he claims he was initiated by an area "witch cult"—one that had quietly survived centuries of persecution. "I was half-initiated before the word 'Wica' which they used hit me like a thunderbolt," he later wrote, "and I knew where I was, and that the Old Religion still existed."

So what had happened between Gerald's meeting Dafo and his initiation? How did this retiree end up naked, bound, and scourged by a secret coven of witches? Version one: Dafo, seeing that they were kindred spirits, introduced Gerald to the "ancient" coven to which she belonged, a group who called themselves "the Wica," and they ultimately initiated him.* Version two: Dafo became Gerald's collaborator in the founding of a *brand-new* "cult" that combined their shared esoteric interests and his Joseph Conrad fantasies, and coated it all with the veneer of *ye olde* historical legitimacy. (Dafo is the only person confirmed as practicing witchcraft with Gerald early on.)

Whichever version holds true—and we may never know—this is certain: "the Wica" would soon be outed.

---

* To be more precise, Gerald claimed that he was initiated by a wealthy landowner, "Old Dorothy," who was the high priestess of the witch cult, but some scholars now believe it's more likely that he used this name as cover for Dafo.

This takes us back to that nighttime scene in the cottage. In 1947, Gerald pooled money to buy land, registered under Dafo's legal name, right next door to the naturist club, on foresty grounds with a view of the Isle of Wight across the harbor. There, they reassembled a sixteenth-century "witches' cottage," purchased from a closed folklore museum. By the early fifties, drawing on the members of the naturist club (and possibly their theater group), Gerald and Dafo's coven was in full swing, with a place to hold regular meetings, or witches' esbats.*

Another critical piece slid into place at the top of the fifties: in June 1951, the Witchcraft Act of 1735 was finally repealed, making it legal for someone to publicly claim they worked with magic or spirits. (Though witchcraft and the occult were no longer considered threats, they had long been prosecuted as fraud.) The very next month, ready to capitalize on this new freedom, the former film producer Cecil Williamson opened the Folklore Centre of Superstition and Witchcraft at Castletown on the Isle of Man. The place was run by the "resident witch" Gerald Gardner (he'd bought a house on the island), billed for the summer tourists as "a member of the Southern Coven of British Witches."

Gerald ate up the publicity. In many ways a product of his era, he viewed himself as a great explorer and a gifted interpreter of lost and exotic cultures. And so he reinvented himself yet again: whereas he'd once made himself into the consummate amateur anthropologist, esteemed in his own mind but less than competent in the eyes of many others (some associates called him "the old windbag"), he now became the high priest of a great British coven. Finally he had esoteric credentials no one could outstrip. When interviewed at the museum's opening ceremony, Gerald spoke of dancing naked in rituals. He told a reporter, "Of course I'm a witch. And I get great fun out of it."

Though a boost for Gerald, the increasing publicity made Dafo nervous of being exposed. One can imagine: it was the early fifties and she was a woman in a small town, a teacher and a mother, secretly taking part in

---

* It seems worth noting that throughout this period Gerald's wife, Donna, herself the daughter of a clergyman in the Church of England and never a practicing witch, was a really good sport about her husband's naked activities alongside his high priestess. (His relationship with Dafo was likely also an openly sexual affair.)

witchcraft rituals. Gerald's magical partner for over a dozen years, she was no longer certain she could continue as high priestess.

Enter Doreen Valiente, a striking brunette who worked an office job not far from where Dafo lived. A dropout from convent school at the age of fifteen, Doreen had long been interested in the occult. During a time when esoteric texts and relics were only available to wealthy collectors, and even a tarot deck was hard to come by, she had managed to get hold of a few Golden Dawn documents. Now thirty, she read a promotional interview with Cecil in which he mentioned the New Forest coven. Intensely curious, she wrote to him, and he passed her letter to Gerald. They agreed to meet at Dafo's house.

The first time Doreen saw Gerald in action as high priest, she was impressed: he was naked and tall, with "wild white hair," swinging the coven's sword through the air. A year later, she was initiated into Wicca by Gerald and Dafo, on the night before they were to take part in a Druid ceremony at Stonehenge. Not long afterward, at the flat Gerald kept in London, she met the rest of the coven—about ten in total.*

Dafo stepped down. In the late fifties, with modest resources, she moved into the home of her conservative Christian niece, resigned to erasing her role in the making of the modern-day Craft. As has been proven throughout history, especially where religion is concerned, men often have less to lose: Gerald Gardner was pleased to become the face of Wicca. Doreen would be his new high priestess.

His confidence bolstered by the attention he'd received through the museum—he quickly bought it outright from Cecil, renaming it the Museum of Magic and Witchcraft—Gerald decided he'd write a complete exposé and guide to the Old Religion. When he shared this plan, Doreen, skeptical of any more exposure, made a remark that's been quoted by witches many times over the decades that followed: "Witchcraft doesn't pay for broken windows."

---

* The coven still exists today in North London—possibly setting a record for longevity. Most covens, I've been told, are relatively short-lived, and five to seven active years is considered a success.

But in 1954, at seventy, Gerald published the book that would trigger the modern-day Pagan movement: *Witchcraft Today*. Posing as an anthropologist who'd gained privileged access, he told the story of the surviving "witch cult" that he'd encountered "in the North, South, East, and West of England today in covens which I know."* With Gerald's flair for the dramatic in full effect, the book opens:

I have been told by witches in England: "Write and tell people we are not perverts. We are decent people, we only want to be left alone, but there are certain secrets that you mustn't give away." So after some argument as to exactly what I must not reveal, I am permitted to tell much that has never before been made public concerning their beliefs, their rituals and their reasons for what they do . . .

He outlined a history of witchcraft and the ways in which it had been misunderstood over the centuries, the witches' belief system (the Craft as a *religion* rather than random dabbling in folk spells), and the specific practices he'd witnessed.

But beyond what was served up for public consumption, what did Gerald's coven practice—in the original nighttime cottage and in his London flat, with Dafo as high priestess and later Doreen? And what's the sense underlying it—the secret meetings, the nudity, the knives, the bondage, all these customs passed down to witches even today?

As I'd already learned, Wiccans, and now Pagans of many stripes, gather on the sabbats, but a coven meets regularly, for every full moon, sometimes even weekly. These esbats are when they perform any necessary magic—maybe a healing or a protection spell—either inside a private home (because it's easy and safe), or outdoors, in nature. This is the beauty of a place like Stone City, decades later: nature is every witch's temple, no matter the exact location. A priestess doesn't need a synagogue or church; she can place her hands on the trunk of a tree—wherever, even in some traffic median—and draw power up from the earth. She doesn't need a white marble sanctuary lined with gold-leaf cherubs; she can take a deep breath and absorb "life

---

* Gardner first used "Wica," or "wise people," to refer to the religion and its practitioners, and the name became popularized as "Wicca" when the movement grew in the sixties.

force" from the air. But power stirred up within a circle is considered the most concentrated.

The basic tools of Wicca, and several other magical traditions, include a couple of blades: the sword, used to "cast" the ritual circle (this belongs to the coven), and the athame, a ritual knife each witch is given at initiation— it's indispensable; every witch has one. The athame is mainly for pointing magical energy in the right direction, or cutting open invisible gateways. (Fulfilling more than a few children's fantasies, a witch might also do this with a wand.) Incense, in a censer, can be used to set the tone, and because the curls of smoke are believed to carry prayers up to the gods. As for the pentagram, or pentacle—the five-pointed star, often misunderstood as "Satanic"—it's a symbol worn around the neck or used in rites much the way a crucifix is used to represent and evoke Christ in Christianity. In the twelfth-century Renaissance, the pentagram stood for the intersection of divine order and mathematics; today, for Pagans, it represents "life force."

In Gardnerian Wicca (Wicca practiced just as Gardner did), a rope is some-times used for binding, and as a scourge for giving dozens and dozens of lashes—though these strokes are gentle enough and largely symbolic, not for causing pain but "to make skin tingle." Gerald had supposedly gotten this idea from the frescoes of the Villa of the Mysteries at Pompeii, which show an initiate being scourged in a ritual "death" before being "resurrected." But Gerald's fascination with the whip was so disproportionate to other practices and, combined with the nudity and bondage, so fraught with S and M asso-ciations that Doreen, once she became high priestess, cut back on the fetish.

Never mind what hipster forays into the occult might suggest (see: late-sixties Mick Jagger and Jimmy Page), no drugs are used in Wicca or any of the major Craft traditions—at least not in any regular, official capacity. Wine might be shared during ritual for whatever reason, but very little. And though plenty of social drinking is likely to happen after ceremony (this isn't really a conservative crowd), no serious witch would circle while wasted. That said, plenty of people interested in magic have studied the effects of psychedelics on consciousness expansion. This is the root of one theory about the classic Halloween image of a witch flying on a broomstick: some say that during medieval times, witches would use "flying ointment," an herbal cream that induced a hallucination of flight, applied to the genitals with a broom handle. This sensational explanation aside—and it's had some traction over the years—witchy broom associations are most likely the remnants of a folk fertility rite: medieval farmers, the story goes, would jump high into the air with a broomstick between their legs to induce the crops to grow. Regardless, brooms are simply not a big deal for witches, who remain, at least while on the physical plane, firmly on the ground.

As for the nudity, this is known as going "skyclad," and it's not intended as a come-on. Instead, as one of Gerald's disciples would later write, it's a "sign of freedom, of a casting-off of worldly things." Mostly, on a technical level—and witches often refer to their magic as "technology"—they go skyclad because of a belief that the human body can emanate more raw power naked. "Power seems to exude from the body via the skin and possibly from the orifices of the body," Gerald wrote. "They say that witches by constant practice can train their wills to blend this nerve force, or whatever it is, and that their united wills can project this as a beam of force . . ." He even cited a rather thin study, conducted at Cornell University in the thirties, that supposedly demonstrated that rays emanating from the human body (a pointed finger, to be precise) were strong enough to kill yeast cells.* Though many American witches wear robes, or drop their robes only for a central part of the ceremony, the principle of working skyclad has lasted for more than half a century.

Beyond nudity, Gerald wrote of how witches "raise" power (or psychic energy) for their magic through clarity of mind, cleanliness of body, and a "spirit of reverence." They also use some very simple techniques, always more effective inside the magical circle: "dancing and singing monotonous chants, slowly at first and gradually quickening the tempo until giddiness ensues"; running around the circle, giving off the occasional "wild and meaningless shrieking"; using the scourge to get the blood circulating. This group whipping-into-a-frenzy is often called "raising a cone of power"—the "cone" being the collective will of the coven, aimed like a rifle at its magical target.

While Gerald passed these practices off as "ancient," I quickly discovered that many were clear riffs on existing sources, while others very likely sprang entirely from Gerald's brain.

---

* To explore the nuances of the relationship between degrees of power and degrees of nudity, Gardner also suggested that a scientific experiment be conducted comparing the magical effectiveness of two different circles of witches, "one team in the traditional nude and one in bikinis."

It's not much of a leap from the ritual knife of Gerald's days in Borneo to the athame, or from naturism to going "skyclad," and even a half-decent Freudian could trace Gerald's sexual openness all the way back to those days with his nanny Com. But there's more concrete evidence that Gerald's rules and rites of Wicca were not handed to him straight from some centuries-old coven: several elements of Wicca's *Book of Shadows*, the central book of spells and rituals he claimed to have copied directly from that of the New Forest Coven, were pulled from pre-existing grimoires, or spell compilations; from *Aradia*, a "witches' gospel" published by an American folklorist in 1899; and even from a poem by Rudyard Kipling.

Plenty of practices were also lifted from Freemasonry—already a huge influence on the secret societies of the time (particularly the Golden Dawn and OTO, whose founders were Masons). Beginning in the fourteenth century, the Freemasons comprised a network of societies of stonemasons, organized around "lodges" throughout Europe; they built all the major churches and cathedrals, blending their own sacred designs into the work. The details are unclear, but over the centuries their focus seems to have shifted from their craft to a mystical ethical system, *the* Craft, and gentlemen and intellectuals were integrated into the lodges. By the early 1700s, England had become the movement's center. Though they survive in less meaningful form today, the Masons now claim six million members worldwide, with just under two million in the United States alone—nearly a third of American presidents have been Freemasons. Since its ceremonies and symbol systems were closely guarded for centuries, Gerald was able to draw heavily on Freemasonry and its claims of "ancient" origins and rites: like the Masons, Wiccans are initiated through progressive "degrees," with initiates bound and blindfolded and presented to the "quarters," or the four directions; like the Masons, Wiccans adopted the pentagram; and just as the Masons came to call their system "the Craft,"* so did Gardner's Wiccans, and Pagans of many traditions.

Then there's Aleister Crowley—without exaggeration, simultaneously one of the most feared, despised, and respected occultists in history. The magician had been running OTO for over two decades when Gardner met him, just before Crowley's death in 1947. In *Witchcraft Today*, published just

---

* In medieval Britain, the word was used, along with "art" or "mystery," to describe any skilled trade.

a few years later, the ritual tools described as belonging to the "witch cult" are basically those of Crowley's OTO. Long, lyrical sections of *The Book of Shadows* are cribbed from Crowley's intricate ritual prose—later deliberately rewritten by Doreen Valiente—as are likely some of Wicca's ceremonial gestures. This marriage of magical methods had a major, lasting influence on the Pagan movement in England and America.

The idea that Wicca was handed down, in an "unbroken" line, from ancient times—an idea Gardner actively promoted—is now recognized as insupportable. But questions of "authenticity" have proved beside the point. Once Gardner's writings about the Craft were published, there was, as an early initiate of his would write, "an almost immediate recognition by many that here was what they had been looking for . . . even if most had not realized they had been looking." Here was a fully formed religion, a new alternative—for many, an alternative to Christianity.

The dam broke: Gerald received letters from all over England and abroad, asking for initiation. Plenty of people wanted a piece of this "world of faery."

Wicca touched ground in America just fifty miles from my hometown of Manhattan—in Bay Shore, Long Island.

In the late fifties, a Londoner and former Royal Air Force pilot, Raymond Buckland, read *Witchcraft Today* and struck up a correspondence with Gerald, wanting to know more. Over a series of letters and long phone calls, the two became friends. When, in 1962, Ray and his wife, Rosemary, relocated to Long Island, Gerald decided that Ray should become his man in America.

The next year, Ray flew to Perth, Scotland, where Gerald had arranged for his training and initiation. Ray returned to the States and established the first official Wiccan coven in this country at his home on Long Island. Over the next decade, he and his wife would initiate twenty priests and priestesses, and from there Wicca spread to the South and out to California— where a handful of the occult-curious had already gotten hold of Gerald's book.

By the sixties, word about Wicca had spread, and many were eager to be initiated, without nearly enough covens to train them. Convinced they'd finally found the belief system to give shape and meaning to their lives, these would-be witches refused to wait. "Wiccan" covens were founded, guerrilla-style, in pockets all around the country, based on improvised spins on the tradition—whatever people could get out of the new Craft books that were out there—and in the most misled, worst-case scenarios, trying to riff off what they saw depicted in the movie *Rosemary's Baby*, with its Satanic spin on witchcraft. In that overeager climate, some Gardnerian covens caved to pressure to initiate more quickly, leading Buckland to write of that time, "Degrees were handed out as though they were so much candy."

Once things settled, America was left with a slew of people, mostly underground, who called themselves "Wiccan"—though many were now part of witchcraft traditions that improvised and expanded on Gardner's original *Book of Shadows* and oral teachings. Some covens gave Wicca a Celtic, Saxon, or feminist Dianic slant; others were brazenly "eclectic," picking and choosing rites and flourishes in the way that only Americans feel entitled to do—and why not? An entire movement had started.

Over the next three decades, that movement fanned outward. The seventies brought the creation of a series of Pagan enclaves, particularly on the West Coast—the predecessors of Stone City. Large ritual gatherings were improvised, along with attempts at a "unified" Pagan liturgy. Brand-new chants and invocations were passed around between far-flung covens and Pagan community groups—and the further they got from their source, the more likely they were to be labeled "ancient" by excited new converts. Throughout the eighties, as the Craft continued to spread, it became more acceptable for a person to "self-initiate"—"solitary" witches could be just as committed as those initiated into covens. And by the nineties, the Internet provided that last great push: the curious no longer had to rely on their local occult shop, or the slim chance of finding an active coven in their area, but could instead approach a mentor or seek out their own magical path online.

I go back to that terrific line that opens Gardner's book: *Write and tell people we are not perverts.* If there was no surviving, centuries-old witch cult—and it seems highly unlikely there was—then who was Gerald writing for? Was he writing on his own behalf, as a man who'd lived far outside English society since he was a small child, and who'd long ago developed an appetite for the "exotic," for rites that connected him to a hidden universe, a parallel world that his own middle-class family would never have access to? This son of a successful Liverpool businessman was, by his twenties, sporting a dragon tattoo, the mark of a social outcast, and walking around Malay villages with a magical knife slung through his belt. He was the perfect voice for the misunderstood and self-educated "perverts" of England, the guerrilla heirs to the Freemasons.

Today, in America, that separateness persists—but it's one that many Pagans cling to with pride. Tell people we are not perverts—although we *are*, if by "pervert" you mean someone who proudly rejects the religious mainstream. Now there are places for Pagans from all around to gather, whether it's a sanctuary as intimate as Stone City or a festival of thousands. Their numbers call for it. An eclectic Pagan underground has emerged.

4

Keep Your Weapons Peace-Bonded!

Fast-forward a couple of years in my timeline, to 2012. For Presidents' Day weekend, I fly cross-country to the San Jose airport and take a five-minute taxi ride through a bland corporate landscape to arrive at my destination: a jumbo-sized DoubleTree Hotel. I've come all this way because it's February and, for Pagans, February means PantheaCon, their major annual "gathering of the tribes" on the West Coast—one of the simplest ways to get a look at the faces of American witchcraft.

Walking through the sliding doors with my roller bag, I am already bracing myself: about two thousand witches show up for this convention each year, and it's a *scene*. Of course, you'd never guess this from the hotel itself, with its upscale-national-chain décor, all mass-produced dark wood furniture and stretches of pale marble floor. An enormous fireplace lines one side of the lobby, and a wall of glass the other, revealing an outdoor pool dotted with preteens whose khaki-clad parents have no idea of the true theme of this weekend.

I hook a left and head toward the convention's registration tables, and now signs of this Hilton outpost's impending Pagan invasion start to multiply. The parade of recently arrived guests features a wide array of aesthetic statements: prosthetic horns, glitter-glued fairy wings, leather-and-lace corsets, brocade corsets, Merry Widow bodices, Victorian waistcoats, knee-high lace-up platform boots, velvet capes, medieval man-blouses, animal bones used as clever hairpins, waist-length hair and nipple-length beards, Celtic tattoos and gothic tattoos, amulets and pentacles of every size made out of jade and silver and plastic and stone. Those who choose to wear lay clothes are either hippied out in tie-dye and florals or in black denim ensembles that are part goth, part emo (all in New York black, these are my kin by default). Pagans dress up for serious ceremonies, much like priests or rabbis or imams; or they dress up simply because they have permission to. I've already come to think of this second category as "lifestyle Pagans," out to enjoy themselves (not unlike the Christians who show up at a megachurch mainly for the PlayStations and Krispy Kreme doughnuts), and many of them are on display this weekend. Every religious community has them.

Regardless of getup, they're all just going about their business right now, fishing cell phones or granola bars or credit cards out of their backpacks, dumping sugar packets into their coffees at the Starbucks bar, or lining up for their laminated passes. It's still only five o'clock, time to get settled in, and people will be arriving well into the night for PCon's eighteenth year. I pick up my name tag and join the herd.

Tacked to the columns by the elevators are brightly colored printouts that read "No Nudity!" and "Keep Your Weapons Peace-Bonded!" I step aboard the lift, holding the doors open for two sexagenarians in flowing skirts and sparkly, tight-fitting tops that reveal plenty of cleavage. On closer inspection, I see that they also have small rubber horns affixed to their scalps.

This weekend, there is no room for judgment.

I am sharing a room with Morpheus, and when I find her there, in what will serve as the "Stone City Suite," she's just finishing rehearsing her stepdaughter Avia for her priestessing debut. A month shy of her eighteenth birthday, Avia will lead her first ritual tomorrow at the Con. In her cartoon tee, pigtails, and Urban Decay lipstick, she listened from her perch on the bedspread as the senior priestess, still in her pedestrian clothes, paced the carpet, giving notes on how to hold the room, take her time, mete out ritual duties.

"We're going to pass the mantle on to her tomorrow," Morpheus tells me once Avia's left, every inch the proud parent. Years ago, she chose not to have children of her own—she said once that her body was for "play," not procreation—but with Avia she assumes the role of adoptive witch-mother. She seems to see in Avia the same ruthlessly independent girl *she* was at that age.

I am less of a novice now—if only slightly. Over the past couple of years, I've observed a few sabbats at Stone City and finally taken part in one; I've met Morpheus's friends and much of her witchy inner circle; I've joined in a few larger Pagan gatherings in different parts of California (this is not my first PantheaCon). At moments, I'm still turned off by the more flamboyant folks on this scene, their florid costumes and right-in-your-face sexuality,* or I'm thrown by the foreignness of the ceremonies, sometimes even embarrassed to be in attendance (so out of place). But I've met enough committed, formidable Pagan priests that, in spite of my reservations, my fascination with this community has deepened. Now that the thrill of the new is gone— I'm no longer shocked by the mere fact of standing in a circle of witches, chanting along with them, drinking from their chalices—I find myself looking for more elemental, more visceral ritual experiences. Regardless of the welcome I've received (or slowly earned), I remain an outsider, and I want to get closer to whatever it is Morpheus has access to.

Morpheus places a boom box on the bureau and spikes the air with California death metal. Straightaway, the instructional priestess transforms into a ball of energy, swinging her waist-length hair and pumping her fists. She zips herself into a corset and pants, both black leather. (The same size as me, she offers to lend me her clothing, but I'm just not ready for corsets as outerwear.) As a final touch, she applies drops of oil from a tiny black vial. "Amber essence," she says—and I realize that its scent, a mix of patchouli and ash and hookahs and flowers that bloom at night, is the scent of everything priestessy.

I ask Morpheus about her husband, Shannon, Avia's father, and she tells me that they're "taking time apart." I'm sad to hear it—though she says he's

---

* Plenty of West Coast Pagans are polyamorous—meaning they openly juggle more than one committed relationship at a time—*and* bisexual. This can make it hard to predict who, among the sexual extroverts, may want to flirt with you.

become more controlling and, until recently, struggled with drinking, a dangerous habit when you live off the grid. "We need a little space," she says—and I'm reminded that in times of personal chaos, no matter how exotic our religion or subculture, we all take comfort in the same banal language.

We head to the lobby bar, a choice spot for people-watching, and soon Morpheus's witchy clique—some of the innermost circle of Feri initiates—has pulled up chairs and ordered martinis and glasses of Bordeaux. This crowd, in their thirties and forties, is particular: they're more likely to be artists, aesthetes, and intellectuals; they're nearly always clad in black and red and purple, with their fair share of leatherwear; they're earth-loving, but far from the hippie type; and most of them share a love of Middle Eastern mysteries, trance, and ecstatic dance. Later on, I overhear someone refer to them as the community's "cool kids."

As we settle in, I spot Thorn Coyle, a priestess with clout, crossing the busy lobby with about twenty people trailing after her. She's sporting her signature goth-androgyne style, in a black suit and white silk tie; her salt-and-pepper curls are cut close to her head, angular and butch. Her crew comes closer still: these are her students from Morningstar, her "mystery school," which, in a confluence of magical and technological streams, is mostly conducted online and through video Skype. They've just arrived from a weeklong retreat, and we can hear them singing a hymn that grows louder and louder—until a hotel guest, not-so-Pagan and dead set on checking out, pushes her loaded luggage cart straight toward the group. A pro, Thorn simply guides the woman through the circle and out its other side, her disciples parting and closing again like the Red Sea. No one misses a note. Everyone keeps on singing.

The more renowned priestesses—or, as some call them, BNPs (Big Name Pagans)—have a shared quality in the way they carry themselves, the effect of this line of work. Part of it is an innate X factor, as with any kind of performer; but part of the priestess mojo, this ability to "hold space," is accrued over time. Thorn has the powerful confidence of someone who's priestessed for thousands of people, moved hundreds of acolytes at a time around in circles, in tongue-tying chants and whirligigs of ecstatic dance, for two decades. "They're like rock stars," a *Rolling Stone* writer friend says when I share this thought. "It's all that time onstage, and the way people treat them afterward. They can't help it."

There *is* a kind of Pagan rock star in our group: Sharon Knight, whose band plays what they call "gothic tribal folk metal." Sharon has the big seventies stage presence of that singer from Heart, with her guitarist boyfriend wailing away on his solos and her bassist boyfriend lending his Germanic death-metal growl. (Morpheus poses in exotic garb on their recent album cover.) Sharon is a Viking—tall, strapping, broad-shouldered, with heavy red curls falling halfway down her back—and tonight she's fastened into a gold-and-black brocade corset with huge leather cuffs around her wrists. She leans into Morpheus now and asks, "Do you ever get people you think want to be your new friend, and then instead you realize they're hanging around waiting to ask for an initiation?"

"Oh, totally. That's so annoying. Forget that."

After a while, everyone heads up to our suite. The mood set with low lighting and trance music, people pass around paper cups of wine and huddle on the floor or the beds.

The conversation turns to ritual sex: it doesn't break out as often as outsiders might think. "Although I was at a ritual for Aphrodite once," Morpheus says, "and fourteen or fifteen couples started having sex around the fire." I'm growing used to this line of talk.

At this point, destroyed by jet lag and with a full slate of rituals and workshops ahead of me tomorrow, I have to get some sleep. I nudge someone off the bedspread, crawl under the sheets, and realize that terrible electronica can be a blissful narcotic.

The Con offers up workshops, meet-and-greets, and rituals for nearly every variation on today's American Pagan: Gardnerians and Alexandrians and eclectic Wiccans and Druids and Heathens and Asatru and Feri and Golden Dawn initiates and Thelemites and nouveau Vodou and Hoodoo folk and Feraferia practitioners and Hellenic Reconstructionists and Celtic Reconstructionists and white-skinned shamans.* Events are wide-ranging, with

---

* This is mainly a white crowd, maybe because of the scene's British roots, maybe because it rose up in tandem with a very white wing of the sixties counterculture. But I soon learn that in some Pagan traditions, the influence of the African diaspora religions (Vodou in particular) transcends race lines.

lessons in Heathen ancestor rituals, Scottish folk curses, Elder Futhark runes, "otherworld travel through BDSM," prison ministry for Pagan prisoners, healing from "our conditioning in Patriarchy," Pagan twelve-step recovery, how "magical tools" can be used in the Occupy Wall Street movement, how to reclaim the slur "warlock," and psychic and magical development for kids. No attendee will agree with everything in the program—many may even feel offended or unimpressed by some of the weekend's offerings—but nearly all will find something to attend that will change their perspective on their magical practice, introduce them to another tradition or future collaborator, or inspire them to take a new approach back to their own coven, miles away. This has always been the intention of these festivals, especially for Pagans who have little community where they live, or who feel pressure to stay in the broom closet.

I'm a bit overwhelmed, so I pick at random: a guided meditation, a talk about Hermetic Qabalah, a workshop on poisonous herbs. And I make certain not to miss Avia's debut—her coming-out ball, as it were.

Avia's ritual, in one of the hotel's huge carpeted meeting rooms, is in honor of the Egyptian deity Bast, "the Great Cat Goddess." With about 150 people in attendance, and Morpheus beside her, she assumes the center of the circle, in form-fitting black, drapey sleeves, and belly dancer's jangly metalwork, with a shiny red sash slung low around her waist and a diadem around her forehead. Readying herself for the role of priestess, she looks so small, so much a child—with the super-thin limbs, puffy, round cheeks, and gangly gait of a teenager—laden with these world-of-mystery accoutrements. But her eyes have the steady look and assurance of a young person who's been trusted with more than the average mainstream kid.

Avia and her ritual helpers make a low sound to quiet the room. A chant—no, a *purr*. In step with their target deity, they purr in unison until the crowd has been tamed. And now she announces, in halting speech, that we will "raise the energy" and "deepen our relationship" with the goddess—an entity, older than Jesus and Buddha both, who will choose to visit us at the DoubleTree this morning. But while Bast is ancient, Avia is not, and the ritual is colored by her own character: sweet, openhearted, still childlike. For her, this cat goddess is just that, a goddess and a *cat*, and just as playful—and so she tosses balls of yarn into the crowd.

To my surprise, the room goes mad, batting the yarn about, using their hands like human-sized paws, the balls unraveling all throughout the circle, the drumbeats picking up speed; the people are winding themselves into the string, dancing in and out of it, some bursting into laughter; and all the while, the new priestess is chanting her tribute.

She chants, and we chant, and at some point it all slows down, and comes to a natural end. And Avia, like a stage actress, resumes her place at the center. "I am the daughter of Stone City!" she announces as loudly as she can. "This was my first ritual!"

The crowd response is instant: spontaneous applause! hooting! hollering! And at this second I realize they are making noise in deep-felt support of a passing-on, a conferral. Because that's what I've just witnessed, for all the morning's peachy yarn and purring. With every young person who takes up the mantle, in this case a girl of seventeen, the community is legitimated. First-, second-, and now third-generation American Pagans. As I head for the doors with the crush of the crowd, I encounter Morpheus, her face beaming. She squeezes my shoulder as she passes: "She *nailed* it!"

In the ground-floor lounge, a collection of striped sofas across from the concierge, I meet up with Ed Fitch, an old friend of Raymond Buckland, Gerald Gardner's ambassador in America. Ed was an early initiate of the Bucklands and a member of their Long Island group, the first recognized Wiccan coven in America. He's in his mid-seventies now, although he hardly looks it, trim in a sweatshirt, with his hair dyed black and a sporty mustache to match; he has the adorably reduced facial features and ingenuous smile of a small kid.

"Hello, dear!"

Ed is of the first wave of American witches, a pack that predates both the counterculture movement and second-wave feminism. (His generation still seems thrilled to be surrounded by liberated witch-girls.) Led by at least as many men as women, his early-Pagan clique was, compared with those who would come in the sixties and seventies, socially conservative. It also— big surprise—included a fair number of military people. In an era before the Internet or even New Age presses, the exchange of ideas—especially the secrets of a "witch cult"—had to take place in person, and work with the air force made long-distance travel possible for free.

Like Gardner, Ed was exposed to Eastern religions at a young age, stationed in Japan as an air force officer in the fifties. During that period, he did more and more research into "exotic" practices and the occult, eventually reading Gardner's *Witchcraft Today*. Back in Baltimore between enlistments, Ed would go to the airport library, where he stumbled across *Sign of the Labrys*, a novel by the American Margaret St. Clair. The book's descriptions of witchcraft practice instantly reminded him of Gardner's cult. Eager to know more, he wrote to Margaret and was invited to her house in Richmond, California. There he learned that in 1966 Margaret and her husband had been initiated by Buckland, Wicca's official representative in America—himself, incidentally, a *British* pilot—who'd flown out from Long Island to perform the ritual. Margaret wrote to the Bucklands recommending Ed for the Craft. While on leave nearby, he went to Long Island to visit, and the Bucklands soon made him a high priest.

Between 1964 and 1972, before they retired to become community "elders," the Bucklands only initiated a total of twenty advanced third-degree Wiccans. But interest in the Craft was outstripping the couple's ability to teach and initiate. And so, in 1969, Ed was part of a small group that created the Pagan Way, a Wiccan group designed to spread the witchy word to the curious without divulging inner-circle secrets. Ed wrote and assembled introductory rituals for the collective that were absorbed broadly into the Pagan community as standard practice. In the eighties, people were still incorporating these texts, assuming—in another instance of spurious lineage—that they were somehow derived from ancient Celtic sources. Sometimes even today, nearly fifty years later, Ed will be at a ritual with younger Pagans and hear them pronounce words they don't realize he wrote himself, as if the chant had been handed down through the centuries.

Ed is mostly inactive now, relocated to Austin, Texas, to live with his son, having retired from a long string of jobs—as a private detective, a shopkeeper at Disneyland, and an electronics engineer. His memories of the early days of the Craft are clearly among his happiest, a time of great invention and possibility.

As I'm about to take my leave, Ed picks up my palm—he's read plenty in his day—and examines it. "Mmm . . . You will pursue two paths," he starts in, "so choose carefully . . . I see you're in a few relationships . . . I see a lot of love and sensuality—"

He draws in his breath. He now looks genuinely concerned. "Ooh, but put some Kevlar over your heart, my dear, because *you* can get hurt. You really should protect yourself."

Ed has touched on an unexpected truth. I'm feeling exposed. Something happens when I spend time with strangers like this, asking them intimate questions: I become vulnerable in return. When you ask people to let you in, you give something up in exchange—it's inevitable. This may be the reason I dream up these projects in the first place, some part of me hoping I'll be forced into a corner, forced to open up. Because I've been planting myself in heady situations for some time now.

A few years ago, while first researching the documentary, I stayed on and off with a surviving Jesus Movement* community in Southern California, one of maybe fifty outposts around the country. The rambling wood-shingled house had about forty inhabitants, and another sixty lived twenty minutes away, on a farm complete with vast avocado and grapefruit groves. I shared a room of bunk beds with the unmarried women and borrowed their homemade clothes, almost Amish in modesty: ankle-length muumuus and long-sleeved shirts. The average day, bookended by folksy hymns and circle dances, could last eighteen hours, with nonstop communal labor and worship. The men worked in their woodshop in town; the women spent their time schooling the children, cleaning the house, and making gross numbers of sandwiches for the men to eat at their construction sites. I swept the meeting room, peeled vegetables, and sometimes woke at five in the morning to milk the goats.

That winter alone, the community baptized nine new people, and I witnessed one young man's "rebirth": at eleven o'clock at night, shining our flashlights on the water, we sang for Yahshua in front of a row of well-appointed beachfront homes as Jacob was dunked into the freezing-cold ocean. He died that night—that's what they called it, leaving your old self and kinships and longings behind. "Are you ready to die?" they'd asked him.

That same evening, one of the men asked me, "Wasn't it dangerous for

---

* This was the name for a Christian offshoot of the seventies counterculture, populated mostly by hippies who decided to reject drugs and free love in favor of staunch religion.

you to come out here all alone, not even knowing us? Isn't that a little bit crazy?" I was struck by the bluntness of his question, as if my logic made even less sense than theirs, with their rigorous constraints and radical baptisms. Then again, from their perspective, I was a wandering loner. I had no community.

Each day I listened closely; I nodded. I respected where people were coming from, even when it was alien to me. And I offered up my own patchwork of beliefs in return: my mother's thoroughly overhauled Catholicism, my long-standing doubts, my gut-level discomfort with organized religion. "I believe in *something*," I would say on cue, "but I'm not sure what." Being there was exhausting: the keeping-up of appropriate behavior, smiling the right smile, always displaying a more-than-clinical interest. But it could be soothing, too: the anonymity; the implicit acceptance; the lack of interest in where I was coming from, what work I did, who constituted my social network back at home. In their minds, it was enough that I'd chosen to be there.

On certain Sundays, we would pile into vans and pickups and make the trip to the farm. Under cover from the sun, all hundred sisters and brothers would listen to a talk by one of the community's wisemen, on a fine point of discourse, and then we'd eat picnic lunches on the green hillside. With everyone spread out across the lawn in tent dresses and aprons, no technology in sight, just clapboard farmhouses and goat pens, I was reminded of some Puritan settlers' scene.

One such day at the farm—bright, open, airy—I approached Othniel, still seeking permission for my film among the inner circle of men. In his late fifties, Othniel was handsome despite a pitted, knobby nose, lean and tall, his chalk-white hair plaited into a short braid. As with the rest of the community's clique of decision makers, the look in his eyes (bright blue) was trenchant, and utterly winning.

"You've got spunk!" he said. "I like that. We've got to get you in with the other women and really have it out. You should hear what they have to say about *submission*, about women submitting to men." I visibly prickled at this, and Othniel laughed—he was enjoying himself. He knew what I wanted that day: to shoot a few minutes' footage on the grounds, for the first time. He did not stand in my way.

"I understand that's how you process the world: through a camera, through some kind of 'project,'" Othniel said. "But one day you're going to let go of all that. You'll see it's just a lot of *stuff.* An obstacle. A way of staying in control. For now, you go ahead and do what makes you comfortable."

Once back in New York City, in my downtown apartment, I got a phone call from Othniel's "brother" Mevaser. He informed me of their decision: permission denied. "What we would really like," he said, "is for you to become our sister. And we think your filming would simply get in the way."

When I hung up, I sat for a long time with my head in my hands, as if it were too heavy for me to lift. I was disturbed, nauseous—and not only because the project had been derailed. I'd been emotionally sideswiped. A relationship, one I'd immersed myself in too deeply, a courtship that had lasted for months, had come to an abrupt end. I looked at Mevaser's number in my phone—stacked between those of a magazine editor and a film-festival programmer—and I could not comprehend that I would never return to the community again. I did not need to make sandwiches all day for Yahshua's army of carpenters, believe me, but my time with them had revealed something hidden: a deep chink in my armor. Perhaps it's a capacity for attachment, a strong sentimental streak, or an embarrassing *need.*

All this is to say: Kevlar would have been a good idea at the time. And it may be a good idea now.

"We are often possessed, and don't realize it," the program description reads. "Come liberate your soul!" Tonight, in two ballrooms combined, an "exorcism" ritual will be performed by the Feri squad, including Morpheus, Sharon, Thorn, and their friend Anaar. I've been hoping for an experience to send a charge through me this weekend—the charge of something new. Perhaps tonight's exorcism is it.

Morpheus's ritual last year had just that effect.

It took place in the same giant space, and the lineup was much like this evening's: Morpheus, Thorn, Sharon—BNPs all. But, unlike the group "liberation" that this year promises, that ritual was as directional as a laser beam: a devotional to the Celtic goddess Morpheus works with, the Morrigan. A goddess of war, death, and prophecy (no lightweight) was to be invoked straight through Morpheus's body. The ceremony promised to "raise the power to feed the Great Queen."

A capacity crowd of about four hundred turned out, forming a ring many Pagans deep around the inner circle of priestesses. The circle was consecrated, I'm sure, and there was some chanting. But there is no completely sensible way to write about what followed.

I had seen Morpheus lead ritual before—but mostly for the sabbats, and not in a display of devotion to the goddess with whom she feels a penetrating connection. I'd also never seen my friend do a possession, and that is what happened—a deep one.

At a certain point, Morpheus's body doubled over and began bobbing up and down as if something was bubbling up inside her. After what felt like a long time, she raised her head—and there had been a change. She took on a voice that was two musical strains at once: her own high-pitched girlish tones and, at the same time, something snarling, a sound coming from halfway down her throat. I guess Morpheus was channeling *her*.

She stalked the edge of the wide circle, staring into the faces of the crowd. She flapped the vulture wings strapped to her arms, more animal now, and everyone in attendance seemed to respond with the rising energy of a gathering pack. The feeling in the room was rougher and less contained—more contagious—than anything I'd encountered before. The priestesses circled closer, tightening around her. Standing by a tranced-out Morpheus, Sharon lifted a heavy sword above our heads. *Take a vow*, she directed us. *But only if it's one you can keep. Don't take it lightly.*

To my surprise, as Morpheus (or the battle goddess) continued heaving, breathing hard, her slender frame so much heavier now, I approached. I stepped forward with the others, raised my hand up to touch the tip of the blade, and took a vow.

Once it was over, Morpheus collapsed, immediately wiped out. She could not talk to anyone, only the ritual crew, turning away even from the people she knew. One Pagan told me that, as soon as the ritual had ended, she'd "wanted nothing more than to curl up in a ball like a little kitten" near Morpheus's feet. Others lingered, too, to be near the priestess—who'd only moments ago been the carrier of their goddess—and her friends covered her head with a shawl just to shuttle her out of the room.

"It happens almost every time she comes into me," Morpheus told me. "When she leaves, I feel dead."

Morpheus had to lie on the bed in our hotel suite afterward, tended to by

Thorn—but she snapped to for a moment when she overheard my conversation. "You took a vow?" she asked. This left her pretty pleased, though I couldn't give myself too much credit. It was probably my lizard brain, and its superstitious thinking, that had made me push ahead of the crowd.

Like Morpheus's devotional to the Morrigan, tonight's "exorcism" is a Feri ritual. The tradition was started in the fifties in southern Oregon by a blind poet and shaman, Grandmaster Victor Anderson, who considered himself a kahuna, a Vodou priest, and a slew of other religious titles, based on the many past lives he could recall in great detail. Though Feri is a "mystery cult," or a tradition whose secrets can only be revealed through initiation, it's a fast-growing spiritual group—at least in California—with its own sects and passionate disagreements about how to pass on the tradition. I knew less about Feri then than I do now, but I could already feel a real contrast, in circle, between a ritual led by Feris and one led by eclectic Wiccans: Feri magic, for whatever reason, is more spontaneous, more primal, more ecstatic.

Nervous about making it inside, I show up a half hour ahead, and a line of about fifty people has already formed. The line will wind down the hall, past the snack bar, and down the stairs by the time they're ready to let us in.

People stream into the darkened double ballroom and find places around the edge of a wide, precisely laid-out circle of folding chairs. The inside of the circle is gently lit; the few hundred participants seem to be accumulating in the shadows at its edges. The circle contains four priestesses, two drummers, a large white orb of artificial light balanced atop an altar. I can also see now that the area has been mapped out with tape, dividing it into quarters, with pathways sketched out on the carpet leading in and out. Everyone is informed that the seats are only for those who cannot stand. The chairs steadily fill with elderly Pagans who move stiffly with their walking sticks, their heavy charm necklaces swaying as they stutter forward to take their spots.

Eventually, the hall attendants pull the ballroom doors shut behind them. The room falls silent.

Anaar, the most intimate student of Grandmaster Victor Anderson, steps forward, in elegant black—and socks. She has the wiry body of a performer, a dancer (I once watched her belly-dance with a sword balanced on her head). She tells us about this evening's ritual, inspired by a North African dance to exorcise negative forces. What *we're* going to exorcise tonight, rather than the bogeyman or the Christian Devil, are the more commonplace specters: "Shame, Fear, Obsession, Rage, and Greed." Anaar shows us how to propel these spooks out of our psyches by demonstrating an aggressive, full-body move "like head-banging." The other route, for the lighter-headed folks, is to fling out your arms, whipping them through the air. "But really *do it!*" she orders us. We will dance out each of these emotional demons one by one.

Getting ready for who-knows-what, I unzip my boots and chuck them under the chair in front of me. If I've learned one thing from a couple of years of Pagan rituals, it's that you can't stand outside the ecstatic action for long. I catch a glimpse of Thorn, in black leather pants, her bare arms tattooed over in obscure symbols. She sits cross-legged by the orb of light, ready to *hold space*; her boyfriends stand at the circle's edge in vigilant support, like long-haired sentinels.

Now Morpheus emerges, in diaphanous beaded blue. Her hair has been brushed out to an extravagant length cultivated only by fundamentalists and witches. Her skirt is slit up the side, and her flat white belly flashes from under a cropped leather corset. She swings a sword to call the four quarters, stalking the perimeter. As with each time I've seen her priestess, something happens: as she gets into a groove, *her light turns on.* Her limbs seem to grow longer, more languid; her steps take on a rhythm; her eyes project a kind of frenzy into the crowd.

Sharon rises to join Morpheus, the sylph and the Viking, two sister-witches with trains of red hair.

"Shame!" Morpheus calls out in her priestessing voice, high-pitched and severe. "It eats away at you . . ."

"Shame!" Sharon calls out as the pair start to stomp through the space. "I'm not good enough . . . Never good enough . . ." It's a theater of the psyche. They take turns calling out, acting out the monster at hand.

"I've *failed!*" Morpheus shouts. "I'll never be enough . . . *Shame* . . ."

The drums pick up, asking us to enter.

I stand by as people begin to trickle into the circle along the paths mapped out on the floor. Soon they are *dancing* Shame, the specter of Shame, banging their heads in heavy-metal style, swaying and thrashing side to side, flinging it out through their arms and the ends of their fingers. People are dancing just to get up and dance—or, as slowly becomes apparent, because they *really need to*, much more than their priestesses do. Pagans of all shapes and sizes are dancing: horned or hippied out or dressed in flannel, barefoot or in rainbow-striped socks. Their frustration and anger and need are palpable. One very obese woman has chosen to go topless: her breasts are so pendulous they hang nearly to her navel, flattened into thick slabs. It is clear she is dancing a word that means something to her. She's dancing it off, waving her arms, her skin rippling, and her long, frizzed-out hair askew. A large-bodied misfit.

"Rage" conjures up the most head-thrashing and guttural shouting, chanting, screaming, pounding of fists on the carpeted floor, all in a disjointed circle around the drummers and Feri priestesses. The dancers come in every incarnation: a voluptuous twenty-something with wild blue hair in a lace nightdress; a guy in long Bermuda shorts, a sun hat swinging on the string around his neck as he bucks his head.

"Obsession" finds Avia kneeling alongside Thorn, furiously shaking out her skinny arms, looking distressed. The scene calls to mind, in a flash, a seventies experimental-psych treatment—say, primal therapy, or something else in R. D. Laing's repertoire. An attempt at mass catharsis. When a religion does not designate you a sinner from birth, when a religion assumes you're already in decent standing with your god (or gods), leaving no reason for penance, then the object of its rituals is left wide open. Tonight is no devotional. We are doing ritual, instead, to improve ourselves: self-help through ecstatic ceremony. And seventeen-year-old Avia continues to rock back and forth on her knees on the ballroom floor.

As I watch this tribe of grown men and women pitch their figures across the darkened space with abandon, relentless, I realize this is one of those moments. I mean, not *many* moments are precisely like this one, that's for certain. But I am talking about how, in a singular situation, at a singular time—at the witching hour, if you will—a person can find herself thoroughly unsettled. At such a moment, the weakest part of you floats up through viscous liquid, up through your gut, your intestines, your fleshy arteries, through the very source points of your wateriest emotions, as unstable as water. Anything becomes possible, and a person finds she is capable of many things.

So this is how I start to dance.

The priestesses call "Fear," and I launch into thinking: "*I* have that. *I* am afraid." Of money, of being judged, of loneliness, of growing old and used up. Part of me wants desperately to snip the wires of my self-conscious brain loop, to stop caring about appearances. I'm here, aren't I? No point in being coy now! And, pushing past my embarrassment, I step forward. I enter the circle. I get into some kind of tribal rhythm, stamping the balls of my feet. I stamp the ground harder and harder, and start pitching my arms out in front of me. I do this until my wrists hurt. The drums don't stop, and the people in the circle don't stop, all these Pagans—and so I keep going. And after enough of this, I have a surprising reaction: I want to sob, deeply, the kind where, if you let it out, it will come for three days without stopping—

Morpheus shouts, "Let the poisons become power!" Is that what the people in this room are doing? *I* don't know how to do that. All I want to do is cry, and I have no idea why.

But some part of me, the scaffolding around my presentation of myself, holds fast, and I don't cave. Having denied myself the release of, I guess, a nervous breakdown, I simply feel uncovered, a lame exhibitionist. What would my people think if they saw me here?

In the nick of time, Fear winds down, and we return to our spots in the outer ring. I am off-kilter.

Now that all these demons, or the idea of them, have been danced out by nearly every combination of the people at hand, Morpheus steps forward with the sword once again. She swings it slowly above her head, tracing a shape in space, to close the circle. Then, finally, grinning, she slides the blade underneath the altar table.

Everyone files out.

In the lobby bar once more, people are toast, utterly exhausted by three days and nights of Pagan derring-do. It's the end of the long weekend's rituals; it's the end of the Con.

It's also possibly the end of a marriage. Across the table I overhear Morpheus talking to Thorn, hand in hand: "I'm trying to hold on to Stone City as best I can." She sees my look of concern. "This is what happens when you dedicate yourself to a war goddess," she says with a sporting laugh. I understand she's talking about the Morrigan—a goddess known in these circles for her demanding nature, for her persistent, aggressive questioning of the status quo.

Thorn is a charmer tonight, funny and tuckered out from the weekend. When not comforting Morpheus, she trades inside jokes with the rest of the clique and consorts with her sweetie Robert. He's in full drag for the evening, in a cream-colored woman's blouse and tasteful clip-on earrings, his eyebrows painted in *just so.*

Thorn's other fellow, Jonathan, is on my left, and we get to talking. A ceremonial magician in the tradition of the Golden Dawn, he's a suit-and-tie Pagan, but he also flaunts about two feet of curly brown hair and a thick hoop earring. He's a few Scotches to the wind, but I can see a thought forming. "You know, we have a grand tradition of anthropologists coming in to study the phenomenon and going native," he says, enjoying himself. If the offer of initiation were ever on the table, would I say yes?

Just then, Morpheus, ready to turn in, stands and leans over me at the table, her red hair falling close to my face, pungent with her signature priestess scent. "You seem to be having fun," she says with a smile. "It's like you're part of the community now."

An hour later, I am asleep. A day later, I've returned to New York, to the acceptable parameters of my daily life. Two weeks later, Morpheus informs me that, bolstered by the Morrigan, she's left both her husband and Stone City, the sanctuary she built over eight long years, and moved in with a friend in the nearest town. Her Celtic goddess has asked her to take up survival training, martial arts, and "fighter" practice; she has also requested that Morpheus formalize a new priesthood in her name.

A few days after *that*, I receive a snapshot by e-mail. In this photo, Morpheus lies topless on her stomach, her hair swept up off her neck. On her bare upper back, along the ridges of her spine, is painfully etched in black and red the outline of a large spearhead. For Morpheus's birthday, the spring equinox, she began this ritual tattoo as a renewal of her oath to the Morrigan. Sharon and Thorn drummed and sang and invoked the goddess into the tattoo, she writes, "and it was a completely ecstatic experience in spite of the pain."

Looking at this image, her perfectly white skin red and puffed all around the spearhead's shaft, I think: This is what people mean when they talk about a *calling*. The countless traditions of this community are narrowed down to one, and then that path is narrowed further still, honed through bodily pain and ceremonial frenzy and voices that only you can hear. And in that process, the shapeless disappointments of pedestrian life give way, and everything you do suddenly has heft and meaning. A clear path of action emerges.

5

The Feri Current

Twice now, I've taken part in massive rituals led by Feri witches and been drawn in deeper than I'd anticipated. I decide to learn more about this strain of the Craft, the tradition in which Morpheus found her calling.

Much as the New Forest called to Gerald Gardner and the redwoods of the Santa Cruz Mountains called to Morpheus perched on her parents' rooftop, the Northwest woods of Bend, Oregon, drew young Victor Anderson away from his family home. One day, walking through the trees—it was 1926, and he was nine—the boy came upon a small, dark-skinned older woman sitting naked in the center of a circle ringed with brass bowls of herbs. She invited Victor, who was mostly blind, into the circle, where he understood he should take off his clothes; then the witch—for this is what she called herself—initiated the boy, sexually and magically. Even without his sight, the ritual sparked a vision: he saw the strange woman transform into *God Herself*, and the woods turn to thick green jungle, and the sky fill with a large green moon. And Victor watched as a slim, feminine man emerged naked from between the trees, towering and horned, cock erect, blue flames wrapping his head like a crown.

The vision passed. The woman rubbed young Victor's body with oil and butter and salt, and told him that he would soon meet others like himself. Now he understood: he was one of her people, of "the Fairy race." He was a witch. Then the small, dark, nameless woman sent the boy home.

Much about this story is troubling—even for some Feri initiates. Setting aside the wildness of Victor's jungle vision, who is this woman who sexually molested a nine-year-old in the woods? How are we supposed to accept this as the bright start of a prominent priest's spiritual journey? And what witch truly works that way, forcing an underage passerby to take part in an intimate ritual usually reserved for adults after years of study? But just as many Wiccans aren't concerned about Gardner's New Forest beginnings or don't feel the need to discern between what Gardner inherited, borrowed, or made up out of whole cloth, many Feris don't feel the need to sweat the details of their origin. A common refrain is: "As long as the magic *works*." Many Pagans today, particularly on the West Coast, view Victor's Craft descendants and their strain of magic with respect: Feris now make up a small but influential clan—like those I'd met and circled with at PantheaCon—with a reputation for being especially intense. Victor's combination of American witchcraft and African diaspora practices with the techniques of the coven he'd discover as an adult in the Northwest gave birth to a tradition more ecstatic and visceral than what much of the eclectic Pagan community experiences at their sabbats.

Victor's genealogy is both exotic and deeply American, combining a few of this country's hidden populations. His father was a ranch worker, as well as a Freemason; his mother's grandmother was one of the storied "blue people" of Appalachia, who carry a genetic mutation that turns their skin bright blue and, some believe, lends them extrasensory perception. The family moved around the West, following his father's work as a ranch hand, carpenter, and fruit farmer, and Victor was often left to play with the children of itinerant laborers who were, over the years, from Mexico, Hawaii, and the Caribbean. His own appearance was racially ambiguous enough that, as his wife would later write, "every culture claimed him as their own." The youngest of six, Victor was delivered by his father in a home birth on a New Mexico cattle ranch where he worked. After Victor's teenage sister accidentally dropped him on the basement floor at the age of two, he was left legally blind. When his mother returned from taking him to a specialist, she was informed that Robert, her oldest, had been killed in a barn fire while they were away. At the news, she suffered a nervous breakdown; she remained emotionally and mentally unstable for the rest of her life.

With extremely limited sight, young Victor somehow managed to get around. More than that, his weak eyes, he would later claim, led him to focus on the development of his "etheric" sight, or how to see the spiritual realm. By the age of five, he'd had one of his first visions: of the goddess Isis (not otherwise known to make appearances in Albuquerque) wrapped in an American flag. While his own family was devoutly Christian, regularly attending the local Baptist church, Victor was supposedly being visited by the ancient Egyptian mother of magic. Within a few years, he would experience his sexual initiation in the woods, launching him down a radically divergent path.

Victor's family moved to Ashland, Oregon, where his father built houses on the nearby army base. During this time, he'd later say, the migrant workers, from Hawaii and Haiti, were inspired to train him, respectively, in native Hawaiian magic and Vodou. While other kids were busy with high school, or working menial jobs, Victor grew into a kahuna and a Vodou priest. (In particular, he developed a close relationship with the Vodou spirit Papa Legba—sometimes a wise old man, sometimes young, horned, and erect—who serves as the gatekeeper between the worlds. Victor would open every ritual by calling him.) He eventually claimed fluency in Hawaiian, Spanish, Creole, Italian, Greek, and Gaelic—languages he said he recalled from his many past lives.

At the age of fifteen, Victor was secretly welcomed into his first coven. The Harpy Coven was a motley crew from all over the country, made up of migrants from the Deep South and recent Dust Bowl refugees who'd ended up in Oregon. (There's an unexplained discrepancy between Victor's age—fifteen upon joining Harpy Coven, in 1932—and the timing of the Dust Bowl droughts—mid-to-late thirties—but so goes the story.) According to Victor, these witches successfully passed as Christians in the community, as do their descendants today. (Later on, when he had initiates of his own, Victor would request that his Harpy covenmates' names be kept secret so that they could remain in the broom closet.) Harpy sabbats had little of the scripted liturgy that Gardnerian Wicca would bring over from England in the fifties and sixties: the rituals were more like local church suppers, with a potluck meal and dancing. Most magical work was low-key, done in the members' kitchens in small groups, and there was no public practice. Through Victor, this subtle style of magical working would eventually spawn a heady, ecstatic American Craft tradition.

By the early fifties, Victor and his wife, Cora, had moved to San Leandro, California, where they would stay for the rest of their lives. She cooked in hospitals and nursing homes to pay the bills. Meanwhile, Victor, who wrote short stories and poetry, read voraciously, regularly borrowing books from the library: anything by H. P. Lovecraft, or on the history of witchcraft. He brought home Gardner's *Witchcraft Today*, which had just been published, and briefly corresponded with Wicca's patient zero. Wicca and its offshoots had yet to take hold in the United States—that would not happen until the sixties—but, sensing a kindred spirit, Victor considered initiation with Gardner. He nixed that idea, however, when he realized he disagreed with Gardner's approach, his hunger for publicity: the Craft should not attract that level of attention.

Still, the rise of Wicca inspired Victor to take on his own students, in *his* flavor of witchcraft. The first Feri disciples began to gather in Northern California.

As Wicca caught on, naming began to seem important, and so Victor dubbed the tradition he was transmitting "Feri" (also spelled "Fairy" and "Faery" early on). He claimed that Feri was first practiced tens of thousands of years ago, by a small-bodied, dark-skinned people out of Africa, the first "Fairy folk"—not to be confused with the winged nature spirits of the same name. According to Victor, these people were were highly psychic and skilled in practical magic. "I was not converted," Victor would say of his initiation in the woods long ago. "I am kin to the Fairy race!" Or, as Tod Browning would put it, "One of us! One of us!"

What Victor himself passed on to his students in the sixties—and what future Feris such as Morpheus and Thorn would later learn—was his own combination of Hawaiian Huna magic, Santería, Vodou, and Harpy Coven practices, built around a few basic techniques he presented as essential witchcraft. As with his former, now-disbanded coven, you didn't have to stand in a consecrated ritual space—magical workings could just as easily take place in your living room. Also unlike Wicca, which is defined by the polarity of the male and the female, and the power of bringing those two separate forces together (Gardner's sex magic was very heterosexual), Feri believes that the dichotomies we're taught in this culture—light versus dark, "good" versus "bad," male versus female—are far more fluid. Put crudely, the universe is a swirling mess, as is every one of us; and life is a striving for balance between these disparate-seeming qualities.

For many in the Craft—and in Morpheus's experience, ever since she was a young girl playing with her blue-haired witch doll—magic is inherently sexual. Even if you set aside the story of young Victor's initiation, this remains particularly true for Feri: as his wife, Cora, would later write, "We are what the missionary would call a sex cult"—if by "sex" you mean, basically, whatever the universe runs on. Feri, like other Craft traditions, requires that you learn to "run" that energy—as when Morpheus learned how.

She was twenty the first time she circled skyclad, almost a year into her Feri training: her witch-teacher, Linnea, had invited her along to the home of an older friend, then a well-known local Gardnerian. Morpheus remembers climbing a staircase in his rambling mansion to a hidden door that in turn led to a secret set of stairs that then led, finally, to an attic ritual room where she joined a group of strangers—Gardnerians and Feris between their forties and sixties. When it was time to begin, she felt a little self-conscious, not because of her body image—she was as lean as she is now, attractive, and confident—but more because she was wary of unwanted attention. These older witches, some of them former or current lovers, were all flirting—something the twenty-year-old was surprised to see came naturally to people in middle age or later—but no one was making a pass. Morpheus realized this was "all part of allowing that sexual energy to rise and bubble up and fuel your magic." That redirected sexual energy felt very effective. "It puts you in this primal way of relating to what's around you," she says. It also makes you vulnerable to the point of altering your state of consciousness. "That vulnerability is pretty powerful," she says, and for magic, "it might be irreplaceable." Whenever she's been in a relationship where there's been a strong sexual connection, she's also tended to be more magically active. "The strongest magic I do usually happens when there's at least some degree of sexual arousal going on."

For most of his life, Victor had a partner with whom he was attuned both in magic and in life. He met Cora when he was in his early twenties; she worked in a shop at the local army camp. He invited her out for a walk and proposed to her that same night (his mother bought her a $5 ring). They were married three days later. The newlyweds moved into a one-room cabin in nearby, thoroughly Christian Bend. Thoroughly broke, Victor went on welfare to pay the bills, eventually finding odd gigs playing the accordion at the local Elks lodge, and later for the Salvation Army.

Victor told Cora very little about the Harpy Coven, and they never explicitly used the word "witchcraft." But while her sister was a traveling Baptist preacher, suspicious of Victor's spiritual leanings, Cora was not a stranger to the Craft: her grandfather had been a root doctor, an herbal healer in Ireland before he emigrated, and her grandmother a "gypsy." She and Victor were psychically connected in ways that surprised him: after a trip into town, he would return home only to have his wife recount to him where he'd been. The couple soon began doing spells together. Victor was the grand magician, a heady presence in the room; Cora was down-home, an equally intuitive "kitchen witch." They were a perfect match: Victor would go off into ecstatic prayer, focusing his work on another plane, and Cora would cook a healing soup, or do other seemingly mundane housework she infused with magic. They were never too up-front about their practices, though they built an altar in their house, causing Cora's mother to comment, "Don't you know that will be of the Devil?" Cora replied with a Bible quote she loved: "Try the spirits and see if they be of God."

Much later, once he began taking on Feri students, Victor became the anti-guru, an elderly blind man, compact and diminutive as the "little people" he claimed to be descended from, with long, oversized ears and thick, demonstrative eyebrows, often sporting the kind of aggressively squared-off eyeglasses that now have a retro chic. He stuck to high-waisted, belted slacks and plain buttoned-down shirts, a pen clipped into his breast pocket. Victor's teaching style, similarly informal and just as hard to pin down, became a thing of legend. If a prospective student rang him up—and if that person was not too timid or overly polite—a series of long phone chats about magical practice might lead to an invitation to the Andersons' house. Once there, you would sit by Victor's rocking chair and listen to him tell seemingly free-form stories about various strains of magic and the fabric of the universe and the divisions of the human soul.

He spoke with a lilt, in a smooth, singsong baritone, and his lessons could sometimes be as elliptical as song lyrics. You could say his teaching method was Socratic: students were expected to arrive with questions, but they would rarely receive a direct answer—not even close. A lot of work with him involved analyzing his poetry on command. Inevitably dissatisfied with the response, Victor would grow impatient, shift in his chair, and pronounce a verdict of "Not really!" He was a "trickster-teacher," one initiate would say: he would tell stories, of true events or merely spiritual allegories, who could tell? Yet *some* lesson was to be absorbed through this telling, slipped into the student's consciousness like a time-release capsule. And when a younger witch was ready—ready for initiation—Victor just *knew*.

While the Craft still had only a very limited following, Victor trained a small circle of witches who went on to found their own Feri lines (Vanthe, which Morpheus studied, was one of the first offshoots). Each of those covens created its own priests, many of whom became teachers as well. And for decades, mostly in secret, the tradition continued spiraling outward.

Unlike Wicca, which initiates its priests and priestesses step by step, through "degrees," Feri has one momentous initiation that shocks your system, welcomes you into the clan, and gives you the right to teach and initiate others—all in a single stroke. For this reason, the ceremony is not entered into lightly. After three years of training with Linnea, from the age of nineteen to twenty-two, Morpheus felt prepared to join the Feri bloodline. "I no longer felt there was a thing that was *waiting*—it felt like it was actually moving *through* me." And so her teacher agreed to initiate her.

Everyone gathered at Linnea's place for the rite. Shannon drove Morpheus from where they were living then, in San Jose, and when they arrived, "the veil was drawn" (as they say). Though he was her husband, Shannon, not a Feri initiate himself, had to remain in the neighboring house, owned by two other Vanthe covenmates, as they performed the ceremony.

Feri initiation has as its key element the passing on of secret names and the magical "current" that is Feri. Traditionally, the priest or priestess initiates the candidate by giving her the names of God Herself and her "consort" at orgasm during sex. If the candidate has her own partner, she has sex with that person before or after being given the names; if she is single, and simply does not *want* to do it with the priest, she is given the names with the understanding that the ceremony will not be complete until the next time she has sex with someone. In Morpheus's case, she walked out of the ritual circle and into the night air, under the redwoods, and stepped slowly, buzzing still, up the path to where Shannon was waiting to help bring the ceremony to a close. Now she knew the secret names of her gods, and once she and her husband finished, she had married them, too. Along with this knowledge came full membership in the coven: she inherited one of their medallions to wear in circle, palm-sized and teardrop-shaped, decorated with the Vanthe emblem in enamel—a poppy with black starry wings and outstretched hands.

For several weeks afterward, Morpheus felt palpably different, transformed. Her senses were blown open—like being a "raw nerve," or not having any skin. And now the other world was as present and vibrant as the physical world. She was plugged into a line of witches going back through history; she could literally *feel* their DNA in her blood and hear them whisper in her ears. She welcomed it. *Yes! This is really real! This is happening to me! This thing is happening.*

In Victor's later years, when he was in his sixties and seventies, he would teach a new generation of Feris—including Thorn, who would become a very influential Craft teacher herself; and Anaar, who would care for the Andersons in their old age, eventually taking on the mantle of grandmaster herself.

I'd seen Anaar lead the "exorcism" ritual at PantheaCon, in her no-fuss, straight-talking style. But the first time I ever laid eyes on her, she was bellydancing at a benefit for Stone City, showing off the life-sized peacock feather tattooed to arch over each hip as she performed her ritual knife dance. Half Midwestern and half Japanese, Anaar was raised on a military base in Japan by parents who were staunch atheists. She now lives in bright, hilly Castro Valley with her husband, a nuclear physicist, growing figs in her backyard and baking her own scones.

After her family moved to Hawaii while she was in her teens, Anaar first heard about the local spirits and saw pictures of real-life witches in a book. But she was not impressed: "I just thought, 'What freaks!'" In her twenties, however, she read about Feri, and "something in my brain lit up." Once her husband relocated them to California so he could work at Stanford, she sought out those mysterious West Coast witches, and after a string of Feri teachers, decided to go to the source. She got hold of Victor's number, and finally worked up the nerve to approach him. They corresponded—he sent her audio recordings of his thoughts—and eventually she was invited to visit the Andersons' house.

By the time Anaar began studying with Victor, in the early nineties, he had been experiencing health problems and, often in pain or discomfort, would stay indoors in his rocking chair. The Andersons were in their seventies then, and kept the house warm and stuffy. While Cora, in a simple housedress, watched quietly from the sofa, rising only to prepare a (literally) magical meal in the kitchen, Victor's students would sit, listening closely to his stream-of-consciousness lessons, taking whatever notes they could, never sure of what he would impart next or what weight his words might have for them later. (Anaar told her kids he was like Yoda. Cora described him as "an Einstein of the occult.") Anaar remembers taking him on trips to the supermarket, for which he'd dress up in a parka with the pointed hood zipped all the way up. "He looked like a garden gnome!" From this reserved older couple sprang a ritual style known in the Craft community for its ecstatic intensity and sexual charge. "Feri has an energy signature," Anaar says. "Like the prickling of the skin right before you get that electric shock—not the shock *itself*, but that current that runs through you just before."

In early 2001, Cora suffered a bad stroke, and Victor grew frustrated with her worsening condition. As a respected priest and healer, he had the idea he could fix her. He watched as his partner was committed to a hospital, then a nursing home, then moved back in with a series of caregivers—and his frustration mounted. What good were all his years of magic—*lifetimes*, even—if he couldn't help the person closest to him? "Victor grew angrier, and people began to float away," Anaar says. "I thought, 'This is when we should all pitch in.' But very few people were solid."

Then, while all the attention was on Cora, Victor suddenly died.

When a religious leader dies abruptly, even the head of a relatively small mystery cult, the tradition is threatened with collapse without its charismatic center. Victor's unexpected death left a vacuum. To fill the void, the initiates moved quickly to transfer the grandmaster title to Cora, the obvious choice.

That move, however, proved problematic: although she had been Victor's magical partner nearly all his life, his widow was now older and mostly bedridden (she would never walk again), and some Feris weren't taking her seriously. Anaar believes there was a slightly sexist edge to some initiates' dismissal of Cora, even within a community of witches. "She was the quiet one in the kitchen, and in this culture you don't take the woman in the kitchen seriously. But it was unwise to underestimate her. I feel strongly that neither I nor many others would have been initiated by Victor without her approval."

With Victor out of the picture, a few people began to take advantage of Cora, who was now very elderly and often alone. Certain individuals put forth false claims of initiation, assuming Cora would not contradict them; as visitors came and went, things started to go missing from her house. While Anaar had no interest in assuming an authoritative role, in order to stabilize the situation, Cora pressed her to take over as grandmaster. "She kept at me—she needed someone younger to stand up." As part of the transition, a small group gathered and held a ritual, and then Anaar sent up the papal smoke (an e-mail statement), announcing the shift to all Feri initiates, and taking up the largely symbolic role of carrying on the tradition and serving as mediator among these headstrong, fiercely independent witches. Magical order was restored.

After Anaar inherited the mantle, Cora survived for another four years, bedridden, insisting on staying in her own house, even if this meant being alone for hours at a stretch. She had a caregiver by day, friends who would occasionally visit at night, and a TV and DVD player installed over the foot of her bed for repeated viewings of the Coen brothers' *O Brother, Where Art Thou?* (the music reminded her of her Alabama childhood). And in this way died the second grandmaster of the Feri tradition.

And now it is up to Victor and Cora's magical descendants to pass on the Feri current, its "energy signature," like the current that runs through you before an electric shock. How many initiates are there today—one hundred? And how many lines have they founded—a dozen?

Initiates and their students continue to study and magically improvise, like artists, like free people. "Just as the poet and musician can create great works through inspiration," Cora wrote, "so we of the Old Religion can make new rituals and services to our Gods. This religion is not a dead fossil, but a living growing human experience." The Craft, as Feri folk see it, is always being regenerated.

6

Diana of the Prairies

As you chant, I want you to put your hands on your womb. *This* is the center of your power!"

This is Ruth Barrett, priestess, and my first thought when I see her—at dusk, in the center of a circle of two hundred women in a forest clearing in rural Illinois—is how much she looks like Wonder Woman's mother.

I can't help it: the image is instant, an arrow shot straight from my childhood, across the years, and into my grown-woman brain. What was her name? Hippolyta, queen of the Amazons. They were all Amazons, Wonder Woman and her people, transplanted from Greco-Roman mythology into the world of American superheroes. Wonder Woman herself was the "warrior princess" of this women-only civilization, and her birth name was Diana. So here is where my first impression makes sense: Ruth is a high priestess of the original line of Dianic Wicca, the all-female strain of Wicca created over four decades ago, when a new wave of feminism was just hitting its stride. Now in her late fifties, she is effortlessly, every inch, the "ancient priestess" from Central Casting: her long gray hair falls in ringlets streaked with black, and she wears a flowing purple dress of distressed cotton, Roman sandals, and a vulva-shaped silver pendant around her neck.

We are at a massive weeklong gathering in the woods, a two-hour drive west of Chicago, in parkland bordered by acres and acres of cornfields—in other words, the approximate geographical center of the Midwest. And though I came here to take part in the tradition of outdoor festivals, a way in which Pagans have networked and swapped magical stylings since the seventies, I find myself confronted with the specter of the women's movement. We are assembled here, women from the ages of six to sixty-something, because we "bleed, will bleed, or have bled our sacred bloods." We're preparing to honor the Goddess, also known as Diana to this crowd, the "fertile Mother/Amazon/Creatrix/Manifester/Maker" who uses her "sacred uterine bloods" to create the world.

Along with the other younger women, in collective singsong, I've chanted—"My body is the body of the Goddess! My body is the body of the Goddess!"—marching to bongo beats in a loose, spirited procession from the edge of the clearing into the ritual circle itself. We, the *maidens* and the *mothers*, have marched between two rows of *crones*—older ladies, the community's wisewomen—as they sang back to us, some of them jangling tambourines or other noisemakers, finally joining us to form the ring.

Ruth is an attractive woman of regal bearing. She knows how to play the crowd with her sense of humor—she calls the Goddess "you who give us the power to tell shit from Shinola!"—but she has a severity to her in the old-school way, honed through her activism at a time when saying the word "womb" could make you feel radical and strong (so far away now). She has us place our four hundred hands over our two hundred uteruses and presents us with a statuette of the Minoan snake goddess, its tiny stone fists clenched, each wielding a striped serpent. But it's not what you might think—in this world, a serpent is not a phallus: Ruth tells us that a *womb* is like a snake, the site of shedding and transformation. She places a cauldron in the sand at the center of the circle, filled with jointed wooden snakes for us to pick up and pass around—to help us "feel our power." Soon these women of all shapes and ages, myself included—I'm here, there's no holding back—stand wiggling make-believe reptiles with our hands.

I am already starting to feel a stab of generational alienation, and the ritual has barely begun. The evening will be full of talk of *blood* and *wombs* and *snakes* and *justice* and *sisters*. Because tonight, second-wave feminism is alive and well in the woods of central Illinois.

I arrive at Pagan Spirit Gathering, two days earlier, anticipating a more mundane brand of alienation: a personal fear of my first massive, multi-day campout. But the opportunity was too great to pass up: whereas PantheaCon's DoubleTree explosion provided an easy shot of West Coast Pagan culture, PSG, slightly smaller,* is a chance to catch a glimpse of the Midwestern contingent. Set in Illinois, the gathering is put together by Wisconsin's Circle Sanctuary (Stone City's older, more rigorous Midwestern cousin), and the witchy folk and families I meet here are mostly residents of those two states, Michigan and Minnesota: a healthy cross section of the region's spiritual misfits.

I'm camping for the week in a raucous "tent village" out under the hot sun—at the edge of a pond, across grassy fields, clustered in the buggy forest, are campsites, organized by clan. But my own clan—I've hooked up with them through a mutual Pagan friend—is fortunately not the back-to-nature crowd. "We're *glamping*," Cara announces as I survey the setup: they've carefully arranged a series of tents around a large dining area shaded by a tarp and surrounded by stuffed coolers. Cara is a slim, pragmatic Minnesotan in a clipped brunette bob; she's in a long-term marriage and, unlike many of the Pagans I've met out west, is a firm believer in monogamy. She's also a Hellenic Reconstructionist, trying to re-create ancient Greek religious practice based on historical evidence. She invites me to take a seat with the others under a large canopy and pours me a grapefruit-and-vodka from a chilled shaker.

I introduce myself to the crew. Heather is a Heathen and, like Cara, from Minnesota, where she works in technical services for a university. Laura and Matt, two eclectics, live in Asheville, North Carolina, in a 120-square-foot house (they're part of the "tiny house" movement). David, a gay rights activist, is also a former PETA organizer who spent three years making guerrilla

---

* With more than eleven hundred attendees this year, the gathering increases the local population—many of whom work for Caterpillar or for the medium-security men's correctional center in nearby Sheridan—by 60 percent.

videos documenting animal abuses by a large traveling circus ("I once saw a trainer punch a Bengal tiger in the face!"). While we sip our mixed drinks in the shade, visitors drop by, en route to a workshop or to prep for a ritual under the trees. There's talk of rain—but the program warns us against any "weatherworking" rituals without consulting the "Weather Collective." For now, the late-afternoon sun is strong.

Eventually, with a slight buzz on, I excuse myself and go for a walk.

I cross the field, heading toward the path that I know winds through the grounds. It's a narrow, dusty road, along which a young mother is pulling a hand wagon packed with three small children: the youngest, an angelic blond in nothing but diapers, is fast asleep on his face. They're a blissed-out, unembarrassed ad for communal living. To my left is the pond, packed with more kids and their parents, some floating on old inner tubes in the ninety-six-degree heat.

At a fork, I turn right into a woodsy area flanked with vendor tents, their handmade wares on display: feathered antlers, pentagrams, wands of every size and material. I spot a lot of Crocs and sarongs, on men and women alike, and at every turn, the bare ass of some older man is visible on the horizon: the festival has a "clothing optional" policy. The organizers have warned us, "Within Pagan culture, remember that nudity is not an invitation to have sex, and should not be regarded as such." And, on a motherly note, "If going skyclad, use sunscreen to protect all your skin from the sun."*

Some campers are stir-frying early dinners in woks or tossing super-market meats onto mini-grills. Many have saved money, taken five entire days off from work, and coordinated a long drive with multiple kids in order to be here; this may be the one time all year when they're able to be openly Pagan among Pagans, to create a village of like-minded folks, a tempo-rary home for their gods and goddesses in the middle of the conservative heartland. Who knows what their lifestyle is the other fifty-one weeks of the year?

---

* Other program tips, in a familiar Midwestern tone: "Please don't block dancers from free movement"; "Please ask first if you would like to play someone else's drum"; and, most delicately, "Sometimes participants, excited by the freedoms and possibilities at Pagan gatherings, get involved in new sexual relationships without considering how these will impact themselves and existing relationships after the festival ends. Take time to reflect . . ."

Deeper into the woods, I hear voices calling out. I come across a huge clearing—this must be the main ritual circle—where about a hundred people are gathered, surrounded by trees four or five stories high. To get a closer look, I step through an archway hung with rainbow-colored rags to join the outer ring of spectators, most of them seated in nylon camping chairs. In the circle's center, a handfasting is taking place, an ancient Celtic ceremony used to join Pagan couples today—not legally binding, but taken seriously by the community. The groom is shaggy and handsome in nothing but a Scottish kilt, his bare chest fit and tattooed. The bride wears a bodice-topped dress in autumnal colors, feathers woven through her long black hair.

Leading the ceremony is Selena Fox, in a gauzy sheath that shows her figure—her pendulous breasts give her the look of a stone fertility goddess (the Venus of Willendorf?)—and a silver diadem crowning her silvery hair. Selena is the beaming, joyful grand doyenne, the sexagenarian mama, the feminist pooh-bah, the high priestess of Circle Sanctuary, and she's organized this gathering for over thirty years. Her persona, as one of the early public faces of American Wicca, has always been that of Glinda the Good Witch—but don't let this fool you. For decades, Selena has been a fervent advocate for civil rights, the environment, and women's rights, and this couple is honored to have her bind them together. *Literally* bind: they clasp hands, and Selena ties their wrists together with braided rope. Now she asks them a series of questions, which they answer in lovely, lilting Southern accents:

PRIESTESS: Will you cause her pain?
GROOM: I may.
PRIESTESS: Is that your intention?
GROOM: It is not.
PRIESTESS: Will you cause *him* pain?
BRIDE: I may.
PRIESTESS: Is that your intention?
BRIDE: It is not.

And so on and so forth, in marriage vows remarkable for their honesty and the absence of threats of "eternity" or "till death do us part." We are watching two young people make realistic promises to each other, in the flexible terms of their new religion, before the inhabitants of their temporary village.

In the earlier days of the American movement, in the fifties and sixties, someone curious about witchcraft could only find like-minded folks through newsletters or their local occult shop. But the festival circuit—and, eventually, the Internet—changed all that. In the mid-seventies, big gatherings were held indoors at hotels (as PantheaCon is today), with some outdoor exceptions in California: in Coeden Brith, in the desert outside Los Angeles, in the Bay Area. These attracted a few hundred in celebration of the sabbats, or even to re-create the ancient Greek Eleusinian Mysteries, but they were often limited to one tradition. A community-wide festival culture was really sparked in the Midwest, by groups in the Chicago area—mostly witches initiated in the British forms of Wicca—who together, in the mid-seventies, formed the Midwest Pagan Council. The council created a joint festival that, at the same time, would not conflict with their own covens' sabbat celebrations. Invitations in underground publications led to the council's first big, sloppy mixer: a giant campout. Within a few years, the Pan Pagan Festival had about six hundred attendees.

By then, Selena had founded Circle Sanctuary: what started as a Pagan farmland commune had by the late seventies been incorporated into an official Pagan "church." She drew on what she'd learned from helping to organize Pan Pagan to create PSG, drumming up interest through mailings and even ads in the back of *Rolling Stone*. The early days, she says, were a "jazz session," plenty of improvisation: the inaugural gathering, in 1980, was on private land in southwestern Wisconsin, without electricity or water, and with a few holes in the ground serving as toilets. Soon they bought their own land, much as Morpheus and Shannon did years later out west—a two-hundred-acre nature preserve about an hour from Madison—and they slowly struck a balance between a getting-back-to-nature vibe and a level of comfort that would keep the city Pagans from freaking out.* PSG evolved into a village structure, complete with morning meetings, workshops, gate

---

* The gathering is now held at Stonehouse Park, former farmland that's uniquely, randomly American: the architect who developed the place in the 1840s once employed the young Springfield lawyer Abraham Lincoln to help defend his property in the Illinois Supreme Court; and today it's used for "living history" demonstrations, Renaissance Faires, Tolkien-inspired live-action role-playing, and modern-day tactical combat reenactment by a band of military and law enforcement guys.

guards, first-aid teams, spiritual counselors (should an unexpected vision mess with your head), and an on-site Pagan twelve-step group.

By the mid-nineties, the number of Pagan festivals grew to about 350 around the country, with many of these temporary utopias pulling in over a thousand witchy campers apiece. Even though only a fraction of American Pagans attend festivals (because of costs), these events have been a huge influence, spreading styles of ritual chants and dress between covens and traditions and across the country. PSG, specifically, now spans generations: each year, a few hundred kids join their parents, some of whom grew up attending the gathering themselves.

In the late sixties, before a real festival scene had emerged, an idea started to catch on: perhaps a *goddess* was at the center of the universe, a creatrix rather than a creator. This belief was fueled in part by the beginnings of second-wave feminism, the environmental movement, and the American Pagan scene's rejection of male-centered Big Religion. There was, however, an essential difference. The core of the Pagan movement, Wicca, at least in its British forms, runs on an even balance of male and female energy, in both its gods and its clergy; but feminist, or "Dianic," Wicca is all woman all the way. Dianics asked why men should be necessary to their magic at all.

Feminist witchcraft—then also called "women's spirituality" or "Goddess worship"—would not come around until two years before *Roe v. Wade*, and about five years before I was born. In other words, this was a long time ago, a time when American women my age had far fewer opportunities and a far greater awareness of the need to force change. Many were sick of being mistreated or abused by partners or employers and finding little legal or social support; others were frustrated at being sidelined by the "pale and male" activist groups they'd given so much to in the sixties. These were women who, in most cases, were desperate to transform their circumstances and those of other women—and here was a chance to build an entire spirituality around that, drawing their magic from the "women's mysteries" of menstruation and the ability to give birth (whether or not a woman chooses to).*

---

* Even a woman who does not give birth or who has had a hysterectomy still has this power, goes the belief, because she was born with a uterus.

Dianic Wicca was born in the small Hollywood apartment of a Hungarian refugee and second-generation psychic, Zsuzsanna "Z" Budapest—the priestess from whom Ruth (my Hippolyta) would eventually inherit the mantle. Born in 1940, Z had come over from the city of Budapest in the fifties, after many of her friends and family were executed during the war. In her twenties, she pursued a career as a professional psychic and in entertainment: she studied at Second City in Chicago, and briefly worked as the "color girl" for *The Ed Sullivan Show* in Los Angeles. There, at thirty, she jumped into the women's movement, and in 1971 she founded the first feminist witches' coven, Susan B. Anthony Coven No. 1,* in a Yule ritual at her place. Z eventually rounded up twenty to forty active coven members and about three hundred more occasional participants. Based on ideas she and her fellow witches had jotted down on a restaurant napkin, she wrote up a manifesto declaring their part in "a changing universal consciousness that has long been feared and prophesied by the patriarchs," their commitment to "defending our interests and those of our sisters" through witchcraft, and their complete opposition to sharing their magic with men "until the equality of the sexes is a reality."

The Susan B. Anthony Coven soon inspired related covens in five other states, some with similar Women's History 101 names—like the Amelia Earhart Coven in New York, the Elizabeth Cady Stanton Coven in Orange County, and the Jane Addams Coven in Chicago.

Born in Los Angeles into a Jewish Reconstructionist family—they believe that women can take part in all ceremonies, even as rabbis—Ruth began meeting people interested in the Goddess when she was seventeen, playing folk music at the original Renaissance Faire in Southern California. The idea of a female creator of the universe made immediate intuitive sense to her. It was at the fair, in 1975, when she was a college student in Santa Cruz, that Ruth met her first teacher and joined her "Goddess group." A couple of years of training later, she returned to Los Angeles, where she met Z and was invited to her coven's Samhain. The ritual was different from anything she'd experienced. The women in the inner circle passed around

---

* Z named the coven after Anthony because she'd once said, "When I die, I shall go neither to heaven nor to hell, but stay right here and finish the Women's Revolution." Z considered her their guardian and collaborator.

a pomegranate (a fruit associated with death, for the season of death), and as each held it, she would take her athame and stab it, in a kind of emotional purge, causing the juice to run—the color of blood. One woman in particular shocked Ruth: so flushed with rage that her face looked nearly purple, she raised her athame and said, "This is for my brother, who raped me"—and plunged the ritual knife into the pomegranate.

Ruth was impressed. This was a kind of spirituality that didn't ask women to pretend, to play a role, but instead acknowledged whatever they might be struggling with, no matter how ugly. Instead of a highly scripted religion led by men, here was a practice dictated by women's own experiences. They could be completely open about their lives, create rituals to cast out their pain and unhappiness; they now had a sanctified place where they could put all that stuff and convert it into magic.

Ruth rose in the ranks, and by the time she was twenty-five, in 1980, Z had handed her the reins of her Los Angeles ministry. She'd eventually initiate a couple dozen Dianics and spawn two more covens. Over that decade, several Dianic Wiccan groups emerged, including lines other than Z's, and both women's and men's mysteries were given their own rituals at festivals like PSG.*

This takes me back to our circle in the woods here in Illinois, where Ruth is separating us by the phases of our bodies. She's asked us for a show of hands: which of us are *crones*?

About thirty-five women raise their arms, many from the earlier days of Wicca in America, many wearing shades of bloodred. Then she calls for the *mothers*, who make up the majority of us: those who've given birth (like this woman next to me, in her twenties, with a baby wrapped against her chest) or who've given birth to "a work of the creative imagination" (like me, I guess). And finally come the *maidens*, "those of you who have just begun to bleed"— an introduction that would embarrass the hell out of most teenage girls on the outside, but here they step forward with their hands held high and their chests thrust out, junior high girls in trendy short haircuts and tank tops with teen-colored bra straps on display, surprisingly comfortable in how they carry themselves. There is even an "honorary nymph," as Ruth dubs her:

---

* This has caused some controversy in the Pagan community in recent years, because of its exclusion of transgender women and men.

a tiny girl of five, with stalk-straight posture and wavy blond hair, wearing a brightly colored sarong.

And all the while, a few women in their twenties ("mothers") stand watch at the edges of the circle and at the forest clearing's outer perimeter. One in particular is the perfect butch incarnation of a Dianic huntress, with long straw-limp hair and a deadly expression on her face; she wears wide leather cuffs and a tightly laced black leather vest, a bow and quiver of arrows slung across her chest. An archer, of course: I remember the famous story of Diana and the Roman soldier Actaeon (I read the ancient Greek and Roman myths obsessively in grade school). The goddess Diana, with her golden bow, led an elite female unit of hunters, and to cross her or her guardians was to meet certain death. To dare to *look* at Diana as a sex object—as Actaeon did when he stumbled across her taking a bath in a woodland stream and was stunned by her naked good looks—guaranteed you'd be torn apart by vicious hunting dogs.

The Dianic relationship to men is a complicated one. Although some have called this "the lesbian religion," Dianics as a group, like the women in our circle this evening, are a mix of straight, lesbian, and bi. (Ruth herself divorced her husband and is now in a long-term partnership with a fellow Dianic, but she says that most Dianics are not gay.) Its rituals may be separatist, but the movement is not anti-men—it's simply not *about* men.* And so, even in the midst of this back-to-nature Pagan gathering, the Dianics feel a need to guard their space apart. Not out of physical fear—not in this setting—but in fear of having their territory taken away from them, of losing the right to gather separately, speak freely and privately, find ways to become stronger independent of the other sex. This is what women fought for in the seventies, and what we pretend we no longer need today.

In 2000, after twenty years of priestessing in Los Angeles, Ruth became a Wisconsin transplant, like Selena, establishing the only major Dianic group in the Midwest, the Temple of Diana. She found herself in a very different part of America, a region in which, unlike in California, the women showed up for circle in sweatshirts and expected to stay seated for the ceremony, like a church congregation. Ruth made a run to the Garment Center to find them clothes at a discount, and taught them to stand up in the presence of

---

* Z Budapest, however, personally dreams of a new socialist society led by women.

the Goddess. But something bigger was at work, a cultural shift: the women's movement had lost a lot of its steam—because of a lack of urgency on the part of my own generation (myself included)—and she could feel it in circle. The women in her rituals were growing more polite, less likely to be outrageous, to toss off their shirts and jump over the bonfire shouting, to let their voices out.

Just the idea of all of us working together—women who are strangers to each other but have that one fact in common, the fact of being women—is a foreign one. Or the idea of taking ownership of the specific stage we're at in our lives, and not clinging weirdly, desperately to our time as *maidens*—a stage we're taught to mourn forever. Whether I choose to make a kid or not, I'm no longer the woman of my twenties: time passes, we change, and who's to dictate to us what moment of our lives is better or best?

Then there's that *word* for what comes next, not around the corner, but someday: *crone*. I find that single-syllable word a little terrifying because of what it stands for—the final stage, the time of life that this culture looks at as post-sex, post-options. But in this place it's a term of respect—shorthand for "lady who's lived longer than you and likely seen more than you, so shut your mouth while she's talking." Among Pagans, crones are respected as "elders," and here at PSG, for the last decade, they've been given a ceremony, created for them in part by Selena. I attended one, at dusk, inside a hidden grove, and witnessed as thirteen crones-to-be, wearing crowns and carrying staffs, many long-haired, in elaborate Pagan dress, their shoulders thrust back, were honored by women of several generations. One by one, they announced their names—magical names like Dawn Walker and Shining Soul—which we repeated back to them, louder than before; and we applauded as they jumped over a broom laid out on the grass, crossing over and into their next phase. They gave us advice, stuff drawn out of decades of living: they told us not to forget who we'd been as girls; they told us to dance more and to laugh at things; they told us to love freely, but not to take men too seriously. Finally, the crone named Seashell, who'd been putting off this ritual for years, never ready, announced, "After this week, with these women, I can tell you that aging doesn't hurt at all." Once the ritual was over, another woman in her thirties turned to me and said, "I want to do this when the time comes." I told her, "I wish someone had done this for my mother."

Tonight, with Ruth's guidance, the crones are dancing around the circle, sending their energy into the bonfire—and next the mothers join in. Maidens hold out bowls of mugwort for us to toss into the fire, and we jump the flames. Then the other teenagers receive us, anointing us each with a bowl of water blessed in some temple. We are in this together, multiple generations, and together we chant repeatedly, heatedly, "Justice for our sisters! Justice for our sisters!"

Once I return home, I will never use this language again.

I want this communion—but I can't relate. I feel embarrassed: this is precisely the kind of dated, pro-women gathering that most of my female friends would balk at, and I don't know how to embrace it. More than four decades have passed since the Goddess movement began, and if you mention that word in this country, "Goddess," you're likely to be dismissed as a New Age lightweight or some sixties throwback. The concept of a female god has very little clout in this culture, and it's worth asking why that might be. Apparently, I've absorbed that message.

But there's more to my rejection of Ruth's world. At this point, after a few years of taking part in rituals—led by priestesses of a range of abilities and personal charisma, with a rotating roster of participants—I can say this: I now have enough of a sense of this landscape that I'm narrowing down what I'm looking for, where my fascination lies. I'm looking for something transcendent, something you can only get at through a great deal of deliberate, specific work and privacy and conviction—and this is not something you stumble across in community-friendly ceremonies that require only a temporary commitment. Whatever magic Ruth is capable of as an experienced high priestess back home in her own Dianic circle, among her own initiates, I won't find out tonight. Tonight, in the woods, she is serving up a ceremony anyone can follow: the inexperienced, those new to her womb magic, her women's mysteries. Most of us don't know what it would be like to dedicate ourselves to Diana, to work with her for years. We won't strip off our shirts tonight to howl bare-breasted at the moon—we've never even circled together before. This eclectic swath of the Pagan community is not high-stakes in its magic. This is a Pagan Woodstock, a hippie throwback, a cheerful embrace of nature.

I want access to the level of witchcraft that only time and training and trust can earn.

Maybe this is my problem, evidence of damage to my own psyche, that I'm looking for something deeper, darker, more layered, harder to live with. Maybe Catholicism, however liberal and improvised the version I was raised with, has left me with unshakable cravings for revelations you have to sweat for. Whatever my stubborn curiosity is about, this much is clear: I need to get at the heavier stuff, wherever a person goes to find it.

7

The Mass

In a promising coincidence, I'd recently decided to spend time in a city much farther south—a heavy place. A place with a dark undertow that could not be further from the Summer of Love Redux I'd encountered in the woods of Illinois. In New Orleans, I'll have the chance to delve into ritual that's thicker, moodier, and more precise—closer, I hope, to what I've been looking for.

It's evening, and I'm headed to the Alombrados Oasis, pedaling my clunker of a bicycle, a red town cruiser, down Dauphine Street. It's a confusing, chaotic tropical city, more dangerous than New York but far quainter in appearance: the downtown neighborhoods where I spend my time—the Marigny, the Bywater, and the quieter parts of the French Quarter—are lined, street after buckled street, with Spanish Colonial–cum–Southern shotgun architecture: tall shuttered doors, wrought-iron balconies, and an array of colors that reminds me of Havana. The grander buildings along Esplanade Avenue have slave quarters in the rear, long since converted into apartments. Everywhere, nature revolts against its colonizers, with every kind of vegetation thrusting its tendrils up through the crevices and the neglected sidewalks—given a foothold, massive banana trees can grow like weeds. The fauna are spread thick and even across the town: mourning doves and slim red finches, small lizards and pink katydids, myriad tropical cockroaches, stinging buck moth caterpillars that fall from the trees in spring, and always, at nightfall, the tinny chorus of frogs.

I quickly learn how eerie the nights can be: though it's a place known for bright streets, loud music, and loud drinking, huge parts of town are barely lit after dark, and completely empty. I can bike through entire neighborhoods and see only one or two people in the shadows. This is a city of hidden rooms, where you could hide anyone and anything, and plenty of people are doing just that.

In its spiritual life, New Orleans is an exotic mutt: a mostly Catholic town, but a place where a nice Catholic girl might consult with a Voodoo priestess. A place where one woman announced to me, "Hoodoo is the new black!"* And then there's the occult underground: Alombrados Oasis, in the Bywater, is the local outpost of Ordo Templi Orientis (OTO), the century-old magical society once led by Aleister Crowley, the man whose boundary-pushing and black reputation have been a live wire running through the last century of occult history.

I pedal across Elysian Fields and over the railroad tracks, a long line of cargo cars to the right, and beyond that St. Claude Avenue Bridge. Just past the tracks, I line up with a young guy on another bike and match his pace, not knowing how to break stride with someone I didn't mean to travel with. Just short of Piety Street, I am nearing Alombrados, and we still haven't diverged. I take a closer look and see that my new partner's wearing black pants and a black tee and has long, stringy dark hair and a goatee—a look that's classic occultist.

We both pull over in front of the same spot: a two-story house, mustard yellow with brick-red shutters and latticed eaves. It towers over its neighbors.

"I think we're going to the same place," I say. (He gives away nothing.) "The mass?" At this, the guy half smiles and pulls open the black gate to reveal a long, narrow alleyway. I follow, rolling my bike along after his.

Mass begins in ten minutes.

---

* Put simply, there is West African "Vodou" or "Vodun," as practiced in Ghana, Togo, and Benin; then the distinct African diaspora practices of Haitian "Vodou" and Louisiana "Voodoo"; and "Hoodoo," African American folk magic as it evolved in the American South.

·   ·   ·

Knowing that Gerald Gardner drew so much from Crowley's writings, and that so much of present-day witchcraft has ritual stylings in common with ceremonial magic, I wanted to learn more. I wanted to dig into its symbol systems, intricate color codes, and seemingly endless lists of secret words—the Hebrew terms, the names of archangels, so many sounds evocative of the cinematic occult. I was ready to leave behind the looseness of eclectic Wicca and try a tradition as unforgiving as it is specific—echoing-through-the-ages, old-as-Jewish-mysticism specific. This naturally drew me into the web of OTO.

Morpheus had provided me with a way in. Aware of my new curiosity and my travel south, she connected me with one of Anaar's Feri initiates in New Orleans, someone who'd recently started studying magic with OTO. (I've since met a few Feris who are also in the ceremonial-magic camp—apparently, crossover's allowed.) A week ago, Mark, the most serious man ever to use the online handle Happydog Potatohead, had agreed to see me downtown, at a nautical-themed beer-and-burger joint. In his early fifties, he showed up dressed in the elegant summer style of older Southern men: buttoned-down oxford shirt tucked into long shorts, capped off with a white boater hat over his neatly clipped ring of white hair. He's married, but his wife long ago excused herself from all things witchy and occult, leaving him extra-eager to meet up with like-minded folk.

Mark's tone was unwaveringly polite and thoughtful, a bedside manner appropriate for someone who used to work with the severely mentally ill. (He's now starting an independent practice as a therapist who helps patients using "magical tools.") Over diet sodas in jumbo-sized cups, he told me about his childhood in mostly working-class Gulfport, Mississippi. His interest in witchcraft was sparked, he said, when an older kid at his Methodist summer camp began warning the other campers against the dangers of witchcraft. This only inspired young Mark, once home, to run to his local library to learn more. A search for "witches" uncovered a book containing photos of skyclad Wiccan rituals.* He was pretty excited. "I was *sixteen*."

---

* It's unclear how a graphic book on the Craft made it into the library of a very Christian town—though I've heard similar stories from a few people around the country.

The appeal of the ceremonial nudie pics, however, did not prevent Mark from continuing in Christ: he went on to pursue a failed experiment with an evangelical group that spoke in tongues, rolled around the floor, the whole thing. "But Jesus and I couldn't make it work, and we got a divorce." He eventually came across one of Selena Fox's ads for Circle Sanctuary in the back of *Rolling Stone*.* This was still in the pre-Internet era. The ad was his only connection to the Pagan community in the Bible Belt, and its depictions of a generous Goddess felt much more relatable than his unforgiving God obsessed with our every shortcoming.

When he moved to New Orleans, Mark finally had a chance to seek out other "crazy people." He found a Wiccan coven to circle with, and eventually learned about Feri. He made contact with Anaar, who became his long-distance witch-teacher. He credits the work with keeping him "sane" after he and his wife were forced to evacuate during Hurricane Katrina: living in a motel outside Jasper, Texas, he practiced his Feri techniques every day. When Anaar finally initiated him—in 2009, in a New Orleans hotel—he became a "citizen of another country."

About a year ago, Mark had added Thelema to his magical résumé, and in a few days, at Alombrados, he'd be taking part in his first Gnostic Mass. Would I come?

Ordo Templi Orientis, or the Order of Oriental Templars, was originally created—in 1906, by German Masons—as an inner-circle group determined to master Freemasonry's symbolism. A school of magic, they used a trio of Masonic rites as their foundation, while also folding in the knowledge of the Rosicrucians, the early Christian Gnostics, the Golden Dawn, the Hermetic (or occult) Qabalah, and several more obscure occult orders. In 1912, Aleister Crowley became the head of the British wing of OTO; ten years later, and for the rest of his life, he took on the leadership of the entire

---

* *Rolling Stone* also sold space to Victor Anderson, who advertised his Feri writings in the magazine. And so Jann Wenner joins the likes of the U.S. Air Force in unwittingly aiding the spread of witchcraft across America.

order, securing its place as one of the major magical societies in Western history.

Born in 1875 (about eight years before Gardner), in a spa town just north of London, Edward Alexander Crowley was raised by strict evangelical parents. After his father's death when Alick was eleven, the boy began acting out. Rather than sympathize with Alick's grief, the teachers at his harsh Christian boarding school used starvation as a disciplinary measure, and Alick was soon sent home because of poor health. Alick's life took a different turn when his surprisingly progressive tutor gave him lessons in drinking, smoking, and girls (not unlike what young Gardner was exposed to during his life abroad with his nanny). Sin, Alick decided, was a lie—and he quickly began enjoying himself.

This was made all the more possible by the inheritance Alick received once he was of university age: he arrived at Cambridge handsome, sexually liberated, and with the equivalent of $2 million at his disposal. Rather than attend classes, he binged on his own syllabus of literature and art, adopted the more lyrical Gaelic form of his name (Alexander became Aleister), and began publishing his own poetry. (He'd go on to become a prolific writer, over his lifetime producing more than a hundred works, from religious texts to erotica.) Aleister also had what was then an illegal six-month affair with an actor—a friend of the artist Aubrey Beardsley, of the Decadent movement (motto: "Art for art's sake")—and decided that he was bisexual.

But Aleister, despite having rejected his evangelical upbringing (he would later refer to himself as "the Beast 666"), was torn over his lack of faith. He left school without a degree, in search of a higher education. Like Gardner, he chose to wander the world, searching for a mystic mentor to initiate him into a secret system of knowledge he believed was out there. After a period of mountain climbing, from the Alps to the Himalayas, Aleister finally collided with London's then-flourishing network of secret societies: a fellow mountaineer introduced him to the decade-old Golden Dawn, an influential group of occultists. There he trained in ceremonial magic, was initiated, and advanced quickly through the ranks. But he wasn't destined to assimilate gracefully into *any* group, and his constant clashes with the Golden Dawn's most celebrated member, W. B. Yeats, meant that Aleister was once again a solo explorer.

That said, history teaches us that visions come most quickly to lone obsessives. And so we arrive at the origin story of Thelema, the magical religious system that Aleister Crowley would eventually spread throughout the world by way of OTO.

In 1903 Crowley married Rose Kelly, the sister of a friend, and on their honeymoon they rented an apartment in Cairo, near the Bulaq Museum. Crowley made one of the rooms into his temple, where he began studying Islamic mysticism and evoking ancient Egyptian gods. The magic seemed to affect Rose. As he wrote in his journals—where ceremonial magicians record all their experiments—it was during his conjurations that she started channeling messages: "They are waiting for you," repeatedly, and finally, "He who waits is *Horus*." Rose knew nothing about Egyptian deities, but suddenly she could tell him everything about that god: how he was conceived by Isis with the dead body of Osiris, how he had the head of a falcon and his eyes were the sun and the moon.

Still unsure of how seriously to take her messages, Crowley brought his wife to the museum to see if she could spot Horus. After wandering past several images of the god without a word, Rose pointed across the gallery: "There he is." In a glass display case was a painted wooden stele that had been discovered in the mortuary temple of the female pharaoh Hatshepsut, inscribed with some of the text of the Egyptian Book of the Dead. It had been painted for the pharaoh's priest, shown in the relief making an offering to a falcon-headed god seated on a throne before a symbol of the afterlife. Above the scene arches the sky goddess Nuit—whom Crowley would later make one of the central gods of Thelema—and just beneath her arched black torso is the winged sun disk, the sign of divinity. The priest below begs to be judged favorably on the other side. When Crowley looked more closely, he knew his wife must be channeling something real: the catalogue number of the stele, the Beast saw, was "666."*

Rose now had her husband's magical trust. He listened carefully when,

---

* Even today, this number is included on replicas of the stele in OTO lodges around the world. The museum staff member who originally catalogued the tablet likely remained unaware of his role in this chain of events.

two weeks later, in a trance, she gave him instructions: For three days he was to sit down in his home temple from noon to one and transcribe whatever came to him. The next day, at noon, he sat waiting with a pen—and heard a voice! It came from over his left shoulder. This, he understood, was a supernatural being named Aiwass who was now standing in the far corner of the room, "transparent as a veil of gauze, or a cloud of incense-smoke." This voice, he wrote, was "of deep timbre, musical and expressive," without affect or accent; it "seemed to echo itself in my physical heart." For three days in succession, Crowley wrote down all Aiwass said to him, and these words became *The Book of the Law*—today a text as significant for many ceremonial magicians as the Bible is for Christians.

The Book of the Law (or *Liber Legis*) announced the dawning of "a new aeon" for all mankind and, as "transcribed" by Crowley, proclaimed the magician himself as its prophet. Through this book, the basic tenets of a new mystical system took form—a system called Thelema, from the Greek word for the will. In Thelema, sin is a lie, and sex is a mystical union that can be used for strong magic. And the central Thelemic law? *Do what thou wilt shall be the whole of the Law.* Every individual is to realize and fulfill his own destiny, his own true will and purpose.

A superhuman entity had made him the vessel through which to share a game-changing message with the world—but Crowley, typically cocksure, was shaken, uncertain what to do next. He had no intention of becoming a proselytizer like the evangelicals of his miserable childhood. For the time being, he kept the revelation to himself.

A lot would transpire—the sudden death of his child to typhoid, his wife's descent into alcoholism, their divorce—before Crowley would dedicate himself to Thelema. Finally, enough had gone wrong that, in keeping with his guilt-driven upbringing, he decided he was being punished for ignoring his calling. He rededicated himself. Aiwass, he claimed, had reappeared to him. He created a Thelemic order, the A∴A∴,* intended to be the heir to the now defunct Golden Dawn; he made public *The Book of the Law.* This coming-out led OTO to his door. Impressed, the leader of the order tapped Crowley to oversee its British members. Under Crowley's influence, OTO absorbed Thelema into its system; by the twenties, he'd taken over the entire operation.

---

* This stands for Argentum Astrum, or Silver Star, but the order's real name is kept secret.

At the same time, Crowley's lifestyle became increasingly decadent, giving shape to the caricature that appeared in the tabloids. Having blown through all his money, he traveled to Sicily, where he converted a single-story villa without plumbing or electricity into "the Abbey of Thelema"—equal parts utopian community, magic school, and debauched hideout. There his magical experiments grew more focused and extreme, as did his reputation. There was sex! (with multiple partners, some married, some soon pregnant); heroin! (he struggled with addiction for several years); animal sacrifice! (this was never substantiated, beyond one Italian cat); murder! (one visitor did die—but from drinking unsafe water). The British press declared Crowley "the Wickedest Man in the World," and stories spread through newspapers in Europe and the United States, leading to his deportation from Italy by order of Mussolini. Things grew more and more chaotic for OTO as well: by World War II, most of the order's bodies had disbanded or been driven underground, with initiates scattered across Europe.

But more than tabloid scandal had spread to America: one last active OTO lodge remained in the world, and it was in Pasadena, California. One of its initiates, Grady McMurtry, met regularly with Crowley while in Europe on military assignments during the war* and became Crowley's representative in the United States. Crowley died, at the age of seventy-two, of chronic bronchitis, after the war ended, but he was destined for a strange second act. More than two decades later, his specter was resurrected in pop culture, with his face on the jacket of the Beatles' *Sgt. Pepper's Lonely Hearts Club Band* and his name in the lyrics of songs by David Bowie and Led Zeppelin.† And just as Buckland was serving as Wicca's official ambassador to the United States during that period, McMurtry stepped forward to keep things alive for Crowley's order, spearheading an OTO revival from America, where the magical society has been headquartered since. Today there are bodies in twenty-four countries on six continents, including nearly fifty in the United States alone, spread across two dozen states.

I find myself standing outside one of those outposts tonight, in New Orleans.

---

* Much like the flyboys who helped spread the first generation of Wicca to the United States.

† Jimmy Page bought Crowley's former house near Loch Ness.

I follow my biking buddy down a Bywater alley and into a backyard with an overgrown lawn, a few unlit tiki torches, and a covered hot tub. We park our bikes and step through sliding doors into Alombrados—well, into a large, collegiate-style kitchen: linoleum floor and Formica cabinets, everything beige, and an assortment of half-dirty glasses and plates all along the countertop. To the right is a jumble of footwear (everyone takes off their shoes here) and a table on which stands a donation jug in the shape of a Janus head. I notice an erase board reminding people of their roles for the mass:

Priest: Josh
Priestess: Sophia
Deacon: Jay
Child: Mark, Rob

I toss off my sandals and step inside.

Just beyond the kitchen, a few steps lead up to another open area: an informal reading-and-meeting room, flanked by bookshelves, a couple of makeshift altars, and a terrarium that houses a snake. It's still early, but people are milling around: a handful of local Thelemites. I say hello to Mark. He's nervous, having scrambled to prepare; he'd bought his ceremonial robe only a few days ago, in a Middle Eastern grocery store.

Beyond Mark, everyone here's in their twenties and early thirties. Tidying up in the kitchen is Andrew, who's tall and athletically lean, with Slavic good looks. He's just come back from blueberry-picking out of town, and offers me some—they're delicious. Of the guy-heavy assembly, I can already tell he's the most at ease in welcoming new people, although they've all become accustomed to the revolving door of occult-curious visitors. Though some rites are completely private—no negotiation—the Gnostic Mass is public, open to whoever knows enough to seek it out.

Seated at the table, quiet and focused, is Jay, in jeans and a wrinkled T-shirt. Jay must be about the same age as Andrew, but even with his golden-blond buzz cut, he looks older, more worn in by the sun, possibly from his years working in construction and carpentry. He's also lived through some hard enough episodes, coming from a huge, modest family and struggling to spend more time with his six-year-old daughter now that he's split with her mom. He's whittling down white tapers, melting them, and fitting them into the wall sconces that will be installed in the temple for ritual. "This is a pretty regular chore," he tells me. Raised thoroughly Mormon in Mississippi, he transferred his allegiance a few years ago, and is now passionately single-minded in his support of all things Crowley. Mark will later tell me, "Jay's just so intense. He's really *found his religion*, if you know what I mean." I think Mark, having left the evangelical fervor of his youth behind, finds this unsettling.

I learn that the guy I'd arrived with, David, is actually the "body master," meaning he manages this oasis, on its way to becoming a full-fledged lodge. (Camp, oasis, lodge—these categories determine what levels of the many tiers of initiations can be performed here.) Each of the bodies around the country answers to the Executive Council of the U.S. Grand Lodge, which in turn answers to the International Supreme Council. David tells me there are about fourteen members at Alombrados—a number I will see jump in the coming weeks—and several friends and "sympathizers" who visit regularly.

More people slowly stream in; they pull up chairs and make small talk. There's punning, and sci-fi and horror references: it's a *very* nerdy scene, which I can appreciate (mostly). Andrew, for his part, mentions that he's been writing a screenplay about a vampire apocalypse in which the vampires have won. "They've taken over everything, and humans are being used as feed for the vampires, living in pens in their own filth." (He can say this and somehow sound very sweet.) Josh and Sophia, Priest and Priestess tonight and on many occasions (Mark told me they are the heart of this operation), are yet to be seen, probably hiding out in their private quarters upstairs.

As people continue to gather, it becomes clear that this is an unusually young group for a bunch of ceremonial magicians, a fact that surprises me. I'd yet to encounter a community within the Pagan and occult scene built up by people mostly younger than me. Others in attendance include: a lanky, ponytail-sporting granola guy from Seattle, new to town; a Texan, in cleaned-up gutter-punk style, who works at a nearby restaurant; and a girl (a visitor) in her early twenties in a flirty asymmetrical haircut and white baby-doll dress, toenails painted in alternating shades of blue, jangly jewelry at the ends of all her limbs.

The most striking later arrival, however, is Dan, the body's rugged elder statesman, maybe in his late fifties. With a shaved head and sharp white beard, he cuts an imposing figure as he lumbers into the house supported by forearm crutches. He wears a white button-down shirt tucked into blue jeans, and a suede safari-style hat that he removes when he reaches the table, leaving a pink ring around his bright white scalp. Peeking out from under his collar, on the side of his neck, is the tattoo of a prowling wolf. A sixth degree—a level reached only through years of study and an explicit invitation to advance—Dan is one of those old-school men for whom the word "badass" was put into circulation. He greets his younger "brothers" in a thick Louisiana accent (he's from Baton Rouge).

"93!"

"93, brother!"*

As for the crutches: about six months ago, he fell down the building's attic stairs, broke his neck, and was hospitalized for five weeks, during which time it was unclear whether he would walk again. But David mentions that when Dan was first laid up, unable to move at all, he did regular meditations based on Qabalah—and he's been zipping through his therapy ever since. The doctors say his progress in just a couple months is the kind it takes most people years to make.

Dan asks what I think about Thelema, and I say that I'm learning right now. A bit unimpressed, he replies, "Well, it's good to take your time."

He looks at me seriously, with his advanced bullshit-detector in full effect, and says, "I've been around, but I can tell you, there's real magic here. You go some places and people go through the motions and nothing really happens. But there's really something here."

"Is it the people at each place? What is it?"

---

* Here even the briefest exchanges contain intricate codes and systems. "93" is the numerical value in Gematria (a Qabalistic system) for the letters of the Thelemic brotherly greeting, "Do what thou wilt shall be the whole of the Law." The same value, 93, applies to the reply ("Love is the law, love under will").

Dan doesn't hesitate. "It's something in this city. And there's *something here*," he says. In this building.

Perfectly quiet, we file barefoot through a darkened doorway, around a corner, and into the temple itself. Impressive and moody, the place has the feeling of history soaked into the floorboards. This used to be a Christian church, and now the walls are painted decidedly occult shades of black and red. A slow Middle Eastern dirge is playing. The high-ceilinged space is dimly lit and, though decorated entirely by volunteers, sumptuous and stately. The altar holds dozens of candles, the only source of light, and far at the other end of the space, mostly in shadow, is an archway in ancient Egyptian style, tall, curtained off. We take our seats in the dark wooden pews on either side, about sixteen of us in the congregation tonight.

The pews face the center of the space, where two plinths stand in straight alignment, one topped with a chalice of burning incense, the other with bowls of water and salt. But my eyes are drawn to the main altar, rising up at the front of the room. Three steps, painted in large black-and-white checks, lead up to the stage; and the stage is surrounded on three sides by heavy red and black curtains, pulled open to reveal the paraphernalia for the mass. The altar table, between a black pillar and a white pillar, is covered in red satin with gold brocade; and atop that are a series of brass plates and a chalice full of wine, its lip covered with a red velvet square embellished in gold thread. Every detail, every shape, the angle of every object in relation to every other object, has value, of course: we are in the realm of ceremonial magic, where no aesthetic gesture is empty: everything is loaded, overloaded, buckling under with meaning.

The wall above is hung with lit candles, and on an ornate gold-painted shelf, in pride of place, rests an ancient-looking tablet, covered in hieroglyphics and images of Egyptian gods: a replica of the stele Crowley's wife had pointed out to him in that museum in Cairo, the stele marked "666."

Crowley renamed this tablet the Stele of Revealing and placed it at the center of his mass, the Gnostic Mass: a ceremony laying out the laws of Thelema, packed with allusions to OTO's sex magic, as played out with swords and chalices and the interplay of priest and priestess. Unlike Catholic or Eastern Orthodox mass, however, this is a statement of belief in self and the power of the human will, rather than a theater of worship and repentance.

The door has been shut; the audience is quiet; the room is warm with the glow of candlelight. Through the music, I can hear the sound of a ferry horn from the distant pier.

Now Jay enters and welcomes us. Tonight's Deacon, he wears a white linen robe and gold silk stole, like those of a Catholic priest. He processes to the center of the floor, a copy of Crowley's *Book of the Law* in his hands. He kisses the book three times, then carefully places it atop the altar. Jay is transformed: the tense, wiry construction worker I met in the reading room now has a clerical dignity.

"Do what thou wilt shall be the whole of the Law!" he calls out to all here, to which our reply is "Love is the law, love under will!" The musky smell of incense is slowly filling the temple, as in the Greek churches of my childhood.

"I proclaim the Law of Light, Life, Love, and Liberty in the name of *IAOoooooo!*" This last name is held as a long, vibrating note, so that it hangs in the air, breathing magic into the letters themselves. It's a word meant to evoke, all at once, the names of Yahweh, Zeus, and one of the spheres of the Qabalistic Tree of Life.

With this, we begin a call-and-response with an absent party: the Catholic Church. Right about now, a Catholic would say, "I believe in one God, the Father almighty, maker of heaven and earth, of all things visible and invisible." But the Thelemite pledges allegiance, instead, to *one Star in the Company of Stars of whose fire we are created . . . His name Chaaaaaaaaos.* Chaos, the formless state before the birth of the universe.

"I believe in one Lord, Jesus Christ, the Only Begotten Son of God," says the Catholic. "Through him all things were made." The Thelemite responds, *I believe in one Earth, the Mother of us all, and in one Womb wherein all men are begotten . . . in Her name Baaaaabaaaalohhhhn.* We were not made by a father figure, separate from us in his holiness; instead, we come from chaos, born out of the same fire as the universe. And from Babalon, the Great Mother, the Scarlet Woman, the bride of Chaos, the destroyer of limits, the ecstasy of living! She is every woman's sexual appetite, woman free from society's constraints. Fearless, she arrives riding the Beast: she reins him in with one hand, and with the other she raises a cup full of love and death!

The Catholic would now talk of how the One God took the form of a man, conceived of a virgin mother, and lived and suffered and died for mankind and rose again. But the Thelemite is not concerned with this story. *I believe in the Serpent,* he says (*we* say), *and the Lion, Mystery of Mystery, in His name Baaaaaphohhhhmehhhhht.* Baphomet! The goat-headed god with a human body that is half man, half woman—a figure that contains within him-her-it the harmony and balance of the universe, the union of opposites. The differences between men and women are "for love's sake, for the chance of union!"

This is Catholic liturgy through the looking glass. While the Christian waits for Christ to return to judge us for our sins, meting out punishments and deciding who is worthy of the kingdom that will have no end, the Thelemite speaks of a belief in *Light, Life, Love and Liberty,* ruled by *Thehhhhleeeeemaaaa.* Thelema, its name meaning "will," its mandate *Do what thou wilt!*

Amen. Auuuuugmmmmn.

The Priestess enters—this is Sophia—and her presence is immediately felt. She is very beautiful, in a Russian or Eastern European way, archetypally womanly, not waifish, maybe in her late twenties, with nipple-length wavy red hair and pale skin—like Morpheus's Thelemite alter ego. She is strapped into layers of jangly belly-dancing gear, with a breastplate covered in thin metal coins; a sword hangs from a sash around her waist. She circles the floor, flanked by the two Children, who serve as grown-man altar boys (Mark looks both proud and sheepish in her presence). In a bold, slow belly dance, taking her sweet time, she snakes her way around the room like a master performer. The men trail after her in their robes.

"Greeting of Heaven and Earth!" she announces in Crowleyite English. In response, everyone gestures with their arms—the Hailing Sign of a Magician—as if we're pledging allegiance to an exotic flag. I watch Sophia the way I've watched Morpheus: she's gripping enough as a priestess to make me wonder how it would feel to be in her position.

At this point, the Priest has emerged from within the curtained archway— this must be Josh—dressed in white, young, pale, and starved-looking, with a trim black beard and large black eyes: some artist's portrait of a "mystic." He holds a silver-tipped lance in his hand, and the V-neck of his robe reveals an elaborate chest tattoo: a cross with a massive rose at its heart. The Priestess wraps him in a hooded cape and places a crown on his head.

Now she kneels before him; the tension between them is palpable. She passes her hands up and down the lance as he tilts his head back and finally exhales. If a truly erotic moment was ever possible between two people in robes and breastplates and a fake crown, this is it—everyone in the pews can feel it.

"So mote it be!" we call out.*

The Priest leads the Priestess up the steps of the main altar and—"I set thee upon the summit of the Earth!"—seats her there, blesses her, kneels in adoration of her. Then he closes the red curtain so that she's out of sight.

The ceremony continues in this elaborate style. We kneel on the floor with arms raised and palms touching, like "ancient Egyptians" in an Old Hollywood movie; people take turns pronouncing Crowley's heady prose. Finally, the curtain is pulled back to reveal:

The Priestess, completely naked, seated on the altar. In her hands she holds the halves of the eucharist: a bronze paten and the glass chalice of red wine. She has her legs spread wide, aggressive: Babalon, the Scarlet Woman, Thelema's holy whore, who contains all the contradictions of women.

This is *great* theater.

The Priest chants as he stands before her:

IO IO IO IAO SABAO
KURIE ABRASAX KURIE MEITHRAS KURIE PHALLE
IO PAN, IO PAN PAN, IO ISKHUROS, IO ATHANATOS IO ABROTOS
IO IAO.
KHAIRE PHALLE KHAIRE PAMPHAGE KHAIRE PANGENETOR.
HAGIOS, HAGIOS, HAGIOS IAO!

I don't know what I'm listening to, but *this* sounds like the language of magic: Because it's precise but indecipherable? Because it has the rhythm of a dark dream?

And now it is time for communion.

While the Catholic believes in the miracle of transubstantiation, the Thelemite, who takes a dose of science with his mysticism, believes in *the*

---

* This magical phrase is used often in the Craft as well, lifted from the rites of the Freemasons.

Miracle of the Mass only *forasmuch as meat and drink are transmuted in us daily into spiritual substance*—in other words, only insofar as every person's digestive tract is kind of miraculous. Here the "sacrament" (a shot of red wine and a gnarly cookie called a "Cake of Light") is not the blood and flesh of a Christ figure, but a celebration of the universe, whose material we're made of, with which we have the right to reunite ourselves. Tonight we consume Chaos, the stuff that predates time.

The Priest goes first: he crosses the host and the wine on the altar and consumes them both. He turns to face the congregation: "There is no part of me that is not of the gods!"

Now the Children step forward and take their places on either side of the altar, each with a tray in his hands. One by one down the rows, the congregants—initiates and visitors alike—rise from their chairs and approach. I watch as Dan takes his turn. He is so seasoned: even in his state, he slips his arms into his crutches, rises without hesitation, and walks to the altar, his wife trailing after him. Looking as if every ounce of his energy is committed to keeping himself upright, Dan waits for his wife to pick up a cake off the tray for him and place it in his mouth. He chews it, keeping his eyes squarely on the Priestess, then downs the shot glass of wine that she holds to his lips, somehow without anything dribbling onto his white shirt. Then, impressing everyone present, he clicks his crutches on the floor loudly and says in a booming Southern voice for all to hear, "THERE IS NO PART OF ME THAT IS NOT OF THE GODS."

The ceremony has me riveted. Despite the dizzying, obsessive details, it suddenly looks simple: these people are trying to exit the mundane and commune with the Sublime. And they get there through a form of self-hypnosis: the theater of the occult. What does it matter where the strings of words and chanted names come from? Whatever it takes to bend and stretch the human mind to get at this fleeting sense of connectedness.

Just as the music drops out, it's my turn at the altar. Slowly, barefoot, I walk past the Deacon to Mark and pick a cake from his tray (his face is stiff and focused). I feel prepared; I want to be here. I place it in my mouth and begin to chew. Only now do I dare look up into the Priestess's face—Sophia's face—pale and round, her eyes rimmed with black kohl. As I receive this parallel-universe sacrament, some part of me is re-creating a childhood experience—but now, instead of a Catholic priest, a naked woman towers over me, her eyes fixed on some point in space. This pellet is both gummy and dry as dirt—but I *want* to take part. I think to myself, "I am meant to chew this until I am ready to swallow. I am meant to eat this and let it dissolve inside me." Then I take my cup and swallow hard.

I turn around now and look out into the darkened temple. Facing the congregation, I stumble—I forget to cross my arms—but I manage to get the words out, loudly and clearly: I tell the people here that every part of me is divine.

What would it take to honestly believe that?

After the mass, we line up to wash our glasses in the kitchen sink. Everyone is quiet, as if they don't want to talk for a little while. I feel a bit drunk on the experience (not the wine), light-headed from the incense.

Jay throws a crimson cloth on the table in the library—"Let's class things up"—and the guys bring out a few bottles: cheap champagne, red and white wine, an Old New Orleans–brand white rum. Coors is also being sold out of the fridge for $2 a pop.

Now changed into a white tee, Jay's considering starting up the backyard hot tub, to help with his back pains: he injures himself at work on construction jobs nearly every day. He shows me his thumb, which has a deep, V-shaped wound in its pad; just days ago, he cut a chunk out of it, picked up the wedge of finger, pressed it back in place, and bandaged it nice and tight. "We'll have to see if it sticks!" he says with a broad, gross-out grin.

A junior member shows up—someone tells me he'd nearly joined a Jesuit seminary—and disappears upstairs to have an esoteric talk with Andrew. A young white woman with black dreads, all in black lace, arrives to borrow a specific book on Voodoo for her "work." Jay now returns from the backyard, having received a healthy electric shock from the misrigged hot tub (he's still working out the kinks). I can't lie—I'm having a good time with this group. They're incredibly geeky, but also close enough to my own age to relate to, and with some attractive people thrown into the mix (this never hurts).

The Priest and Priestess now make their appearance, to mingle with the group: the center has arrived. Josh emerges first, and seen close-up, his face and neck slick with sweat, he's handsome, but his features border on the severe: sunken eyes, blanched skin, and a lean muscularity that's nearly gaunt. As if someone so long focused on the dope- and opium-addled occultists of the turn of the last century has naturally taken on their physique. I can also better make out now, through the open neck of his robe, the tattoo that covers his chest: a large iron cross with arms of equal length and a red rose's head at its center. Fine black rays emanate from it in all directions. I learn that this is the Rosy Cross, a symbol of the Great Work and the advanced marking of the fifth degree, received by invitation only. I imagine the pressure and buzz and pain of the needle pressing insistently into his half-sunken chest, just inches from his heart.

For all his fascinating drama, Josh has the frenetic quality of a super-smart teenage misfit, running around blowing cigar smoke into the faces of the deities whose altars have colonized the house, pouring large shots of rum into a bourbon glass and drinking too quickly. He blows thickly into the face of the two-foot-high Baphomet, with its female breasts and oversized goat's head, flanked by glasses of champagne; then Ganesh atop the bookcase; and Legba in the kitchen. He's not at all the priest he was inside the temple itself; he's more high-strung now, clearly someone who lives a lot in his head and talks a mile a minute and rarely sleeps on schedule, staying up all hours to record his thoughts.

Sophia, in stark contrast, has a steadiness to her. Josh's longtime girlfriend (which explains the chemistry), she reemerges after mass radiant, changed into a white cotton dress and holding a bunch of red roses taken from the temple altar. She hands them around to the women present, as is their tradition. When I first thank her, she is immediately dismissive of the intensity of my reaction, shrugging it off to spare me the embarrassment. I realize that her guard must be up after mass, never knowing what occult-curious stranger has just seen her naked on top of an altar. She will later tell me, when I finally have the courage to ask her about this, how she's developed a method of shielding herself: she does not mingle before the ritual, or even look out into the congregation during the mass itself, because she doesn't want to know who's there. Only once each person approaches to take the sacrament does she register who's in the temple.

Sophia mentions that she'd heard of another OTO body where, during the mass, a visitor actually walked up the altar steps to approach the naked priestess. "I mean, can you imagine?" she says. "I have to trust and feel protected by my brothers and sisters—to trust that if something terrible were to happen they would protect me." She tells me that two Muslim friends came once, young men whom she'd met on a visit to Egypt. "One of them had never even had a girlfriend before, and they're seeing me up there on the altar—and afterward they were really cool about it."

For his part, Mark is thrilled with his first evening as a Child, and gushes about Sophia, tonight's Great Mother. "She would be a serious priestess no matter what tradition she'd chosen." There seems to be a sort of Cult of the Priestess built into the Gnostic Mass. The women think about becoming her (at least I do); the men pay close attention to her, hyperaware of her presence. Fingering a jingle coin on the tabletop, fallen from Sophia's breastplate, Jay says that he once found one on the temple floor and kept it for his private shrine. When he tried to return it to her out of guilt, Sophia laughed and refused to take it back.

Just moments after Jay's story, Mark sees the coin Jay's left on the table and picks it up. "Can I take this?" he asks, then slips it carefully into his pocket. "I'm going to put this on my altar."

8

The Vetting Process

Around this time, I have a dream.

I'm out on a date with my lawyer, a tall, polite Canadian—the kind of stable, practical-minded person some friends wish I would date. In the dream we're strolling side by side in the nighttime air, and he radiates a Zen-like calm, nothing like the chaotic temperaments I'm usually drawn to. But the calm is short-lived. At some point I realize we've entered a large house, maybe in Los Angeles or Marrakesh, the house of a stranger— maybe we've ended up at a party. The place is elaborate, seemingly endless, straight out of those Italian and French exploitation horror films from the seventies: an abstract castle with curving, cream-colored stone walls and high ceilings, the vast rooms marked with faux-medieval details. Without a thought, I leave my date behind and walk deeper into the building, until the string of vast rooms comes to an end, narrowing into a white stone stairwell.

The stairwell is wide and grand and open on all sides, and I can see that it winds upward one or two more flights, and down one or two more flights below. The space is lit by huge wall torches hung high in the recesses in the walls. I hide in one of these nooks and see . . .

. . . a procession of people in long, hooded red robes, their faces obscured, winding steadily down the stairwell. I think to myself, "Oh, these are the *real Druids*." And at just that moment, I'm discovered! Easily, with more of a shrug than a great reveal—as if they'd expected to find me there all along.

I'm taken below, and for some reason I'm worried they'll force me to strip down. (Skyclad, I think, skyclad.) Instead, after some debate, two of the hooded men step forward and lead me into a chamber where the walls are metal and painted in sickly blues and greens. It reminds me of the engine room on a cargo ship, the down-below place in certain gritty films where people are held captive or interrogated or done violence to. Now the men take off their hoods, and I learn they've made a plan: they're going to prostitute me. I suddenly notice a woman in the room as well, an older woman—a *witch*—and she suggests they close the door for privacy, before they "break me in." Already ashamed and degraded, I try to stall the men as they begin to remove their robes—

I wake up in my bed, feeling terrified—then embarrassed and ridiculous.

The next morning, I realize what I have to do. In spite of the cartoonish terrors it's inspired, my curiosity about the Craft refuses to fade. I owe it to myself to try to answer the questions I have. I sit down and write to Morpheus, subject line "The Inevitable Email."

I tell her I want to train in Feri.

I wait for her reply.

Two weeks go by, and no word from Morpheus. The moment I hit *send*, I immediately felt self-conscious, exposed, wondering if I'd crossed a line. This process is not as simple as it might be with, say, an evangelical Christian group: Pagans do not proselytize, and a priestess of a mystery cult does not sign you up at a moment's notice. Groucho Marx would have understood the witches: their clubs do not necessarily want you as a member.

When she finally writes to me, of course, Morpheus is "thrilled." She tells me what I'd already predicted: I will have to connect with a teacher. "The real power and heart of the tradition come by way of relationships between teachers and students," she writes. "Finding the right person is *the big thing.*"

Somewhere in the back of my mind, I'd assumed that she and I might work together, but I know that, with the upheaval in her personal life, she's taken a hiatus from teaching. She has someone else in mind: Karina, a Feri priestess "somewhere in New England" who founded her own line of the tradition, BlackHeart Feri. "She is full of juicy power, a sweet human being, and a demanding teacher," Morpheus writes. She thought of Karina instinctively when picturing me studying with someone. (And this is a community that places a lot of stock in first instincts and mental images.)

Putting aside fears of oversharing, I'd also asked Morpheus for her thoughts on the notion of "being called." I am trying to pin down what's spurring me on, since I've certainly not had anything approaching a *divine revelation*. If anything, I'm fairly embarrassed by my desire to train. On a certain level, this new urge is the equivalent of me waking up one day—me, the skeptic—and announcing that I've found Jesus. I'd written her:

I think of you and your relationship to the Morrigan, and that is not what I'm feeling right now. There is no specific entity reaching out to me directly--it's more the sense of a PULL. The image that continues to come to mind is this: I keep seeing a large, ornate silver box that I only just discovered is inside of my chest. And while the box at first seems impenetrable, I am suddenly able to see that it's made up of individual panels, and if I just tap gently on each panel, in the right way, each will open up for me. But if I do nothing, it will remain just that: just a box.

I wish there were more information contained in this image, but that's it for now. And I know that a woman in white, flowing robes is not going to call to me--that's just not my idea of Her/Him/It. I'm not sure what is.

On this point, Morpheus replies—and what she writes can be said of most witchcraft traditions, not only Feri:

People sometimes say that those who are meant for Feri tradition will feel "called" to it. The reason being that it's got a strong tribal quality, and there's a belief that some people are either born to it and just needed to find their way home, or else they are brought to the tradition because the Gods or the Fey mark them for it. Not everybody believes this, mind you. Some people come to Feri because its practices or energy simply speak to them. But when people talk about being "called" that's what they usually mean. Feri teachers often want to see that a potential student is really suited for, and really deeply drawn to, the tradition, before they want to spend a lot of time working with them . . . Also, some teachers have a practice of resisting the request of a student a certain number of times before they will accept them, just to make sure their interest is genuine and strong.

I also don't think everyone's experience is the same or should be. Just because you may not have had a dramatic moment of being chosen by the Goddess doesn't mean the Gods don't want you, if you know what I mean. And you referenced my relationship with the Morrigan, but that didn't become what it is overnight . . . Over time the relationship deepened to what it is now. So I think it isn't always helpful to look for a dramatic "calling" or marking experience . . . If the tradition speaks to you in a meaningful way, that is a good place to start.

On that note, she offers me a reference, which some Feri teachers will ask for, and sends me on my way. (There is not much New Age hand-holding in the Feri crowd.)

Still, I hesitate to contact Karina. I let the prospect of training sink in, wanting to be certain that I have the right intentions. The cutthroat inside me wants to study for the secrets I'd uncover—writer or not, this is part of the appeal. But I can't approach training in one of witchcraft's great mystery cults on that note. I can just imagine the tidal waves of bad karma that would crash down on me, for one thing; but I also feel I'd be missing an opportunity if I came at this sideways. If there is even an outside chance that the

Craft offers up tools that *work*, then I should not rig the game. I should play it out.

This is the classic launching point of ancient myths and movie plotlines alike: the would-be apprentice petitions the master for training, and, once accepted, she is launched down the path to initiation and a new identity. So how to approach this teacher, who isn't a kung fu master (or whatever)? How does a person approach a *witch* for training? Do I make a pilgrimage to her door and camp out in a tent until she lets me inside? Do I impress her by memorizing Aramaic texts and reciting them backward as I crawl over broken glass? Do I shave my head, fast for ten days, and then tap out a Bat Signal to her in Morse code on my straw mat?

In reality, the answer is obvious: I e-mail her.

Let me be clear: I know almost nothing about Karina. I don't know what she looks like (beyond an oversaturated photo I dig up online: wavy brown hair, puffy cheeks). I don't know how old she is, the tone of her voice, or even what state she lives in. For now, however, this is unimportant. I know nothing about what makes a great Feri teacher—what matters to me is Morpheus's belief in her.

The mysterious, faceless, voiceless Karina does not keep me waiting: she responds the next day. She is pragmatic. "Honored and humbled by a request for training," she now sends me her "preliminary interview" form. There will be no casual phone call, no feeling each other out, until I fill out an extensive, probing questionnaire.

So begins the vetting process.

Karina's questionnaire is part "let's get to know each other" and part psych profile. I answer her questions candidly, offering up intimate information about myself—because she demands it, but also because I know from experience that you can't fake the level of honesty required to form this kind of bond. An intuitive person (and witches are nothing if not intuitive) can smell fakery like a stink. I address her delicately, choosing words with precision and deference. (I also let her know that I'm writing about my experiences.) At the same time, as I fill out the interview—with questions like "What are your phobias?" and the ultra-blunt "Psychiatric diagnosis?"—the cynic in me realizes this would be a neat document for someone to have in her back pocket if we were ever to part ways unhappily. (The Craft priestess-student relationship, though it has its own ethics, has neither the legal underpinnings of doctor-patient confidentiality nor the enforced silence of the Catholic confessional.) So, while remaining pretty candid in my responses, I double-check for any comments I'd hate to have get out. After all, Karina is literally compiling a file on me.

At the same time, this testing, this bonding over long-distance correspondence, is the way in which relationships were built long ago—as if I'd sent a telegram by messenger, carried by mule, to a spiritual leader living high up in the mountains somewhere. I try to instill romance into our functional e-mail exchange, conducted through several rounds of follow-up questions. I tell Karina what I fear most: "Loneliness. Failure—however I'm defining that at a certain moment in time. And here's a new one: aging and not feeling ready for it." I tell Karina my greatest weaknesses: "self-doubt"; "random episodes of unexplained, unpredictable social shyness"; "financial instability brought on by forgetting to make money." I tell her why I'm drawn to Feri: I am "drawn inexplicably to what I perceive to be a darkness" at its core, a darkness that seems connected to "the mysteries" I experienced as a young girl in the Catholic Church. I tell her what I think I'll get out of training: "freedom" and "the ability to tap into a part of myself that feels trapped inside." Finally she asks, "Are you willing to uphold the four-fold way of the Witch? To Know, to Dare, to Will and to hold Silence?" This is the first time I've been asked head-on if I am willing to accept the ways of witchcraft. My answer is yes.

And so, after a month's correspondence, Karina writes to me, "Your words and actions thus far speak volumes, as does Morpheus' recommendation. I am very pleased she sent you to connect with me." She agrees to set up our first phone call for "a live discussion." "Tone means a lot and just cannot be conveyed adequately in an email."

To be frank, on the eve of our first chat, I still have hesitations.

First, there is the question of money, of paying for religious or magical training. I am a little surprised when I learn that Karina charges a monthly fee—the cost of the average smartphone bill. The fantasy of studying with a high priestess does not include billing through PayPal.

"Yeah, the charging for training is a whole can of worms," Morpheus writes after I mention this. "People have, ahem, strong feelings on all sides of that issue . . . I personally don't have an issue with money being exchanged for teaching if it's not exorbitant and if it's done gracefully. Your own instincts and feelings on it should be your guide, though." Money is the source of controversy and dissent in all areas of life, and the Pagan community is no exception. Morpheus charged when she taught, and Thorn has a regimented billing structure. Victor Anderson never charged a fee—then again, he began teaching in another era, and lived with Cora on the edge of poverty their entire lives.

I raise this subject in my next exchange with Karina, in what I think is measured, even self-conscious language. I ask about her "philosophy behind charging," and if I can offset the costs with some form of barter—I make a self-deprecating joke about my writer's "vow of poverty"—signing off, "I ask about this with complete respect for what you do."

Her reply is long and hard. Her note makes me blush—and briefly question whether we'll be able to work together.

I charge for spiritual training because it is my work. I don't do this part time, as a hobby or as an aside to another "real" job. This is my real job. If I were a Priest in any other Tradition, my housing, food, clothing, toiletries, temple and tools would be provided along with a stipend. This money would be tithed to me by the congregation or the larger organization. I have been teaching Paganism, Witchcraft and then Feri Tradition for more than 20 years. In that time I have tried teaching for free, barter, tithing, donation, sliding scale, fixed scale, and now fixed fee. I've settled upon the fixed fee because it works. People understand having a monthly fee. They pay attention to it, pay on time. My kids and I are not (quite) starving.

I understand money is a form of energy . . . My landlord, the utility companies, the gas station and the stores where I purchase the things my family needs do not accept any other form of exchange. Money is not dirty or tainted. It is an agreed-upon method of energy exchange.

I'm not sure where the idea came from that money and
spirituality cannot coexist in a manner that is clean.
I feel it is an immature stance based upon mistrust of
clergy . . . and some very old ideas about the nobility of
poverty. Those who gave up the luxuries of home and family
for the begging bowl were never seen in the same light as
those born to the begging bowl. Those who chose a life of
poverty were usually born to the noble classes and had
completed their "worldly" obligations when they made the
choice. And home (and wealth) were always there to return
to. Finally, we are no longer living in an era where
monastic life is possible, necessary or required . . . One
cannot live on prayer and meditation alone. Our gods do not
require it of us . . . Everyone gets paid (money) for the
work they do in the world. Why is spiritual work different?

Karina's note becomes increasingly personal and intense:

It feels important that you know that I am the sole parent
of two kids. There is no physical or financial "support"
from the father or anyone else. We are far enough below the
poverty line to receive food stamps and Medicare. No one is
getting rich teaching witchcraft to 20 people at $90/month
each. And even if I were living a more financially
comfortable life, would that somehow cheapen what I offer?
Why? Must our Priests be impoverished? Does suffering make
us holy? These are intensely important questions.

I am interested in your interest about my ideas around
money. What are yours? Would you ask these questions of a
college professor? A musician? A doctor? A social worker?
What is it about spirituality that causes these questions
to arise?

This last paragraph makes me blush. I'd assumed that Karina was
middle- or lower-middle-class, but I would not have guessed that she was

the single parent of two kids living partly off food stamps. I assumed this because I wasn't thinking. I'm surprised at the pointedly personal turn things have taken so quickly, but I think over her comments: Karina is making a valid point. If we were living in another time or in another culture, her monthly fee would be paid out . . . how? Through hours spent scrubbing the floors of the dojo or mending the master's shoes or dicing basketloads of carrots for the sisters' lunches. It could take the form of a dowry handed over to the convent, or a donation from a wealthy church patron. There has *always* been payment for spiritual training, in one tradition or another—Pagans simply do not have the infrastructure, the broad and affluent network, to make that unquestionably clear.

A less loaded issue, though just as unexpected, is that of "distance training," which will make up the better part of my first series of lessons. I have expectations of what witchy training might consist of—informed, I'm sure, like everyone else's, by movies or fantasy books from my childhood. A blood oath. Lessons under cover of darkness. Secrets, secrets, secrets. Tools and tricks that can only be learned in a dark room through the passing of hands. And so it catches me off-guard to realize I've been drawn into a long-distance relationship. This begins to hit me when I read a thoroughly detailed document Karina has sent outlining her requirements: I'm to e-mail her weekly, by Thursday night, to be supplemented by occasional phone calls; and I'll receive my lessons as password-encoded online videos. Finally, in a few months, I'm to visit her home, at my own expense, for some actual face-to-face time.

Though Morpheus would not teach this way, it's become common as the Pagan community across the country has continued to expand (Thorn, for example, often teaches through video Skype). Besides, especially with a smaller sect like Feri, geography can simply get in the way: It's that much harder to find a teacher near home through a close personal reference—the approach that's served me well this far. I decide to submit fully, whatever Karina's approach. Any initial doubts are swept aside by her frank parting list of "personal things":

It's really important that you understand at the outset of your training that I am a human being . . . I have not reached a perfected state. I am vulnerable to making mistakes and having struggles of my own. It is not my Way as a Teacher to pretend I'm okay when I'm not. Rather, I stress transparency and authenticity. So, please don't judge me if/when you witness *my* mistakes and struggles toward my own growth and development. Rather, observe what I do while in the midst of it and how I work to move forward. I don't tolerate "pedestals" well. If you need a Teacher you can enthrone upon a pedestal, you will either grow out of that (because I will keep kicking that pedestal out from under me) or we will part ways.

It's also important for you to understand that in order for your Training to actually *work* you are going to have to trust me. You are going to have to make yourself vulnerable. Tell me what's going on in your life--in your relationships, your home life, your job, your social life. What's happening with your health, your diet, your dreams and desires? *All* of these are affected by your Training. I cannot teach you if I do not know what's going on for you. I speak plainly and openly. There may be times when you do not like what I say. That's okay. Align your souls . . . Do your best to see how you might be projecting upon me.

The student-teacher relationship is a very special one. We must trust and honor one another. We must be truthful and ethical in our relationship. The time you spend in Training is a very special time. Respect and honor yourself for having the courage to undertake this! And, have *fun* with it . . .

So Be It!

The first time I hear Karina's voice I realize I'm cradling the cordless phone against my cheek the way I did late at night in high school. The conversation starts out stiff, a bit more formal than I'd like it to be, in the tone of two people who haven't yet figured out when they're allowed to crack a joke. But we're feeling each other out—after all, it's an audition.

I ask Karina what this first "cycle" of training will entail. This phase, she explains, will be about clearing out, cleansing, setting the table for a long-term witchcraft practice. (Much of her approach, especially this early on, could be applied to starting out in other Craft traditions.) She reminds me that Victor and Cora gave different lessons and tools to each of their students, based on a sense of their individual needs. "It's not a cookie-cutter tradition." The goal is to "bring the student to herself," to help me see clearly what my personal advantages and obstacles are—all psychological, of course—and how they'll help or undermine my magic. "One of the things Feri asks us over and over is 'Who are you, who are you, who are you?'" she says. "We examine the blocks inside you that hold memory and determine our behavior. We start clearing those out—the things that derail us—so we can start making choices that were not implanted in us by people who were stronger than us when we were little." The objective of Cycle One, therefore, is to "become self-aware"—a goal some people spend four sessions of therapy a week for years trying to accomplish. I may have just enlisted for therapy through witchcraft.

I tell Karina that I'm already conscious of one mental block. I know that I'm drawn to ritual and the high-mass mystery of spellwork—but I've only begun to grasp the religious side to the Craft. Who is this *Goddess* to me? Do I have a bona fide relationship to her, not to mention the other categories of deities in this many-pronged system of gods of this-or-that? And does this all presume that I have an unshakable belief in *any* kind of supernatural being? I know I believe in something greater than the sum of our quotidian business, but, as I wrote to Morpheus, I do not think that "something" is embodied by a woman in white, flowing robes: to me, that image belongs to the hippies on the Pagan scene, more seventies Stevie Nicks than Creatrix of the Universe. As I discovered in Illinois, right now I cannot imagine growing closer to that woman, that idea—I can only hope there's an incarnation of her that I can relate to.

Karina sort of *phone*-shrugs at this. "What we're doing is realizing our *own* divine nature," she says, and quotes Victor Anderson: "'God is self and self is God and God is a person like myself.' So when we commune with the gods we can commune with them as peers." I tell her this reminds me of reading the Greek and Roman myths when I was a young girl: I was struck by how like humans their gods and goddesses were, with their petty jealousies and ranting and raging. "We're not meant to revere them as beings without fault," Karina says, "but to see that they're no different than we are, and not to martyr ourselves to what they are." Besides, there's no rush: in Cycle One, the cleansing and self-awareness comes first, only then to be followed by "working" with deities. Because this easy relationship to the gods (assuming you can subscribe to their existence) requires a lot of sweat. You have to clear up your own issues so that you don't bring a lot of baggage or presumptions—most likely from the religious system you were raised within—into your Craft practice. Again with the psych talk: you have to get past "false beliefs" in order to avoid having an unhealthy, "codependent" relationship with your gods.

In trying to suss out what our teacher-student dynamic will be, Karina asks how old I am, and I tell her: thirty-four. "That's a great age for this work," she says. "In our culture, we don't even get to be grown-ups until we're thirty. You've lived enough life; you're not going to argue with me like I'm your mommy, like twenty-two-to-twenty-seven-year-olds do. The unresolved mommy struggles get projected onto me, and I hate that. I have my own kids, and you can't pay me enough!" She laughs hard.

As we continue talking, for forty minutes or so, we both let our guards down a bit; she lets herself curse when the urge strikes her, and I'm relieved. She's a straight talker, and she finds parts of this woo-woo witchcraft talk as funny as I do. I'm learning that anyone who cannot laugh about lofty spiritual talk is not someone I can relate to or fully trust. Besides, I like the sound of her voice, and I can tell she's a tough woman: the only disposition I would accept in a teacher.

Decided, I tell Karina that I will start my training next week. I have found myself a mentor in witchcraft.

One topic I deliberately did *not* bring up in this first talk with Karina—it would have been wildly premature—is my fantasy of Feri initiation. At this point, I know only what Morpheus has told me about her own experience, and maybe it's immature of me, but I want to know what she knows. The climactic moment involves the whispering in your ear of the true name, the unpronounceable name, of the Goddess. (*Is* it whispered? That's how I imagine it.) At first this did not sound like a big deal—it's just a word. But, thinking more about it, imagining that precise moment, I see the magnitude of finally hearing a name that only a very small, select number of people on the planet know. A single word you are meant to contain inside of yourself, to whisper inside your head, to dare pronounce out loud only in the most intimate circle—a circle that likely doesn't include even your closest friends or family—for the rest of your life. This is how a mystery tradition treats language: as a secret to be experienced, not merely repeated to others like an instruction manual or facts laid out on a Wikipedia page. And what's more important, Feris understand, is not so much that abracadabra name itself, as sacred as it is, but the shock of hearing it for the first time. A witch learns how to withhold language—and when to release it—for maximum impact.

There's a long list of secrets that Morpheus knows that I do not, and I want in on all of them—because secrecy is intoxicating, but also because this is the only way to understand her experience as either reality or self-delusion. I can still see her clearly that night in the double ballroom, pacing the carpeted floor in her bare feet, gripping her vulture wings, and speaking to the hundreds of people there in a wholly different voice. I want to understand what happened that night, what could not possibly have happened that night, what might have happened that night.

But how might witchcraft initiation, if I got that far, shift my story of myself? Now solidly in my thirties, I spend increasing amounts of effort piecing together my narrative, explaining my past behaviors to myself as chapters along the way to the protagonist I've become. And if this protagonist was revealed to be a "witch," what then? I have always lived as an insider's outsider: raised in a high-end part of Manhattan, but to immigrant, so-called New Money parents; educated at a private school for girls, but one of the few who were not ethnic blondes who rode horses on the weekends; certified by an Ivy League university, but as a "creative type" determined not to take advantage of its business-government matrix; an attractive woman, but with a challenging, overly rarefied taste in "creative" men. At this point, I see that at nearly every step I've chosen a complicated freedom over anything that might look or feel too much like a conventional life or a traditional relationship. In and of itself, this is difficult—but the real threat to myself has come through my unwillingness to *own* my nature, attempting, instead, a half-assed balancing act between the freedom I'm attracted to and something stabler, more comforting.

I don't blame myself: it is terrifying to contemplate an identity as a noncommittal, non-child-bearing woman who's married solely to her art and her travels and her friendships—in many essential ways, an outsider. If that's my true story, my nature, then right now, in committing to train in witchcraft, I'm edging into territory that I've been meant to inhabit all along.

Because isn't that what a witch is? The mysterious solo woman at the edge of town, consumed with her own fascinating schemes and unconcerned about what the townspeople think? She's part enigma, part exile, like most artists. People are excited by her and don't know what to do with her. Of course, she's also *repellent*, the woman the townspeople rise up against and stone to death in Act III. But that's more than I can process right now.

9

Cycle One

I receive my first lesson from Karina in an e-mail labeled "Cycle One Class One," saying "Karina has invited you to view a folder of content"— "content," in this case, meaning oath-bound lessons in witchcraft. I click on the enclosed link and find a series of nearly twenty video clips at an encoded website. I'm supposed to watch each clip in order, without repeat and without interruption, for a total of six hours of class time.

Here are things that I know—that *many* of us know—a witch does: she lights candles, she chants, she charges objects with magic, she pours things in and out of chalices, she waves daggers through the air, she mixes up herbs and powders, she talks to gods and goddesses. By this point, I've tried most of these things on my own, and I've taken part, in my searching around, in enough rituals—rituals open to the still-uninitiated—that I am already at least vaguely familiar with the rhythms in common, the dramatic gestures, the liturgy and invocations repeated across certain traditions. And now I want to know what it would take to cross over, to begin slowly traveling toward the inner circle of one of the Craft's more secretive and ecstatic clans. To learn a piece of what Morpheus knows.

Toward this end, I find myself, yet again, trying to strike a balance between the exotic and the super-banal, positioning my laptop on the coffee table and shoving throw pillows behind my back, the better to sit up at attention. I start playing the clips; as requested, I watch them all the way through, one time only. The look of the videos is simple and as lo-fi as promised, shot about five years ago, in the den of Karina's previous home, by a student with a consumer camera and a tripod. Karina sits—the whole thing's a still shot— with a small circle of students, whose voices I hear, and who sometimes flash an arm or a leg on-camera, but who are otherwise kept anonymous. I later learn that her current students, all twenty-five of them, are in several states—Massachusetts, New Hampshire, Wisconsin, Missouri, Texas, Colorado, Oregon, and California—as well as in Germany (Karina leads Feri workshops there). In this first glimpse of my witch-teacher, Karina's wavy brown hair is cut short and loose, and she wears the kind of comfortable clothes good for getting work done around the house. Her warm, round-nosed face exudes an almost bodhisattva calm as she leads the fledgling witches in exercises, or shares anecdotes about Victor Anderson and other figures from Feri's recent past. Now and then, while she talks to the group, a black cat jumps into her lap, demanding she stroke it.

As Karina had explained, the first training rounds will entail an emphasis on cleansing (your environment, yourself), and on clearing up the obstacles (psychological, spiritual) that every person puts in her own way. Clearing the path to make room for witchcraft. I'll admit that some part of me finds this annoying, the meditation and quiet chants and prayer that are required— none of the flashy stuff that my teen self dreamt about. I get the sneaking suspicion that, as with anything worth knowing, my initial studies will test my patience.

Karina named her line of the tradition BlackHeart Feri, after one of the core ideas of Feri: "the black heart of innocence," it's called, in florid language. This is a nod to what Victor claimed is an African saying: "How beautiful is the black, lascivious purity in the hearts of children and wild animals." Our black heart is the wild, animal piece of each of us, the part that most of us lose sometime in our childhood. Our capacity to be dumb and amazed in the face of beauty, the experience of physical pleasure, the deep intake of breath. Karina talks about "becoming black-hearted again," childish and sexual at the same time—a counterintuitive, even taboo combination. Feris, she says, walk "the knife's edge," that precarious zone where seeming opposites meet—good and evil, light and dark—embracing the whole spectrum of the universe, not reducing it to polarities. (In Feri, the words "black" and "dark" also run contrary to how they are often used in white American or European history: something "white" or "light" is not necessarily "good"; and darkness is not inevitably a source of evil.) Karina's own teacher, Mark, told her to "let the universe play you like a violin, all the notes." The entire range of experience, without self-censorship or embarrassment. I am not there yet.

During the first couple of weeks, I began making my way through the reading list, what Karina rightly refers to as a graduate student's courseload of books on Feri and related magical sources. This, paired with daily practice (as she outlined it for me) and a weekly e-mail check-in with my teacher (my chance to run any questions by her), constitutes my budding magical career. In this way, I begin learning some of the core concepts and practices that, in spite of the divergent lines of the tradition, all Feris have in common.

First of all, there's the key belief that we have not one but *three* souls—and our personal power and health and clearheadedness and connection with the divine depend on their being properly aligned. These souls have many names, but they are known mainly as Fetch, Talker, and the Godself (or Godsoul). Broadly put, Fetch is your animal, or most primal and instinctive preverbal, self—"fetch" after the folk notion that a witch can send a part of herself out into the night to bring her whatever she wants. Talker is a lot like the Freudian ego, the intellect, the communicator, what connects you to others. And the Godself is your personal god, your direct line to the wisdom of the universe, the aspect of every human being that is actually on a par with the gods, in communion with them—Feris say it's a blue sphere that hovers above your head, like a halo. The reason ritual is powerful, they believe, is that Fetch, turned on by the visuals and music and heavy breathing and ecstatic dance that come with these ceremonies, sends that high straight up to your Godself. Every Feri practice is grounded in the alignment of these three souls, uniting your parts. To walk around with your souls unaligned is to leave yourself weaker, unsteady, vulnerable to outside influence.

Though ceremonial magic is intensely cerebral, so many of the fundamentals of the Craft are more grounded in the instinctual, in recognizing and using our ties to the natural world and the life cycle, the rhythm of the seasons, the power of sex. Alignment, Karina teaches me, happens by gathering and then redistributing "life force," or mana, and we take in mana—all of us, even those who will never hear that word—through the simple act of breathing. Something so critical to this form of witchcraft does not require chalices or athames or gothic outfits, just your own breath.

Feris breathe in a prescribed way, in sets of four, and then release that mana to do magical work. This is done through the Ha Prayer—*ha* being the Hawaiian word for "breath." I learn how to do this each morning, following Karina's instructions. After the prescribed sets of breaths, focusing on moving mana through specific parts of my body—I do this until all of me is tingling, until I feel dizzy and giddy from the exaggerated flow of oxygen—I say out loud, "May all three souls be straight within me." Then another set of breaths, exhaling the last one hard, up to my Godself: *"Ha!"* And as I absorb the tingling sensation, I launch into some lines from Victor: "Who is this flower above me? And what is the work of this god? I would know myself in all my parts." In other words, I'm asking myself—me, "this god": What is my work? Who *am* I?

I do this every morning.

And what else? I cleanse. I cleanse my apartment and I cleanse myself. I protect my apartment and I protect myself—through folk spells that are over a century old, not specifically Feri but useful toward our ends. As prescribed, I clean the place obsessively. I burn an incense called "dragon's blood," producing the precise thick, musky smell of Greek Orthodox services from when I was a kid. At night, I take baths in beer and salt. Most mornings, I rub the base of my skull and lower back with an egg and hurl it whole into the toilet. Somehow this is going to provide my body and my home, even my temporary home here in New Orleans, with "a clean slate."

"Whatever works," Karina writes of this folk stuff. "This is a strong principle in my lineage, as it was with Victor and Cora: *Use what works.*" I am becoming increasingly aware that initiation into Feri, and practicing any serious form of witchcraft or ceremonial magic, requires a lot of *work*. You can't simply wake up one day, have a revelation, and be baptized into this.

I soldier through and continue to write to Karina each week by the designated date and time, ignoring my reluctance and feelings of embarrassment, and she responds with corrections and thoughts. Sometimes she replies at length, indulging in her habit of capitalizing certain words in German-epic style—"Souls," "Passion," "Work," "Great Power," "Mysteries"—as if to say, "Let me be clear: *this is what's important.*" Sometimes she replies with, simply, "Trust the process," or even "Yep."

This "process" I'm supposed to trust is packed with words and terms and personal experiments that set off my New Age know-thyself alarm bells—but Karina's straight-talking sense of humor prevents me from feeling completely alienated. In one video clip, she tells her students that we have to function as priests "while still paying our car insurance," "because the policeman doesn't *care* about your black-hearted wonderment." At the same time, her multiple personalities—from Zen priestess to no-bullshit teacher to pushed-to-her-limit single mother—have me on edge. She does not hesitate to write admonishing, sometimes testy e-mails to the group when she believes it's called for.

I've deliberately signed up with a group not known for a forgiving, tree-hugging approach to witchcraft, a community that demands respect, seriousness, and total focus—even if, as in my case, you are training from a distance. The single word that comes up most when other Pagans speak about Feris is "intense"; and when Feri talk about themselves, it's often as difficult, headstrong, highly sexual, sometimes barely socialized people. "Feris are the ones who are of the tribe but *not* of the tribe, of the community but *not* of the community," Karina says in Class One. Victor used to say that when primitive man gathered around the fire to get warm and tell stories and prepare for the next day, the witch would walk away from the gathering and out into the darkness. "The witch would walk into the darkness to understand the mysteries, and bring that back for her tribe," Karina says. "We stand on the borders of the culture." While outsider status is romanticized, the reality of standing apart from the culture is frightening. The tenuousness of being that woman at the edge of town.

I'd told Karina that I knew I had no connection to eclectic Wicca, the broad stuff, because "it left me utterly undisturbed"—and that phrasing is the closest I've come to describing what I want. I want to be *disturbed*, shaken into believing. But does that mean relegating myself to the fringe? Does that mean a life apart? Maybe I'm not supposed to know that answer yet. "You are here for a reason," Karina writes. "It may not be the reason you *think.*"

I'd gotten a taste of that feeling—that kind of personal disturbance—at Alombrados, the night of the Gnostic Mass. It's nagged at me ever since. Through Mark (or Happydog) I'd already learned how beginners take their Minerval, a sort of starter initiation to help you determine whether or not you're ready to be bonded to the order for life. Yes, I'm studying with Karina—but what else might be possible? I know Alombrados is having a "social" this Sunday afternoon, a barbecue for prospective members, a chance to ask questions, so I decide to go.

In the backyard, I roll my bike straight up to Dan, who's sitting out of the sun under a white tarp.

"Well, hello, pretty lady!"

As he leans back in his plastic deck chair, crutches tossed onto the patio beside him, I get a good view of the wolf on his neck. Sophia sits with him, barefoot in a clinging purple dress. She gives me a nod.

Looking for David, the body master, I head into the house, where people are hanging out in clusters, eating plates of salmon and quinoa or waiting for sausages to come off the grill.

The crowd today is a mix of members, friends, and occult-curious visitors. Delia, a striking woman with platinum-blond hair and arms inked in magical symbols, looks the part of an occult biker chick. She tells me she makes jewelry; dangling from her many necklaces are the finger bones of a bear. Chris, a serious Thelemite, drives a pedicab to pay for his degree in philosophy. He shares some wine with me, raising his glass for a toast: "Nuit!" I stutter, then give it right back: "Nuit!" I wonder if these magical greetings will ever stop feeling unnatural coming out of my mouth.

I talk to Lucas, who grew up in New Orleans, partly in Tremé. He has a furry beard and a small upside-down-V gap between his two front teeth, and he wears a backward baseball hat and a large fake-silver braided chain over a T-shirt. His father is a Baptist minister, as were his grandfather and great-grandfather before that, and Lucas grew up going to church almost every day. (At this point, he cannot stand to crack open a Bible.) Though he looks African American, he's also part Native American and Creole, and is ready to have a complex discussion about the meaninglessness of the word "black." He speaks in the overwrought manner of a young philosophy student—intelligent and sincere, but definitely twenty-two.

"I don't believe in any of the spiritual suggestions of Thelema," he says. "It's all practical tools. As a philosopher"—he refers to himself by that title—"I have to remain neutral."

Sophia wanders inside, and I watch her cross the kitchen: she once toured with Ozzfest selling T-shirts, but she's much more graceful than her metal past might suggest. We get to talking about the early days of Alombrados. She became interested in OTO when she started dating Josh—and she smiles at how funny this is, the cliché of following your boyfriend into a major life decision. "A few of my friends were really concerned, like, 'Sophia, you're dating someone who's in a *cult.*'" But Josh was very organized about it—he gave her an entire presentation—and she did a lot of research on her own. "I was finally seeing *in words* something I'd believed all along."

Sophia was raised, much like me, by headstrong immigrant parents. Her grandmother would go to church every day in Berkeley, to a very Mary-centric Ukrainian church where above the altar hung a painting of Mary standing on the crescent, crushing the serpent. "On her *own*, front and center—she wasn't with Jesus. The Ukraine has a long tradition of matriarchy, so I'm used to that."

At this point, she's what is called a "novitiate" or a "novice priestess," someone still preparing for full ordination—which amazes me, since she has more presence and authority than anyone in the body other than Josh. Trying to suss out what makes her such a commanding priestess, I ask Sophia if she's been involved in a lot of theater—but she was never a drama-club kid. She marches in a NOLA noise band with homemade instruments—that's about it. Her presence in the mass, she says, comes after a lot of work: she's put years into understanding each piece of liturgy, each gesture, each ritual prop. At least in this way she's like an actor, uncovering her character's motivation and backstory so that she can deliver her lines with conviction. Whenever priestesses from other bodies visited, she'd ask what they thought of her performance and take note. She needed to learn as quickly as possible: when she first met Josh, his newborn OTO body was not performing the Gnostic Mass at all, mainly because they did not have a single priestess, so she found herself under pressure to step up. She started priestessing before she'd even taken her Minerval—in other words, when she was only slightly more qualified than I am today.

Alombrados can still use more priestesses: it shouldn't simply be the Sophia Show, and the near-weekly mass can be exhausting for one woman to pull off. But there is a twofold barrier to entry: the amount of study, on the one hand; and, on the other, the massive guts it takes to offer up your buck naked body on an altar to an ever-shifting occult congregation. "Josh's attitude is that all female members should feel completely comfortable doing the mass," she says. "But I'm, like, 'No, you just don't get it.' Many sexual assaults happen with someone in your social circle. You have to be able to feel secure and protected. You can't just take that for granted." Two other women in the group recently gained the confidence to step up, and they're now in training.

There were hardly any women in the body until Sophia sat the guys down for a talk. "They were pretty clueless at the time, and just sort of depressed to not have any girls coming around." She explained that blasting heavy metal after every mass might be a turnoff to a lot of women; ditto all the yelling during discussions. "And when a woman shows up who's attractive, you might want to give her a second before you swoop in." Now about five women in their twenties and thirties regularly attend rituals and study groups.

It's late afternoon, and I want to approach David. He's talking with some of the others about his hunt for short-term work. A few of the members pay their bills through jobs in construction, carpentry, or waiting tables (David's posted for electrical work on Craigslist). Not sure what to say, or how formal to be, I ask if I can talk to him for a moment, and we huddle together at the steps to the library. Like any good priest, he knows exactly why I've pulled him aside. Needless to say, this is the first time I've requested initiation into a secret society.

David's a mellow guy from Nashville, very receptive, and he reminds me that the Minerval is a "guest degree." In other words, though the initiation will be serious, the degree is meant as a time of study for people exploring Thelema, a way to make certain that I want to continue on to the next level. "Because, while you can leave the body at any time and never again have any associations with OTO, once you take your first degree you're magically linked to us, and that can never be broken. So it's good to know what you're getting into." Some people choose to remain in the Minerval stage indefinitely, "with no shame attached to that," and others move forward into the order.

The next round of initiations is scheduled for late July, an entire long weekend. "We like to take people outdoors, out into the swamp," he says. "So if you do it now it will be *hot*." This means I'd be going out into the Louisiana swamp for a string of days at the height of summer—something pretty inconceivable to those who've experienced any of this season in New Orleans. Then again, as a war story, it's fairly irresistible. "I did it then, and it's tough. You can always wait until the fall, if you'll still be here." No. No waiting. No more opportunities to second-guess myself. I commit. He'll give me my application.

It has been raining on and off all evening, and it's just getting dark when I catch a ride in Mark's car. On the way, he talks about his love of the old Godzilla movies, the original Japanese series. As a kid in Mississippi, he would come home from church every Saturday afternoon and watch them on Channel 8, beamed in from New Orleans. "To be frank, I don't understand what the fuss is today about vampires," he says with serious consideration. "You put a stake through their heart. Zombies, you just shoot 'em in the head. Werewolves—they're pretty scary, but you can get some silver bullets. Godzilla—you can't stop that. He's like Katrina: an unstoppable force of nature. Now, *that's* terrifying."

Talk turns to mass, and I ask a question I've been putting off, about the sacrament. "Hey, by the way, what's in the Cakes of Light? I've read *The Book of the Law*—is that what's really in there?"

"Oh yeah," he says. "All that stuff."

"So . . . blood?"

"Oh yes," he says.

"The blood of . . . an animal?"

"Well, you can just head to Rouses and pick up a packet of chicken livers that are covered in blood and run that into the pan and burn that up into ash, and then put that into the mix."

"And is there ever blood from . . . a *person*?"

"Well . . . sometimes." He seems to be choosing his words carefully. "Sometimes someone will use their blood."

I decide to go for it: "And is there *semen*?"

"Well, yes, sometimes there are bodily fluids, both male and female. A little bit of Josh and a little bit of Sophia." Loaded pause. "They're really good at being careful at this body," Mark says. "They don't want to kill anyone or give anyone anything, so they're very careful about how they handle it. It's all burnt to a crisp."

So: blood from a not-quite-sacrificial animal, mixed with a small dose of the bodily fluids of the Priest and Priestess—his semen, her menstrual blood.* Such a detail, though repulsive, does not *repulse* me. Instead, as I'm troubled to realize, this thrills me a little—I'm thrilled and disturbed, I guess, as I'd hoped I'd be. Some part of me seems to be saying, Here, finally, is the real stuff of the occult.

Maybe I've always *wanted* magic to contain something repellent, as even small children expect it to, instinctively. The practice of magic has always seemed like the dogged pursuit of the truth—a pursuit that's maybe delusional, maybe dangerous—and the truth often contains something repulsive within it.

If some part of magic's core is difficult, raw, and repellent, I learn that magical practice always returns to *balance*, demands it. All Feri magic requires that the priestess be in a state of *kala*—the Hawaiian word for "light" "pure," or "forgiven"—so that the magic will come from a clean place and not be distorted or impotent. They say that when a person is kala she can ask anything of the gods and they will respond. For this reason, Feris work hard to maintain this state, often performing the kala rite numerous times a day.

As my training continues, I, too, learn how to "make kala"—and this single, simple ritual remains one of the most effective, surprising magical technologies I'm taught throughout my foray into the Craft and the occult.

The first time, I perform the rite on cue from Karina (or Karina-on-video), in tandem with my anonymous, offscreen fellow students. I pour myself a glass of water—as much as I can drink in one go. I follow my teacher's

---

* I learn later that these are dripped onto a single cake, burnt to ash, and then mixed in with the rest of the batter. This is the Alombrados method; different OTO bodies have different methods and may use different ingredients.

instructions, in her soothing, no-bullshit, girl-from-Massachusetts voice. While holding the glass—and *breathing*, of course, always breathing—I'm meant to focus on a "block" or a habit, an anxiety, a pattern of thought, that has me winding a piece of mental thread around some curve in my brain. So I settle on this: the sense, always just below the surface of my confident, functional self, that I am a fraud waiting to be exposed. A fraud creatively (I have no idea what I'm doing, this work is not good), professionally (I have no idea what I'm doing, I may never again pay my rent), in my current personal life (I have no idea what I'm doing, I'm lonely).

I cannot tell if the risks I have taken as a writer will ever pay off; I cannot predict if I will ever live a stabler life (a house with a library and enough room to throw a dinner party); I cannot know whether my string of frenetic partners has awarded me experience (as I hope it has) or possibly derailed me (as I imagine in my worst moments). These are normal doubts, I guess, but whenever I let these fears grip me, they are unforgiving, relentless, unwilling to relax their hold.

But this time, instead of resisting, I do as I've been told to do: I let the fears and self-loathing flood me. I let them run through my blood and soak into my skin until I can picture them leaking from the pores on my arms and my cheeks. It feels terrible. *Sit with it.* More terrible still. *Keep sitting with it.* I feel nauseous. To my huge surprise, I begin to cry—fully, effortlessly. I'm weeping while staring at my laptop screen, holding a glass of tap water, and I want someone to help me.

Now—put it into the water! I direct these very real, very painful feelings into the water until they seem to drain from me into the glass, turning the liquid toxic in my mind's eye, like a thick, dark, heavy sludge. This is what life force looks like when it becomes warped, poisonous. The sickening sensations start to fade.

But we're not going to throw the sludge away—we're going to transform and reuse it. I ask the Star Goddess, the invisible lady I pray to every day, to help me transmute the toxins into something bright. I ask and I breathe and I focus on the glass before me—until I see the water become radiant. No longer terrifying, those self-annihilating feelings have become something good for me, something I can use, something I can drink.

In that moment, immediately, I down the whole glass.

I thank the Goddess for her help—though the ritual won't technically be complete until the next time I piss (the full cycle, I guess).

I'm exhausted, and I feel new. And those impenetrable dark feelings have disappeared. Whatever that proves.

Three months into my Feri training and, in spite of my kala revelation, I find myself stuck. I am reserving skepticism as I start to develop my so-called personal practice—but this requires effort. Greater effort on certain days than I anticipated; sometimes I think I'm burning calories just trying to keep an open mind.

For one thing, I continue to stumble with something as fundamental as prayer. Somehow it never occurred to me that I would have to pray, daily. Can I, *sincerely*? Is daily prayer such anathema to who I am? Why do I buck so hard against it? When I pray—and prayer here is not only the hopeful pronouncement of words, but an evocation of the otherworldly (something the Catholic Church would say is impossible)—some part of me, on a gut level, feels this is for suckers, for the unsophisticated, for those easily conned. For the weak.

I stumble; I sissy out. I hadn't anticipated something as simple as this: an innate refusal to commit to my training. I begin behaving strangely, reverting in so many small ways to some less disciplined, high school–insecure version of myself. I'm supposed to start the day with an evocation of the Star Goddess—but I feel bloated. Or tired. Or too busy. I'll do it later. I'll do it when I feel inspired. I'll do it after I write. I'll do it after I send some e-mails. I'll do it when I'm showered and better dressed. I'll do it when I've got a nicer black candle. Maybe I'll pick up a priestly robe of some fine material, and *then* this will feel right. I'll pray when I feel like more of a grown-up. I'll pray when I feel less like shit. I'll pray when I feel less like a phony. I scrutinize myself in the mirror much more than usual, always coming up short, convinced that my age is finally starting to show (it's not). It's as if the IV that steadily drips self-certainty into my brain now has a pinched tube.

I am losing my sense of self. Either that or all kinds of cracks and weaknesses are rising to the surface and making themselves visible, like an outbreak of pimples—and maybe the next step is newer, cleaner existential skin? I keep thinking back to that phrase in the Gnostic Mass: "There is no part of me that is not of the gods." If I even *believe* in some collection of gods, does that statement ring true to me? If they or she or it exists, what would they make of me?

Finally, in one of my weekly check-ins, I confess my doubts to Karina. Her reply, the self-help-ness of which would normally rub me the wrong way, instead comes as a deep comfort. She tells me that the insecurity and the resistance to this alien undertaking are typical of a new Feri student. At the same time, always with the tough love, she's quick to warn me, "Don't allow the 'permission' to stumble and falter to become an excuse to stop."

Karina tells me that, though I describe myself as "confident," "confidence and worth are two different things! I've met drug addicts and abusers who were very confident but had no sense of self-worth." She asks if I think I've evolved past the hang-ups of my teenage years, or simply pushed forward. "The beginning stages of BHF training will give you ample opportunity to review and correct those places that were forgotten, denied, sidestepped or distorted. We have a lifetime to do this work. It took us a long time to get as entrenched as we are in Who We Think We Are. It's overwhelming to think we need to clear all that in a few weeks or months!"

Who We Think We Are. I think of what the photographer Diane Arbus said about "the gap between intention and effect": it's the point "between what you want people to know about you and what you can't help people knowing about you." Her photos exist within that gap, captured with unforgiving clarity. Who, then, is the essential "you," and who gets to decide that—the subject or the viewer? Is there even a *way* to "clear all that," to scrape off that layer of pretense, of off-kilter assumptions about ourselves? And even if there were a way, what would we find underneath? "Who are you, who are you, who are you?" Karina says Feri asks again and again— the most obvious, navel-gazing question. It's essential—some of us spend a lifetime excavating ourselves in hope of digging up the answer before we drop dead—but this line of questioning can also be paralyzing. It can unnerve us. To linger too long on the question is to open a deep well of emotion, personal confusion, vulnerability. It reminds me of how Othniel spoke to me back on that farm in California, when I was dressed in a muumuu—this is the probing tone, the demand for self-exposure, of successful psychotherapy and cults alike. *Empty yourself out! Free yourself of false ego and "identity"!*

It's also, apparently, the wellspring of magic. I wonder whether I am making myself stronger or weaker, increasingly dependent on something that was not even a part of my life a few months ago.

But who *is* this Goddess I'm supposed to commune with every day? The concept of trying to speak to a god regularly (or at all) still strikes me as deeply strange. On top of that, I've been questioning what links could possibly exist, really, between a "Star Goddess" and my own Latin Catholic and Greek Orthodox backgrounds.

Karina slaps me down, gently. "At the risk of how this might sound: a kindergartner doesn't really concern herself with what college she will attend or what career path she will take," Karina writes. "She learns to count and recite the alphabet. Just now is not the time to be worried about what kind of specialist you will become or what style of Witch you might strive to become. The becoming is in the Self. And the work before us right now is to unveil the Self."

There it is again: the specter of the true Self. I'm to strip myself of adult baggage, to infantilize myself, even (a "kindergartner"), to relearn my alphabet, and in this way to "unveil" what I hardly know I'm made of. And so I scrub my floors and pour ammonia down my drains and burn religious-smelling incense and rub my body with unbroken eggs and place a glass of water at my bedside each night (*not* for drinking!) and pin an *azabache* (an evil eye) bead inside my shirt and start each day by lighting a black pillar candle and chant to the Star Goddess and take in mana and hope that the end result of all this will not be a series of newly ingrained tics and superstitions, not a complete personality crisis, but a cleaner, stronger sense of capital-*S* Self on which to build a magical practice. Because there is only so long you can be curious about a phenomenon before pressing your way in.

But back to the question of the Star Goddess and the many deities in the Feri universe I've yet to learn about. Part of what is so uncanny about American Paganism is the image of mostly white Middle Americans worshipping multiple gods and goddesses: we're a vastly Christian culture, and that means *one* God, not lots of them, and you'd better not forget it. And so, even though I was raised quite secular, the license and prerogative to choose your own gods and goddesses—or to allow them to choose you—remains a foreign thing for me, for *most* of us. There is no pantheon in America, there are no American *gods*, only versions of the One God—at least, that's what the majority would have us think. Our witches disagree; our witches have choices.

The very idea of spiritual shopping embarrasses me, and raises a slew of questions. Does a goddess reach out and tap you on the shoulder and ask you to work with her? Doesn't she have better things to do with her time? Why would she turn to *me*? And how do I know that she exists? To have a legitimate, unpretended connection to God or Goddess or an entire army of godlike forms—to have sincere religious beliefs at all—you have to connect on a level that is more than intellectual, and rooted in more than guilt. A cord has to bind you to those beings (assuming they're out there) on a primitive, gut level that your brain can no longer access or deny or cleverly unpuzzle.

I'm surprised by how hard I have to fight not to dismiss the idea of a *Goddess* at the helm of the universe, rather than a handsome, full-bearded Jesus type. Why does that continue to sound like crunchy hippie bullshit? I should want to pray to something female—I'm her *demographic*. I am a little bit shocked to realize that I may be sexist in my view of the gods. I'm very drawn to the female Catholic saints and to Mary—but, instinctively, I distrust the idea of a female entity at the top of the mystical universe. The image lacks the thundering, epic, Germanic authority of a masculine Super-God. How can I think this way? Have I been so shaped by the Christian mainstream, and the God-the-father and God-the-Son of my childhood?

That said—and in spite of Karina's wrist slap—after compiling other people's ideas and beliefs for a couple of years now, I've found two candidates for my own female god: Nuit on the one hand, and Hekate on the other. These two don't arrive in diaphanous white robes; that version of a celestial being springs from a version of feminine nature I can't relate to even in its human incarnations. Whatever I'm capable of praying to has got to feel strong and dark and complex, light and harsh, good and bad both, forgiving but just as ready to strike out when called for.

Let me offer up two portraits, or two (slightly more exalted) dating profiles—though it's unclear who'll be doing the choosing.

Nuit. In my mind, she is an infinite space that is elegant and silent and all-consuming, a darkness, and a calm that is midnight blue. (Her name is, after all, the French word for "night," even if Thelemites pronounce her name with a hard *t*, almost Louisiana-style: *noo-EET*.) She is the black sky, naked and covered in stars. The Egyptians said that when the sun (Ra) sets in the evening, he enters her mouth; and at dawn, the end of night, she swallows the stars to make way for the day, and then he is reborn from inside her. Nuit is also death: when a pharaoh died, he would enter her body, and she would later bring him back to life. Calm and black; all-consuming and resurrecting. Thelemites say she is the infinitely vast circle of which we are all a part, the circle whose circumference is impossible to determine and whose center is everywhere. Her name comes from *Nu*, which is "space," the chaos from which everything first rose up.

It was Nuit who gave birth to the colossal gods of Egypt: green-skinned, ancient Osiris, god of the dead and the afterlife; Set, the long-snouted, monster-headed god of storms who would have his brother brutally murdered; and Isis, the impeccable mother figure, goddess of nature, and the sister-wife who would magically conceive Horus through communion with Osiris's corpse. These staggering beings, with all their homicidal-incestuous melodrama, all trace back to Nuit.

She is the speaker of the first chapter of Thelema's holy book, *The Book of the Law*, where she says, "I am above you and in you. My ecstasy is in yours"; where she is called the Queen of Space, "bending down, a lambent flame of blue, all-touching, all-penetrant, her lovely hands upon the black earth, & her lithe body arched for love." She is "the blue-lidded daughter of Sunset" and "the naked brilliance of the voluptuous night-sky." Nuit tells us that differences and divisions exist merely for the pleasure of uniting across those divides: "For I am divided for love's sake, for the chance of union. / This is the creation of the world, that the pain of division is as nothing, and the joy of dissolution all."

Some occultists and witches see Nuit standing at the intersection of Feri and ceremonial magic, a sort of crossbreeding: Nuit as the Star Goddess. Perhaps this image will be my way into Feri, a way to see this foreign-seeming Star Goddess in an incarnation that attracts me. I see the upward-pointing triangle, like a pyramid, that is Nuit reduced. I place my finger on the center of the triangle in my mind's eye. Death, Space, Chaos—maybe I could love her, the Queen of Space.

And then there is Hekate.

Hekate is a goddess of the underworld, a "chthonic" goddess; her associations are more specific than Nuit's, but just as weighted. She is the goddess of the crossroads and of crossing over; of keys and borders and doorways; goddess of the liminal, the dark spirit of the in-between. She *is* the veil between the worlds. She is also the goddess of fire and the moon; of magic, witchcraft, and necromancy. Wiccans consider her the goddess of witches, and the embodiment of the trio of *maiden, mother,* and *crone.* In perfect sync with Thelema, her name is derived from the Greek word for "will," as in "she who works her will"—the perfect name for the goddess of spell casters.

In the *Argonautica,* Jason performs a ritual for Hekate as prescribed by her priestess Medea: he bathes in a stream at midnight, dresses in a black robe, then digs a pit over which he cuts the throat of a ewe, letting the blood drain into the earth. On a pyre next to the pit he burns the animal whole, completing the sacrifice—then walks away, never turning back. (Eventually, Medea also *curses* Jason through Hekate.) In Virgil's *Aeneid,* the Sibyl invokes Hekate, performing a necromantic rite in order to lead Aeneas down into Hades:

> *The Sibyl first lined up four black-skinned bullocks,*
> *Poured a libation of wine upon their foreheads, and then,*
> *Plucking the topmost hairs from between their brows, she placed*
> *These on the altar fires as an initial offering,*
> *Calling aloud upon Hecate, powerful in heaven and hell.*

Their necks were slit and the hot blood was collected in bowls; the black bulls' whole carcasses were burned over an altar.

> *But listen!—at the very first crack of dawn, the ground*
> *Underfoot began to mutter, the woody ridges to quake,*
> *And a baying of hounds was heard through the half-light: the goddess was*
>   *coming,*
> *Hecate.*

What a story, what action! So much more strident than the eternal mother figure, always passive and serene, never raging, never intervening.

Sometimes she is a grim, warped crone; other times she is a severe beauty; she is always formidable. She can arrive as a threefold, or even three-headed, apparition—three, like a very un-Christian trinity, or Feri's three souls, or three-headed like the giant watchdog of Hades, Cerberus. The howl of a great dog sometimes signals her approach. Dogs were sacrificed to her, and even eaten as a sacrament in her honor. The yew is also sacred to her, according to the Greeks, and her priestesses draped the necks of black bulls in wreaths of the viscous red berries before slaughtering them in her name.

Whether I work with Nuit or Hekate or some other god or no gods at all, I've found one way to relieve the pressure: I've discovered that, at least for me, the key is to treat everything—the gods, the rituals, the chants—like tools in my hands, a means to an end, a method of playing games with my mind to open myself up. Some occultists and Pagans do not even *believe* in deities, but instead use them as a powerful, primitive, very human psychological trigger for magic—crudely put, a way to hypnotize themselves into accepting their connection to the larger forces of the universe, be they supernatural or purely scientific in a way we don't yet understand. Some say the gods and goddesses are like Jungian archetypes, stemming from a collective mythology that holds powerful triggers for many of us.

This is how David, at Alombrados, looks at the gods: as archetypes. "Crowley himself believed that anything magical that you couldn't prove empirically was worthless. He wrote the Gnostic Mass so that even a scientific materialist could agree with it: you're worshipping Babalon, but that's a representation of certain forces."

That said, he admits that, after eight years of doing this, he's no longer a cool pragmatist:

"There's *something* out there. But I can't say what or who it is or how it works."

10

Morpheus and the Morrigan

In the couple of years since we met, Morpheus has become far more familiar with her goddess—the goddess to whom I first saw her make a quiet offering in her trailer bedroom. Her work with the Morrigan has steadily expanded outward—from that private altar to the highest peaks of Stone City and then the double ballroom of a San Jose hotel, packed with hundreds of other witches. The Morrigan goes by many names—Morrigu, Great Queen, Phantom Queen, Badb Catha, Battle Raven—and now each, when Morpheus pronounces it, is the name of a force that's real. Tangible. Unshakable.

The Morrigan demands of her followers radical independence and self-realization—what her priests call "sovereignty"—and by my next visit to Santa Clara County, Morpheus has taken serious steps toward her own. After fifteen years with Shannon, she's filed for divorce, leaving the future of Stone City uncertain. She's emerged from the Middle of Nowhere and relocated to the nearest town—Livermore, a fairly conservative suburb tucked between wine country and a nuclear power plant. Her Morrigan ritual at PantheaCon the previous year set events into motion that came to a head at the most recent convention: strangers appeared in the Stone City suite to tell her about the visitations they'd had from the Great Queen since. And in the wake of such a strong response—hundreds of people took oaths that day (myself included), and the event was much talked about in Pagan circles on the West Coast—Morpheus felt called to dedicate herself, finally and completely, to the war goddess. Around that time, she wrote a poem inspired by her devotional work, part of which reads:

I am yours utterly
I am your weapon
I am yours utterly
I am your shieldmaiden

She returned home from PantheaCon carrying the sword, and took it up to the spot in the hills that she'd consecrated to the Morrigan. Instead of pouring out cream and beer, this time she planted the blade, leaving it there for a night and a day to let the energy from all those promises drain into the dirt.

That's when, she says, she received a message: *You have brought me the sword. Soon you will bring me warriors. The time is coming.* The Morrigan was asking her to assemble an army, a request that frightened her. As she tried to decipher the meaning of this, she launched a small experiment: she started training in martial arts, and she gathered together a few witches also aligned with the goddess (including Thorn and Sharon) into a "resilience network" dubbed the Raven Kin, for lessons in survivalism and light combat.

More recently, Morpheus, like Victor Anderson, began having visions that she believes reveal a previous life—in service of the Morrigan. "I always try to maintain a bit of healthy skepticism," she says, "but I'm pretty sure that I had a lifetime where I was dedicated to her before, in Gaul." When, in her research of the Iron Age, she was first exposed to the ancient Celtic language of Gaulish, dead for fifteen hundred years, it "stirred something very strong" in her; and she had a peculiar, emotional response to the story of the Gallic wars and the fall of Gaul to the Romans. At this point, Morpheus believes she was in Gaul while it was being assimilated into the Roman Empire, and that from there she went to Britain and took part in the Celtic tribal queen Boudicca's brutal rebellion. She's started studying Gaulish, occasionally posting in the language on Facebook, no doubt throwing their consumer-profiling algorithm into total confusion. (*"Desu ni is Bodúa!"* read one status update.) Using the native language of her goddess is an offering to her, "a gift." "She likely hasn't heard people speak it to her in a long time." Besides, Morpheus says, "everything sounds completely badass in Gaulish."

This is how the Morrigan comes to you: screeching like a banshee in ritual; or as a vison of a bloody-mouthed hag; or as a black figure perched on your chest while you lie in bed, cutting short your breath.* The Morrigan appears in the Irish myths about the Tuatha Dé Danann (the gods of Ireland), where she's often depicted as redheaded, in a bloodred cloak on the battlefield, conjuring up thunderstorms and hailstones of blood and fire. Morpheus has seen her as a terrifying hag—but she usually appears to her as a towering queen, in a cloak full of power and lightning and ravens. This is the goddess I supposedly "met" that night at the DoubleTree, when my friend invoked her into her body: a growling presence that dared us all to take an oath on a giant sword. She—or Morpheus *as* her—was no one to trifle with.

Morpheus—a woman with a loud laugh and an oversized grin; someone who, outside of ritual, can't be bothered to sustain the intimidating-priestess front for long—has spent a great deal of time deciphering her unexpected relationship with this shrieking battle goddess. On an early visit to Stone City, I'd noticed, inside Morpheus's and Shannon's trailer, a painting she had made: this was *the Morrigan*, she'd told me—which at the time meant nothing to me, already inundated with the Pagan name-dropping of gods and goddesses. But the image stayed with me: in the foreground, a woman with long red hair, in a red cloak, stands beside a stone gate just like the one in Morpheus's own Stone Circle; on the other side of the gate, a faceless, shrouded figure kneels in a river of blood; above them both, a winged hag is in flight, carrying human heads in her clawlike hands; and above even her is the massive, stony gray face of a helmeted warrior, her long hair streaming in the wind, dissolving into dozens of ravens. Morpheus had painted this while listening to audio recordings she'd discovered of World War II journalists embedded on combat ships and in landing parties. She would listen to hours and hours of these wartime recordings—the sounds of

---

* There is a recognized form of hallucination that matches this description, known as "the night hag."

machine-gun fire and explosions and terrified grown men—while meditating on Morrigu.

Vanthe, the Feri coven into which Morpheus was initiated in 2000, had a relationship with the Morrigan that went back to the seventies. And though Morpheus had felt a strong, magnetic pull into Feri, she hadn't anticipated the trappings that would come with it—least of all, a magical allegiance to a furious war goddess. After several magical collaborations with the Great Queen in Vanthe's circle, Morpheus felt she needed to learn more about the force she was dealing with. She could never be pegged as conventional, and she'd already, by that point, fought for her independence many times—dabbling in the occult, changing her name, dropping out of high school, initiating into a mystery cult—but Morpheus still thought of herself as "a peacenik-y Santa Cruz hippie." She was disturbed by the Queen's ferocity, and the images of carnage that often accompanied her.

But since she was bound to her, she tried to immerse herself in the Morrigan's nature. Morpheus painted her image and built a statue in her honor and made regular offerings to her up in the hills of Stone City. She also began allowing the goddess to possess her—as a gift to her, like learning Gaulish—and developed a surprising empathy for a presence that had seemed so fierce. She finally received a message from the Queen, revealing her nature: she is not an instigator of war, she told her priestess. Instead, she is part of our transition at death—this is why she has such an appetite for gore. Taking on the form of a raven or crow, carrion eaters, she feeds on the pouring out of life. She consumes life as it passes out of the human body, and then spills it out on the other side. As with Hekate, through this goddess we cross the veil.

But above all, the Queen is the supernatural champion of *sovereignty*, of each person's right to happiness and to choose their own lovers and their own gods and to dedicate themselves to their life's work. Freedom as self-rule. And when those things are threatened, the Morrigan rises up. Morpheus puts it simply: "To value something is to be willing to defend it, right? Warriorship as a way of living."

I land at the Oakland Airport, and Morpheus and her new (and quite serious) paramour, Moon, arrive to pick me up in his car. It's a thoroughly used sedan, and right now it's packed with weapons—from dull medieval-looking blades to pikes made of wood and duct tape. Morpheus helps me shove my suitcase into the trunk alongside a collection of swords. All this weaponry is a new development.

Moon is driving. Classically Anglo-Saxon handsome, tall and square-jawed. His eyes have a far gentler look than Morpheus's, almost timid, and he waves hello as we drive off. His lady twists around in the passenger seat, leaning on the wooden spear shoved between the seats, to tell me the latest. Since I saw her last, Morpheus has joined the SCA, or Society for Creative Anachronism, a group with over thirty thousand members that re-creates the culture and battles of medieval Europe, and the couple have just returned from a "war." About two hundred "fighters" took part; Moon is a veteran, but this was Morpheus's first time "certified for combat." Within her first hour on the field, she got walloped—some guy whacked her with a padded pike, shoving her new helmet (made of very real steel) up into her face—and she now has multiple bruises on her body and a gash in her chin that had to be suture-glued together on-site, in lieu of stitches.

"I didn't want to go to the hospital," she says, beaming. "I wanted to keep fighting!"

She wears a touch of foundation to hide the purple bruising that curls under her chin, and bandages on two fingers. Moon snapped a photo after the battle with his smartphone: it's a bright, sunny California day—the grass is intensely green, the sky a brilliant blue—and Morpheus, her red hair up in braids, stands holding her tunic beside her, the front streaked with chin blood. She is grinning ecstatically.

Moon drops us off at the Livermore home of their friend Meliny, where Morpheus has been living rent-free since she moved off Stone City. "I hope you like cats," he says with a nervous laugh.

The place is a modest one-story stucco building with empty planters lining the façade. Once I'm inside, it's clear that the house is indeed dominated by felines, both domestic pets and feral animals that pass through at will. There are about twelve in all, with names like Ziggy, Tupac, Girlie, and Wednesday. Kitty fountains are perched across various shelves and counter-tops, and a mechanized cat toy whirs away on the carpet, spinning a tiny tail at the end of a wire.

Meliny—a regular at Stone City, a fit fifty-something, and a self-identified "blonde"—works in a nearby lab. She has a degree in biology and recently decided to get a master's in chemistry to go with it. She pours us red wine, and we recline among the cats, cats, cats, and gossip about the growing number of Pagans we know in common.

Afterward, Morpheus shows me her bedroom: her first foray into non-rural, on-the-grid living in nearly a decade. As in the room she shared with Shannon, the fabrics here are all some shade of crimson, from the bedsheets to the wall hangings and the lampshades. Two altars line the walls: by the window, a working altar complete with blue-handled athame, wooden pentagram, glass chalice, small cauldron, jar of salts, candles, mortar and pestle, and collection of peacock feathers; by the bedside, underneath Morpheus's epic painting of the Morrigan, the goddess's altar. This table holds a boline; a statuette of the Battle Raven, naked except for cloak, shield, and spear; and the pair of vulture wings that Morpheus uses in ritual performance. Above the bed, against red silk cloth, a painting of circling ravens is broken up by two bright yellow runes (ancient Germanic letters used for divination); and on the floor lies a stained plywood box painted with runes in white, bookending the figure of yet another black bird, wings outspread.

In a prominent place on the wall, within easy view of the bed, hangs a framed photograph: a portrait of Moon, in classic three-quarter profile, framed by pine trees. He stands in full battle gear: leather neck brace and metal breastplate fastened over a red tunic, slightly rusted gladiator's helmet tucked under one arm. He looks with soft, steady confidence into the camera. The photo reminds me of the favors lovers would give one another during Renaissance times, miniature portraits slipped into lockets, images that were to be looked at longingly in their lengthy absences, until the *idea* of one's object of affection became just as real as who they were in the flesh.

The next night, Moon drives us to Morpheus's weekly gig at a local Persian restaurant. Like Anaar and Thorn, she studied belly dancing, and she's given public performances with both of them. The restaurant is small, maybe twelve tables, and generic in design, but the food smells good. I sit with Moon at a table in the back set aside for friends of the featured dancer. We have a great view from here, and as Morpheus dances to one of her own mixtapes of Middle Eastern tunes, Moon looks on, visibly pleased to be watching.

Officially, Moon met Morpheus about ten years ago, when she was belly dancing with his then wife. But the first time he actually laid eyes on her was when she was the cashier at a health food store near their house. "I wouldn't even be able to *speak* when I saw her," he says in a voice full of awe. "I'd be, like"—he thrusts his hand out—"'Here's some cash!'"

Both Morpheus and Moon, like many Pagans, were in polyamorous relationships, and so they were free to become romantically involved. But their spouses, their "primary" partners, quickly grew uncomfortable with the intensity of the attraction. The love affair, Morpheus says, was "vetoed." They were devastated. Nearly a decade passed until the two were able to reunite, shortly before this year's PantheaCon. This was it, the Morrigan's call for sovereignty realized—sovereignty as permission to put yourself first, after tiptoeing around others for so long. Now they look at each other with eyes full of High Romance, very much a pair of star-crossed lovers finally brought together. You really could not be happier, effortlessly, than the two of them when they are in each other's company. This may well be the reward for their devotion to the goddess they share in common.

Because Moon is also in service of the Morrigan. It was back when he first became involved with Morpheus that he made his involvement with this *other* female official. And their relationship, too, took many years to be fully realized.

When he was about six years old, living in the Philadelphia suburbs, Moon (then Tommy) began warning his mother that there was "a scary witch" in his closet. He had constant nightmares in which a terrifying figure would appear to him, impossibly tall and gray. Sometimes her back would be turned; sometimes she would face him, covered with a veil. Whenever her face came into focus, forcing him to look into her eyes, he'd wake with a start, horrified.

This continued for several years, and his grandmother, with whom he'd been sent to live after his parents divorced, became increasingly concerned. When he was fourteen, she finally sent him to a psychiatrist, who ran a battery of tests. The doctor also noted that the divorce had taken place not long before the nightmares began. The official diagnosis: "abandonment issues, and a strong imagination." Never informed of the results, however, young Tommy assumed he'd been pronounced mentally ill.

In high school, this "strong imagination" crystallized into a skill—Tommy realized he had the ability to help the recently dead complete their crossing to the other side—though a long time would pass before he understood what he was doing.

As an adult, Tommy continued his work with the dead and began to identify himself as "Pagan"; he took the name Moon in honor of his astrological sign (Cancer). He also steadily became aware that his "crossing-over work" was directly tied to a goddess of the transition into death: the Morrigan. He'd finally discovered the truth of his supposed childhood illness: the apparition in his nightmares had been the Great Queen, and his mental illness, his instability, his hallucinations, had actually been growing pains along the way to accepting his larger fate. In the absence of his mother, a much greater female force—a queen, a battle goddess—had been with him all along. So what if she had frightened him? The chosen, throughout history and across cultures, have stories about the terror of being called by a god. And here they were, Moon and the Morrigan, finally beginning to understand each other.

When he learned about the SCA, Moon decided that as the devotee of a war goddess, he should suit up and join in. It may not be real battle—and he had no romantic fantasies of actual warfare or of enlisting in the military—but the SCA fighters go at it hard, whacking each other with full force, in cobbled-together battle armor. He quickly developed a serious reputation as a "heavy fighter."

A few years later, at a "war" in Santa Rosa, Moon was struck full-on in the head with a two-handed sword and his skull cracked. For the rest of the day, he was nauseous and dizzy; two weeks later, the headaches had not subsided, and now it hurt to open his eyes in the morning. He quit his job, and his condition quickly deteriorated. Soon, during a period he refers to plainly as "hell," he became almost unable to walk; he developed meningitis, an inflammation of the lining of the brain and spinal cord; and one side of his face drooped. He'd been a healthy, good-looking man, but now he was debilitated and visibly deformed: he couldn't control half of his face; his mouth would drool if he tried to drink; one eye hung open. And, unable to shut that eyelid, he'd also developed an acute sensitivity to light, so he was left clinging to the dark. Driving was out of the question. He assumed that he'd had a stroke, and that the damage might be permanent. To make matters even more severe, Moon and his wife were then in the process of getting a divorce, and he'd moved to a remote cabin in the woods, with no one to take care of him. He tried to adjust in whatever way he could, each day dragging himself across the house to sit in a hot bath until his joints became slightly more pliable, but he could still move only in painful, measured increments.

Then, one day, about two months in, the inevitable happened: he was alone at home when a black current of deep-penetrating head pain overtook him. He had a fever of 105, and it felt like bugs were crawling around inside his brain. He lay down and thought, "This is it. If I'm meant to go now, I'm meant to go now." He felt himself sinking down, down into the nearby Yuba River: "I believe that I died." Suddenly he saw dark spirits grabbing at him, pulling him up to the surface. That was when the Morrigan appeared. *I still have need for you*, she said to him. *It's not your time. I own your death.*

Within three months, what he'd thought was a stroke—which turned out to be a condition called Bell's palsy—went away after a physical therapist alleviated the pressure in his face. He gradually returned to normal, able to walk more than a few feet at a stretch and look into the light without terrific pain. His entire recovery took a couple of years, by the end of which he had rededicated himself to the Morrigan—and reunited with Morpheus, a fellow devotee.

What does it mean to dedicate yourself to the service of your childhood nightmare and to fall in love with its priestess? Morpheus and Moon and other followers of the Morrigan are not alone in this: there is a long-standing tradition, across several cultures, of people worshipping something they desperately fear—you can find this in Christianity, at least the fiery brand. For many, fear goes hand in hand with the awesomeness of God. Over the last year in particular, Moon has felt his fearful goddess calling to him, calling him out from his cabin deep in the hills to move closer to the city, closer to her priestess, who also happens to be the woman he loves. "Because something's about to happen," he says. He and Morpheus are swept up in her momentum.

At the Persian restaurant, Morpheus dances her way to our table, the priestess in one of her other guises, turning her wrists slowly, continuously, her long hands folding and unfolding in the air around her. Her ultra-white stomach undulates with each step across the tiled floor; her heavy belt jangles; crimson-colored skirts swing back and forth around her bare feet. Flirting with both of us, eyes on one, then the other, she arches her back and lets her long red hair drop closer and closer to the floor, then rhythmically pulls herself up again. She does a twirl and leaves a silver bangle on the table.

Moon doesn't need the token: he is always aware of her presence.

The next night, around eight o'clock, we pull into the parking lot below the BART overpass by the Rockridge station: I'm accompanying the couple to fighter practice. Since his reunion with Morpheus, Moon has returned to battle. He's now determined to become as skilled and high-ranked as possible—a bruiser, a contender, a champion. His goal over the coming year is to participate in as many tournaments and wars as possible.

We get out of the car and start pulling duffel bags and equipment out of the trunk, propping spears and pikes up against the passenger doors. Morpheus looks around at the gathering scene. A collection of about five "rapiers" spar like fencers under the fluorescent lights at the far end of the lot. The war at which Morpheus made her debut was just days ago, so fewer people are out than usual.

Morpheus and Moon suit up. Even for practice, this is an extended process, slipping into linen fighting tunics (in complementary shades of crimson), then strapping on layers of protective gear: enormous metal breastplates, medieval shoulder guards, gauntlets for the hands, unwieldy work boots, and greaves for the legs, in awkward Tin Man style. Last but not least come their helmets, each of which locks the head into an intricate face grille like a sort of iron maiden: Morpheus's is capped with a foxtail, Moon's with the tail of a horse. Standing tall in the shadow of the BART overpass, fully armored, seven-foot pike in hand, his face obscured by so much heavy metal, Moon is every inch a fourteenth-century warrior gone rogue, and I've crossed a wrinkle in time.

Meanwhile, about five other vehicles pull in, and more fighters and wannabe fighters pile out and start gearing up. Mostly newbies are out tonight, about a dozen of them: people who don't own armor yet and are clearly improvising, strapping padding and weaponry to their street clothes. To smooth things over, an older SCA vet shows up with a truck loaded with armor odds-and-ends and passes them out, helping everyone to get half armed and comfortable.

Once the sparring starts—with wooden spears and dulled-down swords and lengths of pipe and shields painted with imaginary family crests—the vet stalks the perimeter in the role of referee, giving tips, telling people to "go for the head" and the women to "get more aggressive." Partners are paired up according to SCA rank and file: when he lines Morpheus and Moon up with another duo, the vet says, "So the first question is: Are you certified?"

They go at it—gently. This is practice, after all. But the wooden staffs connect with a loud crack, and a dull ax smacks a shield with an impact that could crater a car hood. Meanwhile, as he continues to switch partners, all far less experienced than him, Moon holds back and tries instead to share some moves: how to attack head-on, go in for the chin block with your shield. Every now and then, a train passes just over our heads, packed with commuters, their everyday logic incompatible with this scene.

Moon and I pause together for a moment, looking around at the fighters. "This is one of her churches," he says. He's talking about the Morrigan— and he's serious.

On the drive back to Moon's place that night, where I will crash on the couch, he tells me his goal for this fighting season. "I want to make her princess," he says of Morpheus. "I think she'd make a wonderful Princess of the Mists"—the Mists, their principality in the fictional West Kingdom (the Bay Area).

Morpheus turns around in the passenger seat and says to me quietly, "I mean, can you get more romantic than that?"

Morpheus and I spend the day wandering downtown Oakland. We have coffee and eggs near the municipal center and then walk to the park, passing a children's playground. Eventually we settle down on a bench by Lake Merritt in front of a gazebo. She tells me about the people who've approached her—and continue to approach her—saying they've been called into the service of the Great Queen.

"People were coming up at PantheaCon"—this is one year after the oath-taking ritual—"and saying things like 'I had a visitation from the Morrigan, and she said I needed to tell you,' or 'I had to meet you, because I've had these experiences with the Morrigan and I don't know what to do about it.'" Within a couple of months, Morpheus sent out an e-mail to the most devout (or at least the most determined) of the bunch, announcing that she was assembling a priesthood dedicated to the goddess. Their first meeting took place in April.

They named themselves Coru Cathubodua, Gaulish for "Army of the Battle Raven"—or, simply, the Coru. The Coru currently consists of nine members, mostly in the Bay Area, who run the gamut with their Craft traditions and levels of magical experience. Like a band of Pagan superheroes, they bring a range of skills—from those who work with the dead to those who do battle on the astral plane to those who allow the Morrigan to "ride them" in possessory work, as Morpheus does. This past summer, the Coru went high up on Mount Diablo and performed a ritual to bond the priesthood together. The priesthood's insignia, a black-and-red raven with outspread wings, is represented on a large banner in Morpheus's bedroom, and in a tattoo she recently etched into Moon's upper back.

The afternoon is overcast, and as we sit in the park, a murder of crows passes overhead, and then again, and once more. As I watch them circle, Morpheus tells me about her *other* gift to the Battle Raven, beside possessory work: her own blood.

She first became fascinated with blood as a teenager—the power of it, its magical potential—but as a grown woman, and a full-grown witch, her use of it is far more deliberate. Whenever a more intimate offering is called for, Morpheus cuts into the underside of her left arm, always the same section of flesh, always carving the same shape, two inches squared: the Hagalaz rune, the ancient character that represents the hailstone. Though the runes are not a Celtic system, the Morrigan, also a goddess of storms, responds to her work with the Hagalaz.

Sometimes Morpheus will go a couple of months without making this blood offering, but on a few occasions she's "fed" the Morrigan more than once a week. She's gotten to the point where she carves just *one* of the lines, not the whole symbol, so that the next time she won't have to carve over a fresh wound. She uses a razor knife, for a clean cut—she's not trying to disfigure herself or get an infection. I picture her cutting the rune into her soft underarm skin—two vertical strokes and two strokes across, to form a ladder with diagonal steps—and then letting the blood run. I remark on the severity of the act, and Morpheus asks, "Are you saying you find this practice of mine disturbing?"

"Not really." An honest answer.

I wouldn't be the first, she says. Various people have commented on it—including one of Moon's ex-girlfriends. "Oh, she gave him no end of shit, like 'I really think you're going down a dark road.' People are scared by it. But it's an offering of one's own body, and that's a pretty natural thing."

She returns to the rune itself. Hail falls and destroys the crops, she says—but then it melts and helps the land as water. "So that rune is associated with chaos-as-creativity." The chaos of cutting a painful figure into your skin, followed by the creation of—what? She doesn't hesitate: "I was liberating myself from a life in which I felt imprisoned and controlled."

Again the crows pass overhead, louder now.

We make our way back to Livermore, to Meliny's house. En route, we pick up some food—salmon, spinach, a frozen cheesecake—and finally sit down for a dinner surrounded by feline companions. We talk about Meliny's relationship with another Pagan ("He just wants to be 'friends with benefits' "), and Morpheus's upcoming trip with the Coru to lead a ritual in Canada. The meal is capped off with our mostly thawed-out dessert as Morpheus works at mending her proudly bloodstained fighting tunic with a needle and thread.

Meliny pulls out her chemistry homework, and Morpheus and I stack the dishes and head into the kitchen. We rinse and place them in the dishwasher one by one, and it's in a slightly stooped-over position that my priestess-friend suddenly raises her head and announces, "You know, I have a dead raven in a box!"

"What?"

"I have a dead raven in a box. I mean, I have a *spirit* who lives inside a dead raven in a box."

Pause.

"Have I not told you that yet?" She's fully aware that this is news to me.

Meliny enters the kitchen: "What did she say?"

"She has a raven in a box," I tell her.

"It's a spirit. In a raven. In a box."

Meliny turns to her housemate. "Seriously? In your *room*?" I don't know what the Pagan house rules are for this particular situation, but Meliny's excitement is palpable. "No way!"

"Let me introduce him to you guys," Morpheus says, and we trail after her. The evening has just taken on the tone of the world's most surreal slumber party.

We follow Morpheus into her bedroom, and she flips on the overhead bulb, washing everything in a dull, flat light. For a moment, we could be in any suburban bedroom—until the contents of the room come into focus again: the chalices, the vulture wings, the runes on the walls, the general excess of red satin. And the box on the floor. That box! I should have known it contained something of mysterious worth the day I arrived. What witch keeps a two-foot-long stained-wood box painted in runes for no specific reason?

Gathering her velvet skirt, Morpheus squats down next to it and lays a hand on the small knob. We are perfectly quiet. Slowly, she pulls the lid open on its hinge, like opening a trapdoor.

Inside is an impressive sight. The raven is larger than expected—they are long, large-bodied birds—bloated and black, laid out on a plinth of polished, cherry-colored wood. His head and body are covered in short black feathers like fur, but his wing feathers are stiff and straight, neatly folded over the carcass. His thick black beak, as tough as a tooth, is turned over his right shoulder, his one visible eye white, blanked out; the feet are tucked up so that the curled claws peek out from under his left wing. All three of us remain silent, and the silence has a quality to it. I cannot tell whether it's the singularity of the sight before me or actually a new presence in the room, swelling up from the box, that has me dumbstruck. Here, Morpheus tells us, is the last member of the Coru.

She looks up at me from where she sits on the floor. "Oh, Alex," she says. "Just when you thought things couldn't get any weirder."

11

Making Priests

I return to New York and catch a glimpse of my regular life—a life in the mundane world, populated by friends and colleagues who have a different idea of what constitutes reality. But soon I'm traveling again, this time by train, and in five hours I'll finally be face-to-face with the witch I've taken instructions from for the last four months.

The Amherst station is so small that I've only just stepped down from the train car when I encounter Karina, who waves at me from the parking lot. In a T-shirt and blue jeans, she could be anyone's aunt picking them up for a visit. She takes the lead and gives me a hug, but with a certain brusqueness: we're in an intimate situation, in a teacher-student relationship outside any institution of higher learning—I'm about to stay at her home, eat with her kids, sleep on her couch under her extra blanket—but the formality of any teaching relationship still applies.

Karina steers her large gray van onto Main Street and we're off, driving through New England's Pioneer Valley to Northampton, the college town where she spent her childhood. This was once a region of severe religion: here, in 1645, the country had its first witchcraft trial, and Jonathan Edwards kick-started the Great Awakening in 1733. It's also been home to a long line of strong outsider women: this is where Sojourner Truth lived in a utopian clique of feminist freedom fighters (her statue stands in a local park); where Sylvia Plath, and later Gloria Steinem, attended Smith College (Karina herself went to Mount Holyoke); and where the greatest number of lesbian couples per capita of any American city reside today, in what the *National Enquirer* once dubbed "Lesbianville, USA."

But mostly, this afternoon, Karina's feeling the frustrations of her life on the fringe—underpaid and overextended—and she shares them freely. She mentions that the last-minute cancellation of a teaching engagement in Denver has left her without a gig next month, and that any loss of income can mean, say, no new shoes for her kids this school year. I'm reminded of her warning to students: "It is not my Way as a Teacher to pretend I'm okay when I'm not."

Karina has the right half of a two-family house, modest and white-shingled, two doors from an abandoned Catholic church and down the block from a Gothic equal-opportunity housing unit. Across the street is Mill River, which sometimes sends tremors through the floors; across the river are homes that are larger, brightly painted, with catalogue-worthy jungle gyms and swing sets. Karina pulls into her grassy driveway, and when I let myself out the passenger side, an old dent at the hinge briefly has me worried I've broken the door.

A sharp green lawn extends behind the house, and the side entrance (no one uses the front door) is framed with plots of flowers and a concrete statuette of the Virgin Mary. We head up the steps, through a screen door, and into a homey kitchen that Karina recently redid with rust-red walls and cream-colored wood. She's told me a little about her children, and now they stream into the kitchen at the sound of their mother's return with the latest student stranger. Her son, Connor, is eleven and has pretty, sleepy-lidded green eyes. Her daughter, Kim, at nearly sixteen, has the carriage of a teen jock (she's on the track team) paired with a recent full figure. Their father, who is not a part of their lives—Karina says he suffers from a debilitating mental illness—is African American, and both the kids are handsome, with curly hair and bright faces.

Slung straight into Karina's home life, I sit at the kitchen table while she puts a large helping of cilantro into the blender—enough for the gallon and a half of sauce she was inspired to make earlier today, sauce she'll have to can soon. We dice ingredients for tonight's enchiladas, sauté the chicken, then roll everything into doughy tortillas, filling the silences with small talk. Now and again, I follow her out onto the porch and watch her roll American Spirit tobacco into skinny cigarettes that dangle from her lower lip. All the while, her kids play a Nintendo Wii dancing game in the next room, controllers in hand, moving in sync with their cartoon avatars.

At dinner, Kim, though not yet sure what to make of the new guest, talks a blue streak—she's self-possessed and remarkably smart. She says she's on the LGBT student committee, may join the literary magazine this year, and her best race in track is the hundred-meter. She stands up to demonstrate her sprinter's starting stance for me, adopting the pose barefoot on the faux-marble tile. You're supposed to keep your head down to be more aerodynamic, she explains. Her mother watches from the porch, where she leans against the house and rolls another cigarette. A black cat named Monster appears at the screen door, and she lets him in for the night.

Once the kids have disappeared upstairs, Karina and I clean up. She loads some dough into her bread machine, and we sit at the table, talking until late. She laughs at the "really bad business model" she's set up for her work: she rejects about eight out of ten people who apply for training, and of those she takes on, many drop out or are asked to leave well before reaching initiation. Anyone who fills in the psych questions in her preliminary interview with, say, "schizoaffective disorder" or "bipolar disorder" is someone she absolutely won't touch. When I ask why that is, she looks at me in disbelief. "I've known people who've lost their minds doing this training—and I'm talking about hospitalized, put on medication, going to see a therapist twice a week for years. I'm not going to take someone who's trying so hard to keep their grasp on reality and shake that up." Contrary to some of my first impressions, Karina insists that this Cycle One work—all the cleansing and protection—is not *self-help*. Instead, these are necessary baby steps along the way to the real work: serious witchcraft. "What we do is dangerous."

Karina is also quick to dismiss another category of applicant: the power-trippers. One man told her that he wanted to study Feri so he could bend the world to his will. "Oh, I've gotten a lot of those over the years," she says. "At least now I know to tell them to go elsewhere." Age is another reason for refusing a potential student: twenty-somethings are often too young. Karina once had a woman in her twenties write in her interview that she couldn't stand living with her mother and fought with her all the time. "Come back when you're grown up!" she replied.

A generational shift has taken place in how people approach the Craft, propelled by the Internet, and Karina doesn't like it: people are getting casual and sloppy. "I'm old-school, I guess"—her earliest witchcraft experiences were informed by the pomp and circumstance and prescribed hierarchies of the early days of Wicca. When she moved to Providence, Rhode Island, in her thirties, a witch from the local, generations-old Italian Strega scene rang her up "not to get together and have a coffee or anything—just to let me know that *they* knew I was in town." And when she finally settled in Northampton, Karina was invited to a gathering at the home of "Lord Theo," the most senior Wiccan high priest in the area. ("Lady" and "lord" handles were big back then.) The man was carried in on a dais, with all his students and coven members gathered around—and then he offered her the honor of seeing his altar. By the time Karina began studying with her Feri teacher, Mark, she only knew one way to approach their training: with intense reverence, even submission. She wouldn't touch anything in his house that wasn't handed to her; she wouldn't ask questions, assuming that if he wanted her to know something he would teach it to her. "I wouldn't ask why we weren't doing things one way or another, or when were we going to learn such-and-such that I saw on a website."

As an initiate of a mystery tradition within the Craft, Karina has a lot to say about the spread of information online instead of through oral lessons. As we wait for the buzzer to tell us a new loaf is done, talk turns to the ongoing schism within Feri.

Over the last three years, a rift has become more and more pronounced between those Feris who believe in the tradition as a mystery cult and those who would spread it as a democratic, public religion. The divide has been given a name worthy of Greek tragedy: the Sundering. Karina traces it back to Thorn's decision, nine years ago, to publish a book on Feri and to start giving two-year, noninitiatory training in the tradition (instead of the average five years of study until initiation). As a result, the number of people training spiked, and a new breed of "Feri" was created. "That created a mess that may never totally resolve itself," Karina says. Now Thorn instead teaches through her more eclectic Morningstar Mystery School—the people I'd seen chanting in the hotel lobby at PantheaCon.

Karina herself balks at this. She does not buy this rollout of witches—she views them as Feri Lite. "I make *priests*," she says. "I don't make congregants."

Even before initiation, some Feris believe that training produces fundamental changes: Karina's teacher, Mark, told her that Feri transforms people's cellular makeup, their very DNA. I immediately wonder where this lands me. I want a lot of things, but I have no fantasies about reinventing myself as a full-time priest, serving a larger community. I doubt I will ever be a religious enough person for something like that.

The machine makes a chirping sound, and Karina finally wiggles the fresh bread out of its metal tub. A wall of exhaustion is hitting me after the day's travels, so she leads me to the living room and together we make up the sofa, covering its long-faded olive-green print with a bedsheet. She tells me that while they're "a house of late risers," tomorrow I can expect her up by nine o'clock. With that, my teacher retires upstairs.

I look around at the bookshelves packed with volumes on magic and set my travel alarm. Next to a chair piled with plush-toy monsters, a house altar is laid out: feathers, a tall censer of sage ready for burning, a dish of pebbles and inch-diameter mirrors (each window of the house has a tiny mirror taped to it, facing outward, to protect the home).

I lie down, shut off the light, and try to fall asleep. Too nervous. I have the distinct impression that I'm being measured and judged, and I'm not sure someone with all my doubts is in a position to impress a priestess. Through one doorway I can see the kitchen, lit by a night-light; through the other, the heavy staircase leading up to the family's three bedrooms. I wonder what Karina has in store for us tomorrow, and the next day. I turn onto my side, but still no passing out. I can hear the black cat step lightly around the room in the dark.

"Nine o'clock" turns out to be open to interpretation. I do some yoga and eat a cup of yogurt, but Karina has yet to emerge.

I go for a walk past the abandoned church and along the river. I think about something else Karina and I discussed last night: she'd mentioned a series of videos that recently surfaced on YouTube, of a hardly qualified Feri student in his mid-twenties, "a beautiful, sparkly blond boy," sharing some of his training. Distressed, Karina's students had asked her if she planned to take action. She told them, "Oh, someone will take care of that. You don't want the kind of karma that brings." In the early days of the tradition, she said, when all the Feris were out in California, if someone was teaching against the initiates' wishes, they would do "the equivalent of leaving a dead chicken on your doorstep." In this new era, they'll send the troublemaker an e-mail warning—and then "blast him on the astral." By "astral," Karina meant the "astral plane," another level of reality that coexists with the physical plane we inhabit—i.e., a parallel reality or "otherworld." In other words, witches will come after that person in this parallel universe. "This is why I ask my students to keep silence." ("Are you willing to uphold the four-fold way of the Witch?")

Astral travel is one of the skills required of a Feri priest, but Karina files it under "nonordinary realities" that I needn't worry about just yet. "By the time you get to that in your training," she'd written me, "it won't be the weirdest thing you've experienced."

At least for now, however, this phenomenon is the practice I find most alienating and hard to stomach out of all my witchcraft and occult encounters: the idea that we each possess an "astral" body that can travel beyond the constraints of our physical body, on planes or realities that exist in tandem with, but independent of, the "normal," "real" physical world. Even Anaar, Feri's current grandmaster, had told me that the first time Victor Anderson spoke of astral travel her private response was "Bullshit." But then, a few days later, she had an experience, and she never doubted him again. "After that, he could have told me about werewolves and I would have believed him."*

I've immersed myself in witchcraft circles deeply enough for people to speak to me about such major-mental-leap concepts with the assumption of instant acceptance; I've been welcomed into casual talk of adventures in parallel universes—as when, later on, I met Justin, a second-year student of Karina's. Justin would speak with me, as if it were natural as anything,

---

* This may come as a surprise to some, but the witches I've met draw the line at werewolves and vampires. There is a small subculture of "vampires": people who live the blood-drinking lifestyle as a cross between extreme gothic posturing and BDSM—with willing "victims." But that is another story.

about his latest experiences on the astral: the exhaustion he's experienced for months, fighting alongside the Feri guardians (whose names I don't yet know) for hours each night. He calls it "astral warfare," against beings on other planes. Things reached a point, a few months in, where he had to make a pact with the guardians—Karina suggested he do this—agreeing that he would give them four hours a night if they then left him alone for some much-needed human sleep. He even began training in martial arts and CrossFit (on the physical plane) to help him in this magical mission. Sometimes Justin is approached by others asking for help, and he'll do work on the astral on their behalf—as when a friend asked for protection from an unwanted houseguest. He studied the layout of the neighborhood on Google Maps and walked around his friend's block a few times, visualizing his house inside and out—and when he was next on the astral, he strategically positioned the Feri guardians as sentinels to watch over the building.

Then there's Rynn, a member of Morpheus's inner circle and one of Thorn's students. She once told her circle of magical collaborators that while on the astral, she'd found a Celtic roundhouse where they could all gather to worship. A few months later, Morpheus (who'd forgotten about Rynn's discovery) announced, "I found this roundhouse on the astral, and the gods are there!" It was the same temple, at the same parallel-world location.

Morpheus began doing work on the astral with Linnea when she was nineteen.* Linnea would lead her on a "guided journey," asking her to visualize them traveling through a space together: she was training Morpheus to leave her body. Around the same time, Morpheus's future covenmate Anne introduced her to recent historical research about a group in sixteenth-century Friuli, in northern Italy, called the benandanti, who carried on a visionary folk practice: they believed they traveled through town at night, outside their bodies, to battle malevolent witches intending to harm the people and their crops. This kind of "travel" is not a modern idea.

Morpheus described a recent astral experience for me, one she had had with some former students, a trio of pretty-faced blond men in their twen-

---

* Aleister Crowley first learned this technique in his early twenties, through his mentors in the Golden Dawn magical society. Those visions are recorded in his diaries, some of them published in the OTO journal The Equinox.

ties (all of them now Feri initiates), who had moved from the Bay Area to Boston. Missing each other, they decided to circle together long-distance: Morpheus would come to their house, traveling not by plane but on the astral, and join them for a ritual.

To help her find their house—she'd never visited before—her students placed a vessel in the circle: a bowl that was red on the inside and contained an item that had belonged to Morpheus, and a sigil she would recognize. When the ritual began, they evoked the priestess herself, and she set out to join them. She remembers coming in through the air over a town and seeing an iconic building—a big old church with a tall clock tower—and the coastal waters nearby. A sort of beacon, somewhere in the city, was giving off a red light, so she homed in on that. Following the light, she found their house—two stories, white with blue shutters—and could sense what room they were in. She entered through the window, and they circled together.

Once they'd finished the ritual, Morpheus wrote the others an e-mail describing what she'd seen: they confirmed the details. And when she visited them months later, and a friend gave her a ride (on the physical plane), she shouted at him as they pulled onto the street, "It's *that* house! There it is!"

The site up on Mount Diablo where her Coru priesthood, not long ago, took an oath to one another and to the Morrigan is a location in the physical world that Morpheus and Moon discovered in their work together on the astral. While on this other plane, they recognized that they'd ended up on the mountain, and they came to a grove of trees, at the center of which was a stone altar. They headed out to Diablo and wandered around, trying to find the spot in reality. The place had been near some natural caves, and so they drove to that area and eventually found a clearing in which lay a piece of old construction concrete; this, they decided, must be the altar they'd seen on the astral. The Coru has since returned to this spot multiple times (physically) for their ritual work.

Many witches will build temples on the astral, where their collaborators can meet and do magical work. But Morpheus sees her astral travel as travel through the real world—"it's just the *otherworld* part of the real world," she says.

According to her, the world consists of different layers of reality. There's the physical world—the landscape of the earth—and then there's the invisible world, the otherworld, that is overlaid onto it. This otherworld is elsewhere, but it's also *everywhere*, accessed by a shift in perception. "So, when I travel in the otherworld," Morpheus says, "I'm traveling over the same physical landscape, but I'm seeing the spiritual reality of it."

A witch, after all, can unlock other levels of living. She is not bound by the mundane.

Around noon, Karina appears in the kitchen. She stands at the counter, in a bright blue T-shirt and paisley pajama pants, clutching a cup of coffee.

"Don't worry, it's safe!" she says, giving me permission to approach. "This is my second cup."

I admire the perfect foam on her latte, and Karina turns to the counter and bears aloft a metal canister. "This is a hundred-dollar Nespresso machine, and I manifested it for three dollars and fifty cents at the Goodwill! It was brand-new, still wrapped in its packaging. Can you believe it?" We both have a good giggle at this—though, to be clear, she is not kidding. Once she's done laughing, she lets out a sigh. "I manage to manifest the rent money, or whatever it takes to get by, at the very last minute—but financial struggle is still so much a part of my life," she says. "As a witch, that's something I'm concerned about: Why can't I make things work without being in a state of emergency?"

If people are talented at spell casting, it does not immediately follow that their focus is on perfecting their own lives. Many witches are dedicated to using magic to perform a service for others, leaving their personal lives a mess—a scenario that I've seen play out in my own world, with every kind of artist. Morpheus had her own example: "You can have a Harvard professor who's obviously a master in their field, but that doesn't mean that they have a perfect grasp on how to have relationships or whatever," she told me. "Just because you are advanced in a certain skill does not mean that you are somehow a perfectly rounded, perfectly developed person."

I follow Karina out the screen door, and we sit together barefoot on the stoop as she smokes. "I'm an entrepreneur," she says with a certain amount of pride. She runs through a list of self-help business gurus whose aggressive e-newsletters and online video clips she studies in order to better educate herself. Karina believes these strategies just might contain the key to making a better living at what she does.

Karina has had this focused, ambitious streak in her since she can remember. As a young girl in Catholic school in the seventies, she was a stellar student, and very religious—she fantasized about becoming, not a nun, but a priest (it seemed more serious). But at some point in high school, she started drinking hard and realized that she couldn't stop herself. At twenty-two, after a series of twelve-step meetings and a series of car accidents—"It was clear I would die"—she finally managed to stay sober. She started to channel her ambition into AA, becoming a sponsor to multiple women at a time. She learned public speaking, how to organize people and plan events—and this was her reentry into spiritual life. "It was in twelve-step where I learned to pray again," she says. "When I got there, I had an issue with the word 'God.' But they really emphasized in the program that it was a power greater than yourself—and that can be anything from your sponsor to the group to the tree outside your window, whatever. I learned to believe there was something bigger than me."

Newly sober, Karina enrolled in community college. One of her first assignments for an anthropology course was to write an ethnography of a local "subculture." She remembered an ad she'd seen for a witchcraft shop down the road; raised Catholic, she found this extremely exotic. "I thought, 'I'm gonna call those witches!'" The man who owned the shop agreed to meet and talk with her over the next few weeks. "There was a part of me that was really into this as a project," she says, "but then there was a part of me that just *knew*. It was the beginning of my life's trajectory." The shop owner invited her to attend a Samhain ritual, and when she left, she thought, "Wow, something happened. Because they called their ancestors, and I felt the room *fill up*." Karina also took to heart something the shopkeeper had told her, about secrecy: "Try not to talk about this too much, because there's power in silence. If you bring this into the part of you that thinks and rationalizes things, then it loses power."

Like Gerald Gardner decades ago—and, I'll admit, as I'm doing now—Karina had "gone native." She began spending time with other Pagans, mostly women, eventually joining the feminist Pagan movement. "It was pretty radical, exclusionary of men. We would not have them in our circles"—just what I'd gotten a taste of in Illinois. During that time she also read *The Spiral Dance* by Starhawk (now a well-known Pagan author and activist) and started a coven based on the book. Starhawk was a feminist and a Feri initiate, and wrote openly about her teachers Victor and Cora Anderson. Now at Mount Holyoke College, Karina decided to finish school and head out to San Francisco: all the Feris were in California then. (Even today, the Bay Area is ground zero for Feri practice.)

But while she was working on her thesis—on women and feminist witchcraft—a close friend insisted that she meet a man named Mark, in spite of his gender. So she went to his house to interview him, sat down on his shag rug, turned on her recorder, and asked, "So who's the Goddess?" Mark replied, in a childlike voice, "She's my mommy." I cringe a little at this, a grown man using that word, but Karina was moved and impressed. "I thought, 'Wow.' It was a response that wasn't academic, it came from the core of himself." Mark, as it turned out, was also Feri, and had studied with Victor and Cora himself—but instead of being out west, here he was, in her neighborhood.

For Beltane, Mark invited Karina to his house. She arrived expecting a Maypole, but instead found a gathering of beautiful freaks. He was wearing lipstick and had garlands in his hair. She had an immediate reaction. "I believe that I'm a witch when I *say* I'm a witch, and I was pretty opposed to studying under someone," she says. "But I heard come out of my mouth: 'I really need to learn from you; you have things that I need.' We looked at each other as if I had just asked him to marry me." She'd finally found her *teacher*. Soon they began working together on the summer solstice, almost twenty years ago.

When her kids begin wandering the house, Karina grabs her handbag and suggests we drive into town for some privacy. We head to an organic café for lunch. The downstairs room is done in faux-Mexican décor; the walls are hung with Latin Catholic iconography. (Directly behind Karina is a three-quarter-height statue of Christ, bleeding, being taken down from the cross.) We order complicated sandwiches.

I mention Victor's sexual initiation, in the Oregon woods at age nine, and Karina says, "Yeah. As an adult woman, part of me hears that story and wants to say, 'What the hell was going on there?'" Nothing like that is considered acceptable in Feri practice.

Our conversation veers further into dark terrain, to a topic Karina has perhaps wanted to broach, the other deep-seated reason why the Sundering took place: an abuse of the sexual energy underlying Feri, tied closely to the secrecy around initiation. Yes, Feri is openly referred to as a "sex cult"—a phrase that grabbed my attention when I first heard it—but this doesn't imply the decadent B-movie orgies those words evoke. Eight years ago, a prominent Bay Area initiate and teacher, then only a student, came forward and accused his teacher, Gabriel Carrillo (one of Victor's personal initiates), of requiring sex with him as a condition of initiation. Thorn came forward to state the same, blogging (and speaking openly with me) about a teacher (meaning Gabriel) who had sex with her when she was eighteen. Though Feri initiation does involve sex, this rite can be with your teacher *or* with your partner—having sex with your boyfriend or girlfriend or spouse can complete the ceremony (as it did for Morpheus)—and it definitely involves that *choice*. But many of the initiates of Gabriel's Bloodrose line have refused to acknowledge any wrongdoing, remaining silent instead, in protest.

Though Karina respects Gabriel as "a powerful magician," she cannot get past how he handled his students. "I call that rape," she says. "The dynamic between teacher and student is one of power-over—the student *can't* consent." She adds that Gabriel did this several times. She also claims that he would ask students to exchange sex with him for a range of other teachings, or as a way to commune with certain gods. Gabriel died of a prolonged illness in 2007, and some of his initiates carry on his style of teaching as it was passed on to them.

I am struck, yet again, by the inescapable interconnectedness of religion, or spiritual guidance, with power; and of power with sex. In this case, with an esoteric mystery cult, there is not even an institutional structure in place to monitor the clergy—not that that's been effective for, say, the Catholic Church (a flaming understatement). I think of what Cora wrote about the karmic pain in store for those who "abuse sex and throw it around like a baby playing in its own excrement"—but something more deliberate than karmic punishment seems necessary here.

Karina says that she developed an infatuation with her teacher, Mark; she became submissive toward him. "And he never asked that of me! But if he put a glass in front of me and told me to drink it, I would just gulp it down without a word, without even asking what it was. It was that way with all his requests. He never, ever asked anything sexual of me—he *could* have! He was aware of the power dynamic." After she'd studied with him for a while, he finally said, "You know, Karina, sometimes a student can develop a sexual attraction to their teacher, and that's completely normal. But it's a phase."

She looks at me with a gentle smile. "Most of my students go through that phase, that time when they think, 'If only I could be like Karina.' *You'll* probably feel that at some point. But it passes."

On our way back to the house, we stop at the nearby community garden, a large field that's been subdivided into vegetable plots for a collection of residents. The lush green tendrils of Karina's squash have stretched themselves out into her neighbors' patches. "It's running wild!" She also has a panoply of not-yet-ripe plum tomatoes, green beans and red beans, and pumpkins that will be ready in time for Halloween. She collects two bright yellow squash to add to dinner.

Although it's well into the afternoon, the summer heat is still bearing down, and we sit together on the stoop, barefoot again, as Karina lights up. Our time together thus far has been relaxed and free-form in its rhythms. I get the sense that, much as Victor did, Karina is passing on information about Feri's history and practices through conversation. In spite of what's available online, this is an oral, experiential tradition, and a lot must be talked out or physically demonstrated—even though, with a newbie like me, there's still not much witchcraft for us to practice together. I also get the sense that I'm undergoing a general evaluation. And her next words confirm this feeling.

"So are you a witch, or are you just . . . doing research?"

This question is like a kick to the gut—and it's one that keeps arising lately. I've reached a strange juncture with the project: whereas newer acquaintances, upon hearing about the book, used to assume it was purely anthropological, now they ask if I'm a witch myself. Never mind that this question is light-years away from anything I'm prepared to answer—there's also my deep-seated fear of being labeled, shoehorned into a category as a way of diminishing me. This reminds me of when I had a brief high school eating disorder: one of my best reasons for getting healthy was my fear of being labeled anorexic, since that gave people license to see me as weak, a victim, an outsider. And though a "witch" can be many things, she is certainly, by definition, an outsider. My desire to get in on secrets, to earn them, is very separate from this idea of witchcraft as my life's work, as a newly claimed identity. A belief system, a spiritual calling, seems like a life in the arts: if you're questioning yourself, questioning the work, the struggle loses its value, and you've simply exiled yourself to the outskirts of any mainstream life without benefit.

I say to Karina, knowing full well that my answer will have a serious bearing on our relationship, "It's up to me to *prove* to myself whether or not I'm a witch." A look of slight skepticism, or even mild disappointment, crosses her face. "Come on! You know I've been frustrated. I wasn't going to come here, to your house, and announce, 'Hey, wow, I've overcome all my obstacles just in time for our visit!'"

"If you'd done that," she says slowly, "within thirty minutes you would have been in a world of pain. I would have given you what for."

"I'm studying right now because . . . I'm not a kid anymore. And I need to know where I stand."

Now the look on her face says, "Okay. All right." She smiles.

She decides to tell me a story. Last summer, Karina fell for someone and asked the person to move in with her family. Her paramour, however, turned out to be distressingly unbalanced, and Karina was compelled not only to move but to take out a restraining order. It was enough to shake her beliefs.

"After things turned bad, and I mean *really bad*, I'd walk by my altar and just go"—she flips the bird—"*Fuck you. Fuck you, fuck you, fuck you.* My altar's in my bedroom, and I have to pass it to get in and out of bed, and every time I passed it, it was"—she flips the bird again, with great conviction. She shakes her head and smiles to herself. "Here I am, Karina the big priestess, the big Feri witch, and I couldn't see this coming? And I led myself and my children right into this situation?" So she rejected her magical practice completely.

I'm surprised, and ask what she did to change the situation. "I did what I tell my students to do when they're stuck: I cleared everything off my altar and I just burned a candle," she says. "Slowly, I started to practice again. And, little by little, whenever I needed something else, I'd put that back on the altar. This is still ongoing—I'm still recovering."

She's shared this story as a lesson to me. She could see my wavering, the pronounced swerve and jitter in my training right now. She's saying: Here's my own weakness and uncertainty to match yours. I've seen this before—it can be a cult-y technique, a "bonding" strategy—but from Karina it feels genuine. She's extending herself to me. She's being generous.

Early the next evening, we drive to the nearby village of Florence to pick up dinner at A-1 Pizza House. It's the kind of nonchain suburban pizza place that was more prevalent in the eighties: low ceilings and thin brown carpeting; beige contour booths (occupied by a clique of older teens in jeans and ratty tees); an old arcade game; and specials written on paper plates taped to the wall. We put in our order and head outside to wait.

At just this moment, an elderly pixie strolls down the street, carrying a watering can. Her name, I learn, is Jane, and she's about four and a half feet in tall rubber boots, her short red hair mostly hidden under a broad-brimmed gardening hat. She wears a knit jumper and surgical gloves, and her skin is so pale it's more a translucent gray. She has such a sprightly look that I can hardly believe the sight of her. Jane is a Wiccan high priestess, one of Karina's former coven, from her pre-Feri days in the nineties, back when she was still cutting her teeth.

Karina greets her. "I was telling Alex earlier about Lord Theo," she says.

"Oh, wow. I don't know when the last time was I saw him. I haven't been doing group things for a long time," Jane replies. "I just keep to myself. I don't know how things are done nowadays, but I know they've changed." Jane is not a witch of the Internet age, that much is clear.

We excuse ourselves to pop in and pick up our food. As we head back to the van, Jane waves to us from where she's stooped, tending to one of her street planters. I step up into the passenger seat and place the two hot pizza boxes on my lap, wondering at my ghostly glimpse of another generation of New England witchcraft.

During dinner, a kids' paradise of pizza followed by artisanal chocolate bars from the health food store, Karina brings up the annual BlackHeart Feri Samhain gathering. Set for the first few days of November, to coincide with the high holiday of the dead, the event will take place at a castle in New Hampshire, with about twenty of Karina's students and initiates in attendance, including one who will fly in from Germany.

At this topic, Kim lets out a great big sigh—a sigh of the variety only produced by a teenage girl, long and languid and profoundly exasperated. "*So* boring," she pronounces.

"Oh, poor you," her mother says. "Stuck in the tower with all the witches down below, conjuring the dead, chanting up a storm. What a dull life!"

Suddenly Kim perks up, sensing an angle. "Can I bring a friend?"

"No."

"*So* boring."

The next morning, I am surprised to find that Karina has also woken up early and is showered and dressed. She has decided that this is the moment, before I race off to catch the train, when we will do some work together.

In a short skirt and bare feet, Karina sweeps up the house to clean it, then sweeps it again, this time with a broom anointed with herbal essences to "brighten" the space. She "charges" the living room with salt water and sage smoke. Seated across from each other, we perform the Ha Prayer, aligning our three souls, the three parts of the etheric body, the body I'm expected to ride someday through the astral plane.

After the rite is done—this is the first time we've done a magical working together—Karina says she can tell that I am able to store mana. More than that, she could see, when I was aligning, that I was able to expand my etheric body "from a couple inches to a few more inches out." According to Cora, the Talker, your aura—this is what Karina saw—extends nine inches all around. The Fetch, or animal self, hugs the physical body about two centimeters out, with a pink glow and the hum of a bumblebee.*

Karina could see more than that: she caught a glimpse of my Godself, my Godsoul. She says, "Your Godsoul was very bright"—then laughs. "I thought, 'I can see her haircut!'" (I have a carefully shaped bob.) "I only looked

---

* Fetch also contains a "phantom" version of the genitalia of the opposite sex, making each of us equally male and female, if you combine the planes on which we exist. In a passage to make Freud's head spin, Victor wrote that from every woman's clitoris "extends a sexual part that is like a phantom penis!" And within every man's scrotum "is a replica or 'X-ray' image of the female vagina!" (The exclamation points are Victor's, anticipating the reader's reaction.)

from an angle, you know, because Victor said that if we were ever to look directly into our Godsoul, we'd be blinded."

The night before, after the kids cleared the dishes, Karina and I had lingered at the table, getting onto a conversational roll that lasted until late. We finally had a real rapport, comfortable cursing in front of each other and telling lame jokes. We waved our hands and banged the tabletop and generally talked like ourselves, sometimes face-to-face and sometimes on either side of the screen door as Karina indulged in another smoke. Could I have something in common with this woman who claims she can see my astral self?

I think about what she told me, about the ways in which personal turmoil can stomp out belief. When that happens, you wipe everything off your altar and start again. Burn a candle—simple. And little by little, each time you require magic, you search for the right spell and go from there. Everything in increments, as dictated by need and the drive to keep living.

And just a few weeks later, I remember this conversation when I wake up and discover that I need help. This is one of those times, I decide, to go in search of the right spell.

12

The Binding

From: Morpheus Ravenna

To: Alex Mar

Subject: Re: In need of a spell (that's right)

OK. Here are some options.

1. Freezer spell. Freezer spells are helpful for shutting
someone down. The essence of the spell is to take something
representing the person, dress it with appropriate
materials, wrap it up in foil, and stick it in the freezer.
This is commonly used to stop someone who is causing harm
by manipulation, malicious gossip, etc. For the strongest
version of this spell, it's recommended to use a tongue (like
beef tongue you can get from butcher shops); there's an
obvious symbolism there with stopping their malicious and
manipulative speech. You slice it open so you can insert
something representing her inside it. If you can get a
photograph of her, and write her name on the back, that is

best. If you can't get a photograph, write her name on a piece of paper. Across her name at a 90-degree angle, and on top so it covers her name up, write out what you want to do to her. "Shut X's mouth so she can no longer manipulate anyone with her lies or hurt anyone with her malicious behavior" or however you want to put it. Just be as specific as possible. Then dress the photograph or paper with any mixture of these things: mustard (for disruption), red and black pepper (to make ill words burn in her mouth), cloves or slippery elm bark (against malicious talk), and the most important one, alum, to stop her tongue. You can hold the dry materials in by folding up the paper or photograph with them inside. Then, insert it inside the tongue, and pin or sew it closed. Nine pins is traditional. Wrap it in aluminum foil and stick it in a freezer so it freezes solid. While you're putting all this together, you should of course be focusing on your intention for the spell. Speaking your intentions as a prayer or incantation is good too. Burning black candles doesn't hurt. :)

2. Binding spell with a poppet (as an alternative to the freezer spell). A poppet is a little doll, your classic witching tool. The idea is to literally make a representation of her that you can do work on. You can make one out of anything—shaped wax or clay, sticks tied into a person's shape, cloth sewn into a shape, whatever you can think of to make a little doll out of. The important thing is to link it to her. If you can get a piece of hair or bit of thread or cloth from her clothing, that's ideal. If not, pin or glue a cutout picture of her face onto the face of the doll, and write or carve her name onto the doll somewhere. Name the doll out loud. "I name you so-and-so. You are so-and-so. Anything that happens to you, happens to her." Now, you can do all sorts of things with the poppet!

I'd start by making a little oil or concoction you can dress it with. You could use basically the same ingredients I mentioned above; hot pepper is especially important. Poppy seeds are another good one, for causing confusion so she becomes ineffective. Graveyard dirt adds power to any work like this. Mix whatever herbs or materials you're using into a little bit of oil. Dress the mouth, hands, heart, and sexual area of the poppet, for stopping her from using her speech, actions, emotional influence, or life energy to manipulate or hurt. Take some pieces of twine and bind the poppet around the mouth, the heart, the hands, and the feet. Tell her she is bound from manipulating with her lying speech, bound from using emotions and energy to hurt others, bound from reaching out to your man in word or deed, and bound from coming near him. Wrap it up in something reflective like tinfoil or put it inside a box lined with mirrors facing inward, to reflect all her harmful intentions and negative energy back to her. Then you should bury it somewhere not too near where you or he live. A crossroads or a graveyard is the best place. If you've got any relatives buried nearby, you could bury it near them, and ask them to help you with the work.

3. Whatever work you do against her, you should take a cleansing bath afterward just to make sure you are free of any negativity remaining from the work. A bath with a little salt in the water--and if you have any herbs or oils such as hyssop, eucalyptus, or cinnamon, put some of that in the bath too. Neat little trick: burn two white candles by the edge of the bathtub, and when you step out of the bath, step out between the two candles.

Oh, and in the same vein, I recommend doing a really thorough kala practice before you start any of this, and again after. It is especially important before you begin the work, because you need to make sure that you are free of the things you are targeting her for. Because the way I understand it, any magic we do we are pretty much doing to ourselves first, so when you're hexing someone you need to make sure you aren't guilty of the things you are targeting them for, so your spell doesn't "stick" to you on its way.

. . . OK, I'll stop there. :D Got any questions?

love--M

I'd asked for this. I went to Morpheus for a spell—a "binding" spell—and she came through in spades.

I'd become involved with someone new, a filmmaker. He'd pursued me, I'd relented, and soon we were staying together in sublets on both coasts. He was reclusive and intensely talented, a planet rotating his Work—and I felt I had no choice but to spend time on that planet for a while. The attraction was very strong. Now and again I'm reminded of that theory, that people partner with those who look like them in some way—not necessarily a racial but a tribal kinship. And Shawn's face was so much like mine that it was uncanny, like seeing myself reflected back in another human.

At the same time, however, he was in desperate recovery from a painfully recent (*too* recent) breakup with someone who'd apparently done all the things women do to men in country songs and worse. And then, one day, using work as an excuse, she began reaching out to him, at an intense pitch.

I described things to Morpheus:

The man I'm with now, who I'm becoming more serious about, has a former lover who's doing her best to manipulate his life at the moment. From what he tells me, she's a pathological liar, weaving a web of deceit and emotional voodoo from a distance—and, unfortunately, she intersects with his professional life over the coming months (she stars in a movie he made and is now using the upcoming premiere as a playing card). As far as I know, the chick's not explicitly witchy, but the energy she's sending out at the moment is clearly powerful and destructive. (He's started to lose weight and get red in the eyes from exhaustion, as if something's being drained from him.) I've had enough of this, and would like to take some kind of action that could counter what seems to me to be a form of assault through *massive*, concentrated amounts of negative psychic energy.

The end of the relationship was due to duplicitous actions on the woman's part, and the sting is still there. And now she's emailing and texting him multiple times a day, compulsively, calling and leaving unanswered voice messages.

I'd like to protect him from the energy coming from this person. I'd like to make her irrelevant, so that her possible presence and words and input can no longer take any emotional or psychological toll on him. I want to sap her power in relation to him. He's such a skeptic (he was raised deeply Christian, left the fold, and now believes mostly in "science") that I wouldn't be able to draw on the power of his own belief in the magical working. If I could be just as effective without asking for his permission, that would be great. If I could help stabilize things as soon as possible, I think it would be a real help.

And so, for the first time in my life, here I am, seriously considering a magical intervention. I choose the freezer spell: folding a cow's tongue and sealing it with nine pins, or maybe sewing it up with a large needle and some thick red thread—two and a half pounds, the whole tongue, cut from way back in the animal's throat. This becomes the plan.

But in spite of how fed up I am with the "emotional voodoo," I realize, in writing out my shopping list of ingredients, that I can barely imagine going through with the spell. I become wary of not being "clean" enough entering into it, not being completely honest with myself as to why I want to get involved (anger? impatience? greed?). Besides, within two days of my deciding to turn to witchcraft, the situation seems to subside, to calm, to slowly resolve itself. I congratulate myself on my restraint.

And this is what eventually happens: after everything we go through together, and all his visible suffering and stress, and this woman's bent, compulsive outreach, he will reunite with her. And when asked about it, he'll say, "She wore me down."

"I've had many people ask me for advice over the years," Morpheus tells me, "but most of them don't go ahead and do it. They either get too nervous or they start to see the situation differently. And sometimes I think it would have been better for them to have *done it*."

Part of me wonders if things might have ended differently had I let go of my nerves and my skepticism and gone ahead with the spell. I was *embarrassed*. I was embarrassed and afraid of getting caught practicing undeniable witchcraft—and using it to influence not only the life of my then boyfriend but also that of his ex, a woman I'd never met. How could I explain an action like that—not only to him, if he had found out, but to myself? And I was doubly embarrassed by my own need, because that's what an act like that proves: your neediness, just how deeply you care. Giving your lover that level of importance is risky enough; giving a woman you don't even know that level of attention—clipping out her photograph, chanting over it— is hard to stomach.

That said, I was excited by the idea of taking action, tired of simply watching things run their course, ready to rise up and do something dramatic, even absurd, on the off chance it might tip the scales in my favor. Since so many of us have little or no ritual in our lives, inserting that element can seem extreme—unlike for Morpheus, who integrates ceremony into all levels of her life as if it were utterly natural, another bodily rhythm, like breathing. And maybe this is a way in which the rest of us, in the ultra-civilized world, the skeptical world, hobble ourselves, prevent ourselves from ever discovering whether witchcraft can have an impact.

Then there's this: even if I believed completely in the effectiveness of witchcraft, believed it had undeniable muscle, I'm not sure I would have been happy with a forced result. To force someone's hand runs contrary to who I am and how I set about getting what I want. I have a complicated relationship to the idea of Fate. I have an intuitive sense that there is meaning to the structure and sequence of events, and that while we can tip their course slightly, nudge them in what we believe to be the right direction, to truly tamper with the elements in play would be to miss the larger story set out for each of us.

This instinctive view on my part surprises me: as a thinking person, and someone raised to have empathy for others, I'm well aware that Fate works best as a concept for those born into comfortable circumstances. The modesty of this perspective also confuses me: I've never thought of myself as a person who underestimates her own abilities or lacks ambition. But a dose of Catholic guilt was injected into my system long ago, and that feeling prevents me from simply *taking*—instead, I have to *earn*. Or else a reward must have been laid aside for me by a larger force, and then my job is to uncover it. It's my right to seek out and claim that prize—a great success! a great love!—because, you see, it was mine all along.

Maybe this is where Fate lines up with Magic. I think of how Crowley defined magic, as "the Science and Art of causing Change to occur in conformity with Will"—Will, in its capital-W Thelemic definition, meaning each individual's epic purpose in the world, each person's alignment with the universe. Crowley held, as do many witches, that any magical working that steers circumstances into that preexisting alignment is 100 percent karmically okay. But if it requires a more unnatural *shove*, then you're in dangerous terrain and must take ownership of any dark consequences.

So how to know where the line should be drawn, both in magical practice (if you believe in it) and in our mundane desires? What karmic rules to subscribe to? What larger forces might be at play? In casting my freezer spell, in purchasing my couple of pounds of raw flesh and placing another woman's name inside and, black candles lit, doubling that thick tongue in on itself and sewing it shut, could I have gained something under false pretenses, something I did not ultimately want, something that could hurt me deeply even though I now "possessed" it? Or is this passive, guilt-ridden Catholic thinking? (When I first asked Morpheus about magical ethics a few years ago, she didn't pause: "If I have to cast a spell that goes against someone else's desires in order to protect the people I care about, so be it.") But knowing what I know now, I see my ex and *his* ex as more perfectly suited to each other than I could ever have understood—a frantic, paranoid union that I would never want in my own life.

From the day I met Shawn until the day it was over, it lasted six months, during which we were sometimes in the same city and sometimes apart—but when we were together, it was in close quarters and relentless. His work's like a fever for him; mine *should* be for me—but instead I allowed myself, happily, to sink into his world, his problems, his state of constant emergency. His creative process seems to require a level of panic that mine simply does not, and there was a peculiar relief in letting go of myself that way, getting swept up. "Time off" was often regimented and repetitive (featuring trips to the same clothing outlets and supermarkets); most movies were out (a waste of time), as were books (too demanding). The major topic was work (his). For the time being, I decided not to question things. I decided we were on a dysfunctional mission together.

I realize now that Shawn was not unique, in the course of my personal history, though the depth of my feelings insisted he must be. As I've already confessed, I have a strong dose of the "religious impulse"—but instead of signing up with a group, I've repeatedly sought out cultish relationships. That's putting it crudely, but it rings true enough: a string of creative men, sometimes several years older than me, always focused inward on their self-induced crises, living inside their own weather system. Religion maps sense onto chaos, and humans crave sense and meaning. So in the absence of a religious system—and especially if, like me, your personality falls on the "naturally devout" spectrum—we seek out a substitute, other rules by which to map our behavior. In this way, the sometimes cultish rhythms of work and relationships become strange surrogates for God. My relationships with the more charismatic men I've dated have had elements in common with what's drawn me to Morpheus or Karina or Josh or even that Jesus Movement community out west: each has access to a kind of magic I covet. Because to fall for someone is, in some ways, to claim his powers as your own.

I want to stop sublimating this religious drive and instead embrace it, pitch forward into it, see how it might better serve me. Stop being this spiritual dilettante, a professional "seeker." If I have a natural talent for belief, I must be a natural fit for something to believe in—some system somebody has laid out somewhere. I imagine a near future in which all my parts might align. For the first time, I find myself surrounded by people who assume just such a thing is possible.

13

Proof; or, The Creeping of Your Skin

Josh, the frenetic young priest at the heart of Alombrados, would never have worried himself over a binding spell. Not with a poppet, not with an animal's tongue. He doesn't care about the concept of Fate—he demands an active hand in how events play out around him. He is greedy for results.

It was this desire to master his environment that led him to a life in ceremonial magic.

Josh grew up mostly in Albuquerque, New Mexico, an army brat (his father was in the air force). Like many who are eventually drawn to the occult, he had an appetite for religion from a young age—but his mom, though a devout Bible reader, did not attend services, and his dad was more or less an atheist. So, by the fifth grade, their son started joining his mountain-biking buddy's "really out-there" Christian family in their search for a local congregation. He was most turned on by the Catholic church they attended: the soaring architecture, the fine dark wood—the aesthetic was awesome, the mass elegant, solemn. But Catholicism was too spooky and visually lush for his friend's family. The mother, like Josh's own, rejected the ritualism as "pagan."

Relegated to the family's chosen Christian youth group, Josh was confused by his youth pastor's harping on sexual sin. Thirteen and now masturbating, he developed a pronounced concern about eternal damnation. The question he'd return to over and over was that of Good versus Evil: how can a forgiving God, a God who believes in the possibility of salvation for all, cast out certain angels as "demons"? It did not compute. He asked, "If we can be forgiven, why can't we forgive the demonic forces? They fell because they disobeyed God—but *we're* doing that constantly, right? Is there no way for them to come out of the hellfire?" In asking forgiveness for demons, he suddenly found himself ostracized.

In a way, Josh began to relate to these fallen angels, these ultimate outcasts, and though he wasn't allowed to watch horror movies, he spent much of his private time drawing demonic figures and monsters—horns, crowns, exposed intestines, made-up sigils, you name it—filling entire notebooks with the stuff. Eventually, his parents sent him to therapy to avoid a full-blown descent into delinquency. The concern wasn't entirely misplaced: by the age of fourteen, beyond getting kicked out of his Christian youth group, Josh had already been initiated into the West Side 40 Crips in a gas-station bathroom (mostly this involved having the crap kicked out of him). All the while, he continued to read the Youth Bible alone in his room. "I felt like I was reading a book of *power.* I read the stories looking for some special formula. It wasn't even religious for me—it felt magical."

After high school, Josh jumped from reading magic into Christianity to reading texts that were actually *intended* as magic. His family moved to Olympia, Washington, and he enrolled at Evergreen State College. The ocean and the persistent fog and rain made him feel as if he were in another world, "totally psychedelic'd out by the giant pine trees." That was where he encountered the occult, through goth kids and acidheads who brought him to abandoned cemeteries. A new friend of his, Tim, had a girlfriend who claimed there was a malevolent poltergeist in her house—plenty of teenage girls have ideas about the supernatural, but she was *convinced*—and she turned to the boys for help. Jumping at an excuse to embrace the weird, Josh and Tim went to a local occult shop and asked for a book on "demon conjuring." The polite Pagan at the counter—"he had the look on his face like 'Oh, not *these* kids'"—handed them a copy of the seventeenth-century grimoire *The Lesser Key of Solomon.* A regular reference for many serious ceremonial magicians, the first section of the book is the "Ars Goetia" (or "Goetic Arts"), a catalogue of the methods of demon evocation used by King Solomon, who is believed to have trapped the spirits and put them to work.

Nothing much would ever come of the girl's poltergeist situation, but the boys had walked out of that store with a major magical text. The knowledge that, for centuries, generations of magicians had used these methods, these spells and invocations, to systematically conjure up the superhuman, that these affairs extended far beyond the realm of teenage fuckery, was truly radical for Josh. There must be real power in this spellwork, stranger and more impressive than anything his youth pastor or his therapist or these goth weirdos had ever known. The stakes had changed. The gates of his mind flew open.

This curiosity, combined with drugs and an outsider's view of the world, led Josh to pick up magical momentum. Soon he and Tim were diving headlong into wild, unguided occult experimentation. They had started a band (industrial metal), with Josh as the frontman, and they divided their time between music and magical research. Together they rented an apartment and outfitted it like the occultists' den at an imaginary zoo, packing it with stolen Masonic tombstones and graveyard flowers. Their place took on the scent of rotting irises, a cemetery smell. The atmosphere was thick.

They began attempting Goetic spells from *Key of Solomon* inside the apartment, not thinking twice about it. Things turned dark fast. College friends claimed to see a huge stork, tall as the ceiling, moving around Josh's bedroom; Tim began to have regular visions of a dead woman; a visitor claimed something tried to choke him in the shower. The duo developed a local reputation, hosting radical parties that occasionally culminated in orgies—one involving an improvised ritual to Babalon, the Thelemic goddess (in late-nineties Olympia, kids assumed it was yet another "goth party"). Josh remembers how a woman who worked at the nearby Barnes & Noble became very upset the next morning over her sexual escapades: she was convinced that an entity that had been in the house that night had made her do those things. He found this encouraging—one of his first confirmations that they were tapping into something powerful.

Josh became increasingly ambitious. He decided to take a major leap into Enochian magic: they would evoke an angel. He and Tim hiked deep into the woods until they found a small clearing around a tree stump. In the dirt they drew their circle, and inside its boundaries they laid out their tools, including a bowl of oil Tim was prepared to scry in.

They recited the Enochian "call" to bring in the spirit—and Josh heard a *roar*. It sounded like a motorcycle. The wind blew through the trees, and they sensed a presence. "It was massive, like someone standing behind you on all sides, everywhere. I felt *engulfed*." Josh felt small, dwarfed, terrified. He froze. "You know when they're talking about 'the angel of the Lord' when you're reading the Old Testament? They're not 'Oh, angels—pretty! World peace!'—that's *not* what an angel is. Whatever an angel is, is scary."

Now that they'd conjured up something huge, they had no plan for what to say. They'd wanted to do something for their band—"Robert Johnson nonsense, like 'Help us make connections so we can get a deal'"—but that suddenly felt petty. "I realized this was the kind of thing where I could be, like, 'What will happen to mankind in a hundred years?' and I'm asking to get a *band contract?* I felt embarrassed." Josh managed to put in their request. But after that night in the woods, he started taking magic much more seriously. After that encounter, he was all in.

Just days later, at a show the band played in Seattle, someone approached them—Josh says he was the touring guitarist for Ministry. The guy asked to produce their first album; they'd record in the Seattle studio where Nirvana made their first album. This was just what they'd asked for. They decided an otherworldly patron must be at work.

Under these changing circumstances, Josh's larger perspective began to shift: he started to believe you could gain things in life regardless of whether or not you'd "earned" them or been "good." "For me, sorcery's a real thing, and if you do it the right way, you'll get everything you want," he says. He no longer believed in destiny—or at least he believed he'd learned the secret to overriding it. "Your fate becomes different from other people's fate."

He began to enjoy himself. His band was drawing crowds to their shows, and he had three or four girlfriends at a time. Josh started to match his musical ambitions with new, magical ones: he got involved with the OTO lodge in Seattle, found an older mentor there, and took his Minerval initiation—then his first degree and his second degree. He wanted to legitimate his magic; he wanted his work to be recognized—and how else to do that but through Crowley's own society, some of the only people on the planet capable of understanding his experiments?

Meanwhile, Josh was beginning to feel that the mellow weirdness of the Northwest was "not Wild West enough for my taste." An OTO brother began talking up New Orleans, and building up "this dream of what it would be like to live in this idyllic shithole." The city sounded decadent and dangerous; apartments were cheap. And Josh was intrigued by the fact that this place, known in part as a haven for eccentric outsiders, was currently without an OTO lodge. "I had my own vision for what an OTO body could be, and I thought I could do a better job than a bunch of yuppies," he says. "That was my arrogant way of thinking about it." So he and his then girlfriend (a Minerval of barely legal age) threw everything they owned into a car and drove across the country.

Shortly after they arrived, Josh created a Yahoo Group, hoping to attract any underground Thelemites (or the Thelema-curious). He soon heard from locals, as well as some folks in Baton Rouge. They created a "body-in-formation" (an OTO group pending official approval), holding small outdoor rituals, and regular meetings at the St. Charles Tavern. Soon he and Andrew and David, three serious young magicians, moved into a two-story building on Gallier Street in the Bywater. "We were so young, we wanted it to be a monastery," he says. "It was more like a terrorist cell. We had 'Silent Tuesdays,' where no one in the house was allowed to speak to each other. And the rest of the week, people were constantly doing ritual." They built a temple inside and a space for Gnostic Mass out back, complete with the necessary magical gear. Josh's mentor would fly in from Seattle once a year to assist with initiations until Josh himself became certified. Finally, after a few years, with a core group of occultists assembled, they moved into a larger, grander spot: Alombrados's current home, a converted Christian church. Now Josh is the charismatic center of OTO in New Orleans and sleeps in an antique four-poster bed above one of the more impressive temples in occult America.

But he's yet to give up the scrappy Goetic habits that got him started. One night, when Josh was giving me a tour of the upstairs at Alombrados— the living quarters he shares with Sophia and Andrew—I noticed a sealed brass urn on a corner table, inscribed around the lip of its lid with Hebrew letters and wrapped with a length of red string and a feather. A *vévé* had recently been scratched on top—just the kind of drawing my mother had warned me off of when I was in college.

"Is there someone in there?" I asked Josh with a smile.

"Yes and no," he said. "There's nothing *in* there. But it contains someone, if you know what I mean."

Josh had made a mess of a Goetic working he'd done, and he was still attempting to rectify the situation. So he'd killed a black rooster, poured its blood into the urn, and tied one of its feathers to the lid. For the next step, to complete the corrective spell, he'd have to travel to a remote spot in the Louisiana countryside.

"You can't do it here?"

"No, I have to go out where there's no one—so it will appear to me and I can confront it."

"It," I understood, was a demon.

I may not have a magical identity yet, but I already know that Josh's boundaries are further off, and his ambitions more enormous, than my own. For the time being, my occult aspirations are more like fantasies. Again and again, I attend Gnostic Mass, imagining myself as Sophia (I mean "Babalon") up on the altar. I've developed a talent for swallowing down the nearly inedible host, and I now say it out loud with confidence, that loaded double negative: "There is no part of me that is not of the gods." The ritual is almost always followed by a late-night, booze-fueled talk with Andrew and Josh about the finer points of Thelema (and obscure music and horror films), and the following day is spent weighing my next step at Alombrados.

Right now I feel as if I exist in a liminal place, a borderland between two zones: one occupied by smart, upwardly mobile agnostics, and the other by possibly unbalanced super-devotees of obscure practices. I am lost in the middle, still unclaimed. Unlike Josh and Morpheus in their earlier days, I haven't found a way to be completely myself while testing this divide.

Earlier on, Shawn had pressed hard with his questions, demanding I take sides. After all, he'd been raised as an evangelical Christian and long ago traded faith for what he calls the "perfection" of mathematics.

"So do you believe in magic or what?" he asked. Each time I held firm at "I'm conflicted"—which is to say, I have no answer. This frustrated me almost as much as it did him. For a person with strong instincts, this question mark—which persists—was perverse.

"What do they do about the lack of evidence?" he asked (more than once).

"What do you mean?"

"What do they say to justify the lack of proof of their 'supernatural' abilities?"

Though rooted in Shawn's fairly advanced skepticism, this is a decent question. Some part of me has been trying to uncover proof since day one. But the question also *presumes* that no proof can ever be presented—whereas Karina, for instance, claims that evidence will be revealed, in stages, over an extended, rigorous period of training.

"That's an *unanswerable* question," Morpheus says when I eventually pass it along. "And the reason is: magic works primarily through nonphysical means that we can only observe in subjective ways. And that means that its manifestations can almost always be explained away, if that's your goal. So that line of thinking is a trap. Skepticism can be really toxic, because it makes you not trust your own lived experiences, the evidence of your senses, without outside verification." She considers her sensory experiences to be "prima facie evidence." This is what some Pagans refer to as UPG, or "unverified personal gnosis": the idea that a person's subjective spiritual or magical experience need not be proved universal to remain valid. (Critics enjoy calling UPG "*unverifiable* personal gnosis.") It's similar to a "private revelation" in Christian circles, and just as complicated: on the one hand, you're offering up utterly subjective experience as the basis of knowledge, which puts you on shaky ground; on the other hand, isn't *all* faith based on unverified gnosis?

That said, Morpheus tells me there *are* checks in magical practice. It is every witch's and magician's responsibility to remain aware of the difference between their "actual sense experiences," she says, and "the interpretive process of forming a story about what that experience means. Because that's where you can get tripped up."

She gives the example of invoking a deity. Early on in her training, Morpheus had a hard time believing they were real—as I mentioned before, not all Pagans do—leaning on the possibility that the gods are psychological archetypes the mind plays with to work magic. The question was always "Did this deity really show up, or am I imagining it?" She developed a checklist to run through after each ritual. "My sense experiences might be images and messages and thoughts that come unbidden into my mind, like they're coming from outside—those are all pieces of sensory evidence. I don't need to have someone else in the room who's seen the same thing—otherwise, it can't be real. But I want to look for: Did I have evidence that affected more than one of my senses? Is it in line with other experiences? Does it make sense in a larger picture? Am I making assumptions?"

The nebulous quality of these encounters was something she learned to accept. "When you're chanting, reciting poetry, or doing whatever you're doing to invoke the deity, and then they arrive," she says, "it's not, like, in a flash of light and a bang and a puff of smoke! Our culture, particularly with movies and TV and stuff, teaches us to expect spectacular displays of phenomena. So for a lot of people, the subtlety of how this stuff actually operates is a problem at first. It's a change in the air; it's the entry of a presence that is signaled by the creeping of your skin or a shift in your awareness. We have been taught to dismiss our sense perceptions, so then we're not sure we're having an actual experience. And then we ask ourselves, 'Well, am I just *wishing* this was real, so I'm talking myself into it?' It takes time to recalibrate your expectations. It's a matter of learning to trust your own perceptions, and to say, 'You know what? I didn't give myself goose bumps. I didn't talk myself into having that picture suddenly arise in my mind—that *came* from somewhere.' I realized I was having experiences that were real and that were changing my life, that were *claiming* me." This subtlety Morpheus describes is just what my mother spoke of when I asked what it was like for her, as a girl, to receive a message or a visitation—something I'd long assumed she'd be reticent to talk about, tight-lipped, defensive. I was wrong: she answered with ease. When someone is there, she said, "you can just *sense* it. It's like one of those double-decker buses is passing by, and someone is looking down at you from the top."

I mention to Morpheus one of Shawn's requests: that a witch levitate, or do something similarly spectacular, to demonstrate once and for all that magic works. She sighs. "Any time you try to use magic to work against a really strong, physical, natural law, that's going to take a ton of energy and a ton of skill, and very few people have that. You hear tales about Tibetan wizard priests being able to levitate and shit like that, and I believe it—but to do something so badass that it will allow you to overcome gravity, you have to dedicate your *life* to mastering that ability. Most people aren't going to get to that level, and that doesn't mean that they aren't doing real magic." Then she gives her more succinct, personal response: "I actually don't have to prove it to you. To come up with fabulous displays for your edification—that's not what magic is for. That would be a giant waste of my energy and effort."

She pauses. "You know, I *have* seen stuff that's as visible and spectacular as the movies—but it's really uncommon."

She tells me about something she witnessed one night while at a Pagan gathering in British Columbia with part of her priesthood. After a long day of working with ancestral spirits, and then a nighttime ritual in which she encountered the spirit of Queen Boudicca, she sat with her friends around a fire near a large lake. At some point, the lake began to appear to her as if perfectly still, a surface of glass rather than water; she felt the glass was a giant gateway that spirits were reaching through. She wandered off farther along the lakeside, with Moon following, and they sat down on a rock promontory. "And I started channeling the *feeling* of what was going on with the spirits," she says, "and I felt like there was something going on with the dead that needed to be honored. So I started singing to them, and I went into a trance." She was channeling their grief—maybe these were spirits who had never been mourned—and her singing became a keening funerary chant. Finally, she closed her eyes and lapsed into silence, until she heard Moon speak. "Are you *seeing* this?" At that, Morpheus opened her eyes, and the whole surface of the lake, which had been completely glassy, was now rippling toward them. And there was no wind at all. She was overwhelmed.

As they left to rejoin their crew, they ran into a Pagan friend who'd walked that way because he'd noticed something was happening to the water. He turned to Morpheus and asked, "Was that *you?*"

Morpheus likely assumes I'll accept this story, because we've become friends—and because she knows that I've been training with Karina, and looking into Thelema. But she does not expect most other people to take her seriously—nor is it important to her that they do.

"Being a magical practitioner involves some level of accepting that not everyone is going to believe you," she says. "That's just part of the deal. When someone has not experienced magic on a level that was persuasive to them, I cannot expect them to understand in any visceral way that it was real. And they can think I'm nutty—they're allowed to—and I don't have to be worried by that, because my experiences are my own. It actually takes a lot of strength of character to accept that who you are is not dependent on who other people see you as." In other words, that gap that Diane Arbus talked about—the gap "between intention and effect," between how each of us wishes to be seen and how we *are* seen—does not even matter. This is what it's like to have *any* kind of faith.

"There are gonna always be some people that think you're a *fool* for seeing magic as a real thing, and that's okay." She laughs. "That doesn't mean you *are* a fool."

I show up on a bright Sunday afternoon to hand in my Minerval application. People are streaming out of the temple in sweatpants, having just finished yoga. In the library, Andrew and Sophia lean over the crossword together, deep in focus. When he notices me, Andrew looks up with a big smile. "Hey!" He knows exactly why I'm here today.

I hand him the paperwork. This includes a waiver stating that I'm participating "voluntarily" and I accept risks, including "heart failure; stroke; spine and neck injuries (either of which could result in paralysis)," as well as "drowning and contracting of communicable diseases." It continues: "I also realize that as a participant in the activities of Ordo Templi Orientis I could possibly incur non-bodily injuries, including, but not limited to: emotional, psychological, and social injuries; and damage to, or loss of, personal property." When David originally handed me the form, he made sure to say, "I mean, it's really, *really* unlikely any of this will happen."

Andrew takes my documents and signs on the line with a flourish.

He introduces me to someone else at the table, Nick, a youngster— "Born in 1989," Sophia announces in disbelief when she reads his forms— with shaggy black hair and a patchy growth on his chin. He sticks out a pale, skinny arm and shakes my hand. "We'll be doing our Minerval together!" Apparently, it will be me, Nick, and Lucas out in the swamp together. At first I'm shocked that I'll be initiated with two such young guys—but then again, why not?

David (my other cosigner) finally shows up and takes his turn signing my application. He stacks it with the others.

When I turn to head out, he stops me. "Just so you know," David says, "once the signatures are on the paper, the process has begun." He and Andrew look at each other and grin. "You may find things start *happening* in your life."

14

Coru Cathubodua

For the Coru, the raven came last.

First, after a decade apart, a near-fatal illness, and two divorces between them, Morpheus and Moon came together through the Morrigan, and they deepened their commitment to her, as her dedicated priests. Then, in a collection of dreams and nightmares and secret messages passed on during ritual, the goddess pushed a handful of other followers, with surprising urgency, into Morpheus's path, until enough were gathered to build a priesthood, and the priesthood took a name: Coru Cathubodua, Army of the Battle Raven.

They gathered from across the Bay Area, some relocated there from as far away as Texas and upstate New York and Florida, having been raised all along the spectrum of religious belief: by Episcopalians, Mexican Catholics, New Age hippies, conservative Ashkenazi Jews. Ranging from their early twenties into their forties, they have jobs in public relations; at a nonprofit theater; as a physical therapist trained in Chinese medicine, a singer of traditional Irish songs, and a white-hat hacker.

The Morrigan appeared to them in rituals, surprised them in their dreams. For some, this first happened years ago: the goddess offered protection from their traumas—abuse by a mother's new boyfriend, a destructive romance, PTSD that refused to relent. For others, this happened when they caught her attention, in the immediate wake of the oath-taking at PantheaCon. To all, she gave marching orders, and, one after another, they showed up at Morpheus's door, until there were eight: Morpheus, Moon, Scott, Amelia, Ankhira, Hannah, Rynn, Rudy.

The ninth was the raven. Or the spirit inside the raven inside a box.

The raven was discovered high up in the hills outside Nevada City by a local Pagan, a friend of Moon's. While out collecting magical plants, he'd found the bird where it had fallen dead on the road, likely struck mid-flight by a passing truck. Having once made a botched attempt at "vulture magic" (magic using found animal parts), he didn't want to risk wasting the beautifully intact creature—a bird with heavy magical associations. So he took it back to his garage. There he built a hinged plywood box, filled it with natural preservatives (cornmeal, salt, mugwort), and stored the raven inside. He was willing to wait: he had a hunch that one day the right person would come calling for it.

Three years later, Moon began receiving a specific message from the Morrigan in his dreams, informing him that one of her "warriors" would soon come to him, and giving instructions as to the ritual he was then expected to perform. But he had no idea what she was talking about. Then one day he was sitting with his friend Jon at a Nevada City coffee shop and he decided to share some of the experiences he'd been having with the Great Queen, and about the early days of starting a priesthood. Jon, in turn, shared the story of the raven. "Now that you've told me about what you're doing," he said to Moon, "I know it belongs to you." A transfer of ownership was arranged.

Morpheus and Moon announced to the as-yet-unnamed Morrigan priesthood that a new ally wanted to present them with a special gift, and that this would take place in a ritual in the Sierra Nevada foothills, just outside Nevada City. The ceremony was already mapped out: the Morrigan had laid out the details in Moon's dreams.

The band—whoever could make it, along with Jon, the gift giver—met up that morning and drove together into the low, rolling hills that lead up to the Sierras, hiking the last half hour along natural pathways through the high-chaparral terrain. Finally, around noon, they reached a spot with enough space for a ritual circle, at the top of a ridge overlooking the valley.

Once they were set up—they had put out offerings of cream and beer (the goddess's favorites) and laid the raven on a warrior's shield—the circle was cast, with Morpheus at its center. The group chanted a song Morpheus had just taught them, and chanted and chanted and sang and sang. Using a utility knife, Moon carved a rune shape into his arm (once again, the Hagalaz, the hailstone), dipped a fingertip in the blood, and bent down to smear it across the bird's beak. And now, with everyone chanting still, the priestess went through her changes, doubling over: the Morrigan had entered her body. She downed the beer, she downed the cream, and then Morpheus-as-Morrigu put her hands on Moon and drew him close to her face. She held him there for a moment—his goddess and his girlfriend— then leaned in to lick the remaining blood off his arm.

Having made their offerings, the young priesthood turned to their own affairs. Moon spoke slowly: "Queen, we've brought you here to receive one of your fallen warriors." And then Morpheus-as-Morrigan approached the raven. She crouched down over the dead black bird and whispered to it— strings of words that no one could make out, and which Morpheus herself does not remember—and placed her hand on its chest. She straightened up again, stepped back—and there was a palpable shift. They all looked at each other as if to ask, Did you feel that, too? And then they turned to stare at the bird once again—because it was *breathing*.

No longer could they dismantle it into parts—they'd planned to make its head into a necklace, its feathers and claws into magical objects—because something inside the bird had made itself known. The solution: to induct the raven, or the spirit of the raven, into the priesthood. It was now a member, as much as its human counterparts.

Morrigu's face began to soften and seem more and more like it belonged to Morpheus. Once they'd taken a moment to gather themselves, everyone returned to the cars, carrying with them the Queen's new warrior-priest.

In the weeks that followed, after Morpheus and Moon took the raven home with them, they learned more about it. First of all, *it* was a *he*—a man Moon felt he'd had a relationship with in a past life, or in past *lives*. His personality was so familiar—and, more specifically, slightly *obnoxious.* "We realized," Morpheus says, "he's kind of a little punk."

From what they've discerned since, the bird is inhabited by the wise-cracking spirit of a recent American war veteran who died young, likely while serving in Iraq over the last ten years. His reincarnation as a raven, who met the similar fate of a sudden death, makes sense to the Morrigan's crew: after all, corvids are her animal, and they feed on the battlefield. Sometimes when he appears in Morpheus's dreams—do witches ever get a simple night's sleep?—he is in human form, and she can see what he looks like, no older than twenty-two and still in military fatigues. He's shared his name, or the name he wants to go by this time around: Cruach, Gaulish for "bloody."

The priesthood also announced their name: Coru Cathubodua. This was it: they were all assembled—all nine, with their special skills of possession and Feri witchcraft and intuitive magic and knowledge of past lives and ability to talk to the dead or communicate from the other side. They held meetings in one another's houses; they asked questions and discerned their goals.

A priesthood needs a secret oath. With this in mind, this past summer, about six months after Cruach's welcome, the Coru took an oath to dedicate themselves formally to the Queen and to each other. They spent the week-end on a hilltop of the Diablo Range—sacred territory for many local Native American tribes—camped out on national-park land. They pitched their tents in the intense heat, went for walks through the woods, and on the first night fried up a lot of bacon and passed around Costco shepherd's pie.

That Saturday evening, just after the sun went down, taking the temper-ature down with it, they were ready to start.

At the camp, they removed their clothes and formed a circle around an empty cauldron. And one by one, each took a turn standing inside the vessel and being anointed into the priesthood—anointed by every other member—until the group had been bonded together. And then they wrapped themselves in layers and began the mile-and-a-half hike higher up the mountain, hoping not to be discovered. It was already ten at night, and they made their way by strong, clear moonlight to a secluded grove: the spot Morpheus and Moon had discovered on the astral, with its ready-made stone altar. Everyone felt it: the Morrigan was hovering over them in the woods, waiting for things to happen.

At the center of the clearing, Morpheus, who had fasted for several days in preparation, invited the Morrigan into her body. Then, through her slim, pale frame, bred in the mountains of California, the new priests each visited with their Celtic goddess, stood close to her, took a turn confiding in her, making her promises, receiving their own private message.

As after the oath-taking at PantheaCon and the induction of Cruach, Morpheus did not remember any of this experience—or very little. In possessions she is "not really there." She can recall her goddess's slow arrival while she prepared for the evening, feeling as if "a hood is hovering over my head, and it's starting to descend—a *looming* feeling." By the time the circle was formed, the Morrigan had become very present for her, and shadows were gathering all around and above her, causing her to "get the shakes— like stage nerves, where your limbs feel lightweight and tremulous and a ton of energy is running through your body." At that point, her vision started to distort: "The detail of the world around me becomes very sharp and clear—but it's like I can see *through* it, and everything is just spirit, kind of shadowy and gray." Then nothing but glimpses, "flashes," until she regained her human self on the other side.

But before Morpheus was allowed to return to her body, the priesthood needed to make their oath of dedication to each other—Pagans of divergent backgrounds and magical tics, some of whom had circled together only a handful of times—as priests of the Morrigan. "Sometimes you have to be the fool," Ankhira says, "the one who takes the leap of faith and steps off the cliff, praying that the bridge will appear beneath his feet." Rudy, too, saw it as a cliff jump: "I just tossed my whole being over the edge." And so, in the presence of Morrigu, a new liturgy was spoken and the commitment made.

What Rudy did not realize that weekend at Mount Diablo was that she *was* about to toss herself—or *be* tossed—over that edge. After dedicating herself to the Morrigan, she was met with a year of personal chaos: she and her husband lost their house, he lost his job, and she herself was unable to work, newly pregnant while still breastfeeding the last baby. Finally, the marriage disintegrated. She believes her relationship with the goddess was a direct influence on the breakup. "I think that's what needed to happen. It's all part of the plan somehow," she says, sounding like so many others who've recently found their religion. Rudy, like her fellow priests, has come to accept a dose of adversity—a kind of initiatory ordeal—as the price for self-transformation. During the split, she says, "I was so distraught that sometimes *she* would come in and take over my body so I didn't have to survive it. She's intense on both sides, the Morrigan: it may be ecstatic pleasure, but it may also be more pain than you've ever conceived of. She's in your life, she's in your business, she's in your *everything.*"

For the Coru, their goddess is no archetype, metaphor, or psychological trigger: she is real enough to dismantle whatever's keeping them secure. But she is also the name—Morrigu, Badb Catha, Queen of Phantoms—that they've given the thing pushing them, driving them, demanding more. And what if all of us thought of our ambition, our transformative drive, as something *outside* ourselves, a huge force spurring us on, terrifying but irresistible? Then each of us would feel we had the right to change our life, upending it if necessary, to stake out a new identity—because a Great Queen was ordering us to do so.

15

Three Nights at the Castle

Samhain is approaching: the season of death. The time of year when, the witches say, the veil is thinnest, the veil between this world and the realm of the dead. And I am to spend this Samhain with my new coven—incredibly, I seem to *have* a coven*—in a castle in the woods of New Hampshire. Karina had invited me that night, over dinner at her home, to the BlackHeart Feri Samhain Gathering: three days and nights (emphasis on "nights") of circling, trancing, banishing personal demons, and bumping up against the dead. Since I've been a distance student of hers for the past six months, this weekend in early November will be my first time spent with other apprentices, as well as her personal Feri initiates. This also means my first round of private, coven-only Feri rituals.

Justin, the second-year student who'd told me about his battle on the astral, volunteered to give me a ride the couple of hours from the train station. (He lives in Northampton, near Karina.) I find him waiting by an old gray sedan in a leather jacket, Afghan scarf, and tight gray pants. I compliment him on his black boots, half unlaced. "They're my shit-kickers," he says.

---

* I should say that Karina herself prefers the word "family."

It's a clear afternoon, and as Justin drives, he talks happily, incessantly: about how he's the son of a Christian pastor, raised in a tiny farm town in Ohio; how coming out to his dad at fourteen made him the target of a church intervention that same Sunday; how he struggled with "preacher's-kid guilt" when he first discovered the Craft (in college, through gamer friends); and how, in his thirties, he's been with his partner, Travis, a middle-school science teacher, for thirteen years. Travis, after rejecting his Catholic upbringing, has started asking Justin questions about witchcraft and is currently making his way through some of Karina's recommended reading.

After a couple of pit stops for Dunkin' Donuts coffee—for all his Feri-based personal cleansing, Justin loves his coffee and cigarette—we finally cross over into New Hampshire. We drive through the small main street of Rindge, turn down a dirt road, and continue on for several minutes, past suburban homes, then woodsier homes, then just woods. At some point, surrounded by dense evergreens, we look to the right and see it: a castle on top of a hill. It simply *appears*. At first glance, it's a castle in the German countryside, all tan-and-gray brick, set above a few hundred acres of land, capped with a series of turrets and a single tower that rises above the rest of the sprawl; but as we continue to approach, driving up the hill now, I realize the complex is completely modern, boxy—a perfectly American nouveau-riche faux castle, a nineties special. The brick is actually a veneer, and a multicar garage is camouflaged against the main building. We're one of the first to park in the lot-sized driveway.

With weekend bags and ritual stuff in tow, Justin and I pass under a stone griffin to enter through the Romanesque front door. A pair of aluminum knights stand guard in the foyer and on the landing of the main staircase, peering down at the just-arrived guests, flanked by replicas of the Unicorn Tapestries. We have rented an immense house, with stone arches and alternating slate and hardwood floors, five bedrooms and three parlors done in suburban-Renaissance décor, and specially designed "secret" passageways where Karina's kids will hide out. Through the windows are views of Mount Monadnock; just through the sliding glass doors, an outdoor hot tub overlooks a vast lawn that rolls down to a tree-lined lake. Oil-painting portraits and photographs of family members, images from the forties through the nineties, can be found throughout the upstairs in gold-painted frames: they're a conservative, mostly blond clan (someone later says the family is "in politics"). Occasionally, over the course of the weekend, the house phone will ring, bringing the outside life of this family (is it an old friend calling? a golf partner?) uncomfortably close to an abundance of witchcraft.

But first, people stream into the ultramodern kitchen: a lot of harried priestesses, dragging in suitcases and pulling off hats and scarves and multiple sweaters. Some of the crew is very everyday American, in T-shirts tucked into jeans, and the rest are draped in dark, flowy fabrics. All around, there are charm necklaces and heads of abnormally long hair. There are about twenty-five of us (including a few non-Feri spouses), from New England and Florida and the Midwest and Colorado and even Germany, and accommodations require some improvisation: we've been assigned shared beds and sleeper sofas and futons and sleeping bags and beanbag chairs and even a small trampoline with a pillow. We haul our things to our designated corners and begin laying out clothes and toiletries and wands and talismans. The three-story castle is now brimming with witches.

Everyone crowds around the big kitchen table and countertops for a buffet dinner, and I get a good look at who's here, nearly all the members of the BlackHeart Feri coven, my *covenmates*: grade school teachers and grad students and graphic designers and massage therapists and copyeditors and theologians and purveyors of arts and crafts. The meal, heavy on potato and cheese, was prepared by Holger, who has a mustache as thick as his German accent and wears high-waisted corduroy pants with diagonal zippers. Throughout the weekend, he will chase us out of the kitchen unless it's our turn to wash dishes. Holger's a Feri sympathizer who flew in from Germany with his wife, Margit, one of Karina's first initiates.

Then there's Asherah, a massage therapist and acupuncturist from Leeds, Massachusetts: a white woman maybe in her thirties, with long brown dreads, a permanent smile, and lots of jangly Indian jewelry. There's also Shen-tat and Jade, who have a coven with its own temple in the Denver area. She is full-figured, with piles of lush black hair and cleavage on display in a fitted black top; Shen-tat, with a buzzed head and tiny glasses, looks like a medieval friar. Ray, a suave older gay man, works in interior design (he'll sport a colorful scarf nearly the entire weekend). Don, a rotund fifty-something, has elegant long white hair and "Boston blue bloods" in his family. Kiya, another new student, dresses like an Orthodox Jew, in long skirts and high-collared shirts, her hair always covered with a kerchief—but unlike any Orthodox woman, she often refers to her "husbands": she's in a poly relationship with her high school sweetheart and another couple, all sharing a college town house in Massachusetts. Katie, a grade school teacher with a tiny face and gap-toothed smile, speaks openly about her ongoing custody battle. Like me, she's a new distance student—but, unlike me, she already has a fully formed identity as an intuitive witch: as a girl, she'd accompany her grandmother at night to gather ingredients for spells, and now she herself teaches local classes in "earth magic."

In the parlance of *Rosemary's Baby*: "All of them witches."

All of *us* witches.

Is that true? I *have* traveled many miles to be here for a multi-day magical gathering—but the label still doesn't feel natural to me. I'm unable to shake my doubts about my Feri practice, to let down my guard, some part of me always observing, apart. I continue to hold myself at a secure distance from this alternate-reality version of myself, the woman who would call herself "witch" or "priest."

Before the gathering, we each received a packet over e-mail outlining the weekend (it continues to amaze me how much oath-bound witchcraft is made possible by the Internet and Yahoo Groups). In reading it over a few times, I was struck by a defining quality of most rituals I've taken part in: the setting of expectations, and the role those expectations play in the group's experience. The packet included a request for four volunteers to "tend the circle" during Saturday night's particularly high-energy ritual, "keeping a Witch Eye open for uninvited guests" (i.e., unwelcome spirits), and an additional six to act as "spotters" or "tenders" for the newcomers. In another note, under "Ritual Etiquette"—a section reminding us that our rituals "are not 'celebratory'" but instead "have deep purpose"—Karina wrote:

> Both the Friday and Saturday Night rituals will be Very Intense. You will need to use every ounce of Life Force you have and all you can contain to withstand these Rites. You will see things, feel things and experience things unfamiliar to you. You may become overwhelmed. You may feel ill. Let your Tender know. They are there to help you. This is expected to those new to these energies. There is no shame. That said, we will not hold back

the Powers in order to make it comfortable. So . . . [she pauses for effect] consider yourselves forewarned.

In other words, we've been told way in advance that the ritual will, undoubtedly, blow us away, and we've been asked to help prevent fallout from such powerful magic. It's not that I believe Karina is being consciously manipulative, but you can't deny the power of suggestion—as when she writes that "possessory experiences are an expected result" of the Saturday ritual; or that it "is expected" that newcomers "may become overwhelmed" and need help.

I think of Leon Festinger's handy theory of cognitive dissonance, in which he pinpointed that people change their opinions or stories about an event in order to avoid conflicting with their group or devaluing something in which they've invested a great deal. In other words: most humans, once they get in deep enough, will dig in their heels and commit to the value of an experience, because to change their minds and become, instead, openly critical involves a cutting off, a loss, that's more than most of us want to bear. And that loss is calculable: the loss of the bond, the group contract, created when all of us study with the same teacher; the effort and cost to be here (about $450 before travel), and to study (about $100 per month, plus tools and supplies), in order to have an ecstatic magical experience. There's pressure not to disappoint the group or ourselves, and it colors our individual results, the stories we'll later tell of circling together. We're each here, in part, out of a desire to share secrets with the tiniest of in-groups, and if none of this—this specific tradition, or magic in general—is real, then *we*, the participants, have just forfeited a shot at being special. And we've spent valuable time on a "practice" that's undeserving of it. And, taking it a step further, everyone in this coven is a wack job, or at least doing a great impression of one. All religious communities, to some degree, function in this way, bolstered by the collective's dream of specialness—a specialness spun out of practices whose value can never be verified in the practical world.

While people finish up dinner, Karina announces that we should "make kala," because the opening circle will begin shortly. Soon all twenty-odd of us, at the kitchen table or perched on stools or retired to corners of the house, are gripping our glasses of filtered water, breathing breathing breathing, raising the glasses to our foreheads, and then exhaling! suddenly! like a burst of air, and guzzling the liquid, turned bright and glowing in the mind's eye.

I do this along with the rest, of course—but once I've drunk from my glass, I find myself staring at the others. I see a desperation in their focus, the intensity with which they clutch their glasses or water bottles. And for a flash of a moment, this coven looks cultish to me. Something about how we're all grasping at this technique—the only tools required being water and a glass, ridiculously mundane—as if our lives depended on it. Something to do with how so many of the faces around me look either inexplicably serene or pinched with the barely concealed pain of someone who *needs this so much*. (Then again, how is this different from being surrounded by people repeatedly making the sign of the cross? Any discomfort I feel must not be with Feri, specifically, but with an all-in subscription to *any* system.) I can't yet tell if these are expressions of an impressive lack of self-consciousness— the ability to throw yourself completely into the "technology," give yourself over to magic—or the polar opposite, a nagging awareness of being in close quarters with your witch-teacher and covenmates and what they expect of you.

Once the powerful puffs of exhalation have died down—the sound of so many individuals blowing imaginary feathers upward (to the Godsoul!)— people wander across the hall into the ritual room. Just a couple of hours ago, this was the living room of a conservative New England family, complete with grand piano, love seat, and plush Oriental carpet—but all that's been moved aside for our intended use of the space this weekend. With the space cleared, we remove our shoes and, in bare feet or socks or stockings, form a witches' circle. Someone turns the lights way down. Karina has requested that this opening circle be "low-energy," Feri Lite, since we've traveled today. But regardless—in spite of my doubts, and in one of the many sudden emotional shifts that will define my weekend—my pulse picks up tempo in anticipation: my very first private Feri circle. My first time circling with the coven.

We breathe in and out repeatedly, deeply and loudly, building up a group rhythm; I immediately notice Shen-tat, who moves a lot during ritual, swaying and weaving his hands in and out. Tonight, our first night together, Karina takes the lead. As the group continues to breathe and sway, she casts the circle; and I realize that this is the moment, right now, when she will call the Guardians by name, names whose secrecy so many Feri witches have fought over, through poisonous disagreements and "witch wars." We're surrounded by our own moaning and heavy breathing and chanting, inviting all seven in one by one, these ancient intelligences out there in the universe who, for whatever reason, are driven to teach humans magic. If an outsider really wants to find their names, she can; but I waited to learn them the old way, through the mouth of my teacher, and I won't repeat them here. They are shockingly simple, child-simple, like names in a folktale; and each is evoked with the right gestures and tone of voice, conjuring up that spirit's spirit. One is of the earth, dark; her territory is deep knowledge, and in calling her into the circle our voices grow low and sexual. Another is pure receptivity, and we reach her through a groping for the stars above our heads in a childlike, tippy-toe way, in a blissed-out baby-voice of amazement, with a lack of self-censorship that I've only felt during the most out-there acting exercises.

That's what this is like, the embarrassing wide-openness that witch-craft requires: a movement or voice or improv class, in which the actor is expected, required by her work, to throw herself all the way in. To make a flailing mess of herself as the only route to truer performance. (Meisner called it "living truthfully under imaginary circumstances.") As a student, full of angst and confusion about my prospects, I was able to throw myself into theater productions, propelled by a powerful desire to leave my own body, my own life, to disconnect from my world and be somewhere else, a place of escape—and the more depressed and adrift I was, the more con-vincing my performances. I was *good* onstage—until I started to enjoy living in my own skin. Maybe the past several months, since beginning my training, have been a search to see if I've still got that in me, that part of me willing to walk away from my high-functioning, socialized self in order to connect with something bigger. Willing to tap into my personal chaos, to let buckle my scaffolding, in order to get at whatever's behind the panels of that silver box inside my chest.

Not much more happens tonight, mostly the inauguration of the weekend—and also this: Karina takes a moment to point us out, the "new-bies." As she called the guardians, she now calls us each by name: Katie, Kiya, Daniel, Stephanie, Alex.

In this way, she marks the beginning of something.

. . .

I wake up early and head downstairs to find some breakfast.

It will soon be time for an official coven meeting (Karina calls it a "salon"), and a few people shuffle through the kitchen in puffy socks and bathrobes in desperate search of coffee. I'm most impressed by Shen-tat, who makes his entrance in full-on priest robes: brown-stripey monk's garb with a thin leather apron. He wears this as naturally as the others wear their oversized comfy sweatshirts. I grab tea and toast and step through the sliding doors onto the back patio, where Justin and Jade are standing, zipped up in jackets, hands in their pockets, Justin with a first-of-the-day cigarette. The air has that crisp, cold New England smell, and the morning-wet lawn is an extra-green carpet rolling down to the woods below. Beyond that, a low light plays off the surface of the lake.

The salon is held in the sunny, carpeted third-floor playroom, most of us still in our early-morning clothes. Even though it will consist of a lot of business talk, we cast a circle together first—the equivalent, I guess, of a Christian youth group saying a prayer before discussing the upcoming fund-raiser—after which we take seats on the carpet or on beanbags, Karina in one of the few upright chairs, our chief in repose.

It plays out like a State of the Union–cum–town hall meeting. Karina gives a motivational talk about the robust life of the coven, then transitions quickly into a rundown of logistics for the gathering. Amy, another of Karina's initiates (three of the five are here), frequently jumps in, a round, pint-sized force of nature with Irish-pale skin and short red hair, in a large black tee and silver pentacle. (She's the frenetic office manager to Karina's CEO, her right-hand gal, here since the early days.) The big topic, a half-hour discussion, is a sensitive political one: the recent ousting of two Black-Heart Feri students who were far along in their training. Karina had sent out a mass e-mail breaking down the decision, and, as hard as it is for those who were friends with the exiled, most members are reassured that the coven has "standards" (as someone put it); everyone's expected to meet those standards; and there are consequences when you don't show sufficient respect for your training and your teacher. For me, this emotional talking-it-out simply confirms my sense of the larger Craft culture as closely tied to self-help and alternative therapy, to that kind of group-mandated wide-openness.

Karina returns to the present, and Saturday's "caravan" ritual: a "mash-up" of Feri circle and Sufi devotional *zikr*, something she developed five years ago. It's designed to build energy in a rhythm like the female orgasm, "rather than the male-ejaculatory model of building a cone of power." (Hard to be surprised by talk of orgasm when training with a self-proclaimed "sex cult.") I doubt the Sufis believe they're approximating the female orgasm, but I assume this means the energy will come in waves, with plenty of opportunity for peaks along the way. As Karina had warned us in her pamphlet: "We run very Hot and High for a grossly extended amount of time."

On our way back downstairs, I once again pass the wall of family photographs: there's an officer in the 1940s, cigarette in hand; smiling blond children in suits and pressed dresses; a formal Christmas gathering of the entire clan, in dinner jackets and red velvet. But below, in the family's living room, *Karina's* clan arranges the photos of its ancestors on improvised altars, in remembrance of their dead, both blood and Craft relatives—including, of course, Victor and Cora Anderson. (Before the weekend is out, Gerald Gardner will also be evoked, and Doreen Valiente, and so many other Anglo witches of the past century.) At the center of the altar for "blood ancestors" Kiya places a wooden incense boat, to represent the bark the ancient Egyptian dead rode into the afterlife. Since it's Samhain, we've each brought along a photo of a family member we wish to remember and possibly invite to commune with us; that's how witches across the country use this time of year.

I decided to bring a photograph of my grandmother Josefina while she was still in Cuba. I've always loved this picture, taken somewhere out in the countryside in Gibara, at the edge of a field of sugarcane, my grandmother, still so young then, maybe in her mid-twenties, standing on top of a cart, surprisingly barefoot, with bare legs and a dark cotton skirt that just covers her knees, a white kerchief tied loosely around her wavy black hair. But this is not a worker's portrait: her naked feet connect at the heels in a perfect V, like a dancer's; she holds her moon-shaped face (so pale she used to walk the island streets with a white lace parasol) tilted up into the sun, lips painted and eyes gently closed, one hand on her hip, her carriage radiating ownership and an easy grace. Perhaps Josefina was visiting a nearby ranch, more spectator than worker, her style of dress less practical than a statement of personal freedom. I've asked my mother, and no one seems to know when this photo was taken, the precise moment it captures in Josefina's life. I like to think this image came—barefoot, head tossed back—before her life started to twist in on itself, knotted up by the strange luck of being born in a small-minded provincial town, a young woman starved for experience, covetous of it. For a couple of years, when I was traveling the country researching new projects, this photo was on my phone, as if maybe she deserved to come along with me, to make up for all she'd missed.

It's appropriate for me to include this photograph here—Josefina has supposedly reached out across the veil a few times before—but it's also highly inappropriate. Put bluntly: my mother would not appreciate me dragging the family into witchcraft business—or at least magic that labels itself as such. I do, however, think that my *abuelita* would get a kick out of the proceedings—or perhaps she'd humor me, my spirit of adventure. She's at the center of one of the most momentous stories in my family about communication from the other side; and she was also in some ways a liminal figure, existing between two worlds while she was alive, a personality that didn't fit, someone who wasn't able to realize herself. I taped her photo to black paper and surrounded it with glass stones from a crafts store, in watery island colors. The quality of her presence is one I can conjure up easily, in my mind if not in reality: the powdered scent of her skin and her hair, the always gentle look in her eyes when she took care of me and my brother—a look of clear, uncomplicated affection, since we were too young to know anything of her frustrations, her string of unhappy relationships, her much wilder past.

A few hours stretch out ahead of us before tonight, with its elaborate dinner and Samhain ritual, and I decide to go for a walk by the lake. I pass the stragglers chatting on the back patio and quietly—as if I'm sneaking off—head down the sloping lawn, which narrows into a series of paths into the trees below, opening onto views of the lake and the great span of pine trees on the other side. I go deeper and reach a tiny boat dock, abandoned for the wintertime, where I take a seat on an old deck chair. And I have a small realization: even after a few years inside this community, and my deepening relationship with Morpheus, and the months of studying with Karina, and my taste of Thelema, the nearest I've come to a spiritual sensation is outdoors, as here, looking out at the dusty-green pine trees across the blue-black lake, smelling the damp earth, the cut of the cold in the air each time I breathe. The quiet is piercing and unhuman—so simple, but so alien to regular life—and it's an opportunity to feel vast and miniature at the same time.

It reminds me of Edmund Burke's writings on the features of "the sublime and beautiful": anything so vast in size or sequence that your eye can't take in the edges of it, like nature, points to the infinite. And a sense of the infinite triggers both excitement and terror—that one-two punch of the sublime. To experience the sublime is to become fixed on the spot, utterly still inside and out, both amazed and terrified; the mind becomes "so entirely filled," so "astonished," that it cannot think of anything else; it loses its ability to reason. "Astonishment is that state of the soul in which all its motions are suspended, with some degree of horror." This is a more convincing religious experience, this injection of the sublime out here in the natural world, in stark contrast to the regular stuff of my daily life, than anything I've experienced in dozens of rituals—and it couldn't be simpler. This is the closest I've yet to feel—not just today, this afternoon, but at many moments when I've found myself alone in a place like this—to anything like God, or God Herself, or the Star Goddess, or Nuit, or whatever you want to call him-her-it. Is the rest, all the human noise and effort and striving toward "initiation," just so much window dressing?

Slowly I turn back, away from the lake, along that path through the trees, to the foot of the lawn (I see it looming up ahead, our faux castle)—and the quiet is already broken. I hear a sequence of guttural grunts, in the steady rhythm of a locomotive, echoing across the property. I look to the left and realize where these sounds are coming from. "The pumpkin massacre"—I'd forgotten about this—is a holiday-themed exercise in emotional release. A middle-aged blond woman, one of those most broken up about her ousted fellow students, is whacking away at a pumpkin with a huge ax.

Back to the castle of alternative therapy.

Personally, I'd skipped the "massacre"—too much for me even under the circumstances—but the "dark mirror" is a requirement, and something I'm curious to try. After all, scrying through a so-called black mirror is a long-standing folk-magic technique, and the phrase itself is so evocative, like the title of a macabre film passed around on VHS tape.

This mirror, oversized and installed in the castle basement, was made by Ray, as he'd announced, with some "full-moon magic." I find a sign taped to the basement door that reads "The Mirror Is Available": it's my chance. Slowly, closing the door behind me, I head down the stairs—it's remarkably quiet in here, despite the kids playing upstairs and the Craft talk in the nearby kitchen—and reach the bottom floor: that familiar basement darkness. Following light strips laid out on the ground, I wind around the hallway into a large, even darker space that must be the family rec room: covered pool table, boom box, an old-timey Coca-Cola machine. And then I see it, across the room: in the far corner, a ceiling-high shroud is hiding something. I step around to see a black velvet seat in front of an immense darkened mirror, carefully framed with purple drapery. Two heavy silver chalices stand before it on the floor. Getting the idea, I sit down and settle in for a long look into the polished glass.

I sit in the dark and I wait—for a long, long time. Five minutes, ten minutes. And finally, to my genuine surprise, a scene appears to me, a scene I've played out before: a clear throwback to the dream (or nightmare) of months ago, that night before I decided to reach out to Morpheus and begin my training. I see now, in the full-moon mirror, a parade of the hooded figures from that dream—those tall figures in red robes, lit by torches against that winding stone-wall interior, descending deeper and deeper into the belly of that strange estate. But this time their robes are white, and they move in a line in the distance far behind my blacked-out silhouette, a straight-lined procession through the shadows (there is nothing behind me in reality, just drapery); and the basement, in a subtle visual shift, has become the belly of a castle—a real one, centuries ago, maybe in Spain—many stories below ground. Whereas that night months ago I felt in immediate danger, frightened, humiliated, now I'm uncertain. These people in white, no longer Druids (are they Spanish? they're definitely magical people)—am I hiding from them? Am I their resolute prisoner? Am I resolutely waiting for them to arrive and capture me? Or are they coming to me to receive a message?

After a couple of minutes in this haunted state, I snap out of it—and, in a kind of *Wizard of Oz* postscript, the "torches" become the reflected Christmas lights that line the edges of the floor, and the space becomes a dimly lit rec room once again. But that image was *very clear*, and I am left with the sensation that, for months now, I've been asking myself the wrong questions. If I'm a witch at all, if even a piece of me skews magical, and if I carry around inside me a parcel of what seems to run in the women of my mother's family—and these are *enormous* ifs—then maybe my witchcraft does not match the style of the priests and priestesses in this house. Maybe I have come to the wrong coven.

Before the Samhain ritual, over a beautifully set meal under the low light of the dining room's glass chandeliers, we are asked to consider our Craft ancestors, blood or not. And so I ask myself (what a question) who in my family I might count as a witch. My mother? An intuitive witch, maybe—though she would *never* use that word. And among our family dead, her mother, Josefina? If I believe my grandmother reached over from the other side to save her daughter's life, does that make her magical? What about my great-aunt Norma, the pragmatic woman who *received* those messages, without ever second-guessing herself? On the other side of the family, we trace back to Minoan Crete: could there be some yet-unnamed faces from that time? The question, for me, is not whether I can ever prove that their magic *worked*, but whether they were *engaged* in magic, whether they practiced a form of witchcraft by whatever name. Just that would be enough to reckon with.

Whoever we claim as a magical ancestor, Karina says, is someone from whom we'll be making a request: for a magical power or tool or talent that we lack. Because tonight, on Samhain, our ancestors will be very close, just across the veil, and they will be listening to our appeals.

That's what most prayers and spells are, after all: painfully sincere pleas for charity from the other side.

We gather in the ritual room and form a circle. The space is nearly dark. The sliding glass doors look out over the hillside, now perfectly black. On every side, pushed against the walls, are altars—to our blood ancestors, to our Craft ancestors, to the Feri gods Sheitan and Dian y Glas and Melek Ta'us—loaded with mirrors and photographs and food offerings and peacock feathers. Karina asks those "cleared to cast circle" to come forward: thirteen people move toward her.

"Wow," she says. She turns to Amy, her early initiate: "I remember when it was just you and me, and I dreamed of this day."

Karina now tells the thirteen to step back, and asks the five newbies to form a tight inner circle, and both circles to "align your souls." We all hold hands in our own rings, inner and outer, and breathe "blue fire" (a kind of magical energy) until we're full. And now we newbies close our ranks tighter, and throw our arms around each other, while the rest—the more serious witches, initiates among them—go about the business of casting circle, sealing us in for the night. We on the inside are surrounded by heavy breathing and moaning, and then the chanting of the names of the guardians, and the arm raising and baby voices and sexual sounds that come with it.

Eventually Karina asks us, the greenest, each to "form a pentagram" with our bodies. As we stand like this, arms outstretched and legs apart, she approaches us in turn, holding a bowl of consecrated salt water. Finally she arrives at me. "Alex!" she says—and everyone in the room chants:

"In the name of Sex"

(She anoints my head lightly.)

"In the name of Self"

(She anoints my left hand)

"In the name of Passion"

(my left foot)

"In the name of Pride"

(my right foot)

"In the name of Power"

(my right hand)

"You . . . are . . . blessed."

She saves the most water for my forehead: I can taste the salt as it runs down my face and into the corner of my mouth.

People continue chanting—more free-form now, and growing—and the chants change, and the rhythms of the circle change. More moaning and heavy breathing fill up the dark. And now we invite the Craft ancestors to join us, and our own blood ancestors to mingle with them. And so I invite *my* people in: Josefina, Norma, Eduardo, Stephanos, Ana. I say their names aloud twice, but softly, privately, as all around me people recite *their* names. I'm getting a little dizzy, crowded into the dark with these people I barely know, everyone muttering aloud now, like a scene in an asylum where patients wander the crafts room having conversations with themselves. But I force myself to focus—and now I see them. I see them clearly: my relatives, watching me. And, as in life, I sense the emotions that passed between us—especially among the women.

That's it: I focus in on the women who believed they had some kind of sight—Josefina, Norma—and slowly I turn my mind to what I might ask of them. At this moment, I manage to drag three short words out of my brain: to—own—myself. I ask these women in my family line for the magical ability to own myself.

What does this even mean? On the surface, it's embarrassing cult-of-self-help language; but I'm also being honest. I have been glossing over my fears and weaknesses—the cruelty of my own vanity; my avoidance of the fact that I'm well out of my twenties, and I had better claim whoever it is I'd like to be already; the painful confusion of my creative life, at least as fraught as my romantic life has been. I realize this is exactly what these women I loved were unable to do themselves: to have ownership, to each be and own herself completely. So this is something I could do for them as well; and, over any disapproval they might feel for my dabbling in American-born Craft with these strangers, they would want this for me: to be independent in the most frightening sense of the word; to lose my fear of outsiderness; to be able to stand apart from the normal, calculable world with purpose.

I am meditating on this, a stronger, clearer, diamond-cut sense of who I am—which is what the Morrigan is about as well, sovereignty—when someone else joins my women. Interrupts them. A third woman jockeys for position; and while my family, though palpable presences, were free-floating and abstract, she takes me away from them and pulls me into a fully realized scene. She is not much older than me—she could be a wilder, harsher, less forgiving version of myself—and I know immediately that she is a priestess. She's pausing on her way along a rough and rutted pathway in the mountains in Crete. There's a cool wind coming up from the water, and cypress trees behind her, and craggy, steel-gray rocks. A priestess in Crete—Minoan Crete?—with long, strikingly black hair and pale skin, dressed simply, in a rough white robe or tunic. She's waiting: she expects me to follow her. She has my attention, and so she starts walking again, uphill, and I know intuitively that she's walking toward a temple, that she's the priestess there. And once she's there she'll bathe in the fresh blood of a black bull (a bull for Hekate: that's what she likes). And when I'm deepest in this vision—or hallucination, or trick of the imagination—and she is still walking through this open, cold, island-mountain landscape, my brain *gives* it to me, hands me what I've asked for without knowing: a scent. I *smell* the air on that hillside covered in white rock, and the cypresses, and maybe the slightest trace of smoke and the Mediterranean blown uphill by the low wind. For a moment, I smell these things as clearly as I can smell someone's skin.

But just then the sounds in the room—the actual room I am standing in—come crashing into my moment. The chanting shifts and changes. The moaning and the ring of Karina's finger cymbals and all our percussive, pelvis-swaying movement give way to the bland rhythms of some neo-Pagan-sounding, Celtic-style sixties tune about "ancestors," nothing *my* ancestors would be drawn to—and immediately the mood is broken. That scent is gone, dissolved in an instant, and I know it was nothing like the smell of this tightly shut, low-ceilinged nouveau-riche living room packed with barefoot American witches weaving between one another, raising their arms and twisting their wrists in the air. *My* scent was something else entirely. But no one will believe me—no one outside these witchy circles—and I'm too smart to think otherwise.

After the two-and-a-half-hour ritual, I am visibly exhausted—Feri ceremonies, for their ecstatic quality, are known to go especially long—and Ray makes me drink a glass of water and eat something from the leftover bowls of carrot sticks and dinner rolls. This is how you "ground" yourself afterward: you drink and you eat and you accept the kindness of others. I don't know what to make of tonight—but I do know that, long before we were done, the circle had worn me out, ground me down, and exhaustion can leave a person vulnerable and distort the mind.

Later, Justin will tell me about last year's Samhain gathering, his first with the coven—actually, his first ritual of *any* kind. He left just as tapped out as I am now. "I walked out of there: 'OMG, what the hell did I just experience?'" He wandered around the castle for an hour. And as he struggled with how to process the events of that night, he became skeptical. "The doubting mind came in, the rational mind, putting definitions to everything I'd just experienced. I thought: 'Well, they were just pretending. They were putting on a show for us first-years—I can deal with that.' We'd talked about pushing the energy around the circle, and I'd really *felt* the air moving, but I thought, 'No, I must have imagined that.'" It wasn't until he heard another first-year talk about her ritual experience that he thought, "Holy shit, this is *real*." That night, he learned how to contain his incredulity, to "quiet the part that doubts."

Justin believes that these sensations, these encounters, have been real—but I'm not ready to come to any conclusions. I am much too open to influence right now, for better or worse, and so, as some of the group strip down for the patio hot tub, I make my way upstairs to pass out.

More happens that weekend: a wave of four or five possessions that runs around the circle like a contagion; a four-hour ritual orgy of ecstatic dancing. But what stays with me, and unsteadies me, is the woman I saw, or *thought* I saw, on Samhain night; and what I saw, or *thought* I saw, in the black mirror in that dark basement rec room.

Regardless of what I experienced that weekend, I understand that I do not have a connection to Karina and her vein of witchcraft. To continue to train with her would involve lying for the first time in this experiment.

So we break up, over the phone.

"Your path may not be signing up for five years of self-analysis and a lifetime of purification," Karina says. "When you came to visit, you told me you grew up in a house where magic was happening, so I *think* there is magic within you. But whether you're a witch or not—that's something I would never, never answer for anyone."

And that's that.

In the meantime, with or without a witch-teacher, I haven't forgotten the smell of the wind coming up that mountainside in Minoan Crete, centuries ago.

16

The Small Question of Satan

While my split with Karina has left me rattled, I refuse to let it bring my magical life to an end. And so I find myself, on a thick night in New Orleans, sitting huddled in the dark with about fifteen others, all of us clutching red candles. As our lungs fill with heavy incense and tobacco smoke, we chant over and over and over:

> *Santísima Muerte! Beloved of my heart! Do not abandon me without your protection.*
> *Defend me from my enemies, and grant me a peaceful death.*
> *Oh Holy Mother, hear my prayer! Amen.*

Each time it's called for, we repeat these phrases ten times. Fifty times throughout the ninety-minute ritual, each time, it seems, at a greater pitch. We are at Alombrados—but upstairs, in Josh and Sophia's quarters, tucked into narrow rows of folding chairs in the hallway that curls back from the top of the staircase—and as the space continues to fill with smoke, it becomes harder and harder to clear my throat and recite along with the others. The sheer repetition is exhausting, and maybe the intention is for us to reach an ecstatic state this way, from the incessant chanting and the inhalation of smoke and the sense of the ceremony's never ending.

Tonight Josh is introducing us to Death; her name is Santa Muerte. And in this increasingly foggy state, I begin to wonder: The group Josh has assembled, most of us with no experience with this saint or force or whatever she is—are we his devotional offering? Are we unknowingly underwriting his latest request to his patron? Sometimes I think I might be shooting too much from the hip, brushing shoulders with stuff I don't understand.

In this city, it is *always* the season of death—Samhain is year-round. Death suffuses everything: she's in the weather, the heavy tropical weight of the summer air, the lingering threat of the months-long hurricane season, the waterlines from previous storms (all with women's names) still visible on some of the scrappier buildings downtown. Death is in the air here, hanging low, like those nasty April caterpillars and the banana-tree blossoms, surprisingly fat and purple and syrupy.

Not that she—Death with a capital *D*, the dark stuff of the Romantics— is always a bad thing. A creeping awareness of death-as-destiny feeds people's ambitions, and she can teach a person how to be festive, in a throw-up-your-hands kind of way—as in, It could all wash away tomorrow, so . . . ? Living here, you roll with things. After all, you could view life—our greedy metabolisms and the constant decay-regeneration-decay of our cells—as death in motion. Everything ambling toward that hungry, bone-thin lady, Saint Death.

Santa Muerte, like the many Voodoo spirits Josh works with (out of respect for the home team), is not part of the OTO pantheon. She is a deeply controversial saint, venerated by outcasts, the desperate, those living low. She is worshipped in much of (very Catholic) Mexico, and wherever there are large Mexican communities in the States. Her cult has grown wildly over the last thirty years—in the wake of the Catholic clergy sex-abuse scandal, and as a kind of rebel uprising by the poor and those on the violent fringe, disappointed with how little the church has done to improve their lives. The Mexican church labeled her followers Devil worshippers; more recently, the Vatican's culture minister dubbed them blasphemous. But the adoration of Death, the embrace of her, is natural in Mexico: on Día de los Muertos, people flood the cemeteries and skeletons fill the streets.

Santa Muerte herself takes the form of a skeleton draped in a long veil and robe, often a wedding dress. To most Americans, the sight of her would be horror-movie terrifying—her face a fleshless skull (she's also known as the Skinny Lady), her bone-fingers gripping a Grim Reaper's scythe—but in Mexico she is a champion of the down-and-out and a reprieve from Catholic guilt. You can ask her for *anything*—health, money, sex, revenge. She does not judge. For this reason, she is the saint the cartels pray to—men who cannot claim to be Catholic, but who know that Death herself won't turn them away. Josh has insisted to me, however, that she is not dark—if anything, his description reminds me of Hekate or the Morrigan. "She's the most natural component of death—it's just *life*, which is dynamic. She's right on the liminal point of the creation and the destruction of things." Santa Muerte is not a force of moral judgment, but a force of nature. She doesn't mete out justice; she metes out the inevitable.

Josh's altar table stands against the wall at the head of the staircase, and above it he's built a large shelf on which are laid out the multiple incarnations of the Lady of the Shadows. Santa Muerte is three ladies—La Negra (in black), La Blanca (white), and La Roja (red). La Negra is off the table from the start: Josh makes an announcement forbidding us to work with this black-magic incarnation, known for her protection in more extreme, violent circumstances—unless we'd like "a world of pain" to rain down on us. (This is the incarnation *he* works with, and that's a risk he's willing to take, as an experienced occultist.) So, putting aside La Negra, we are left with the twins: La Blanca, who offers purity and health; and La Roja, who accepts entreaties for the entire range of desires, from love to money and business— whatever pleasures and satisfactions you *want*, *want*, *want* in the material, carnal world.

We raise glasses of tequila and toast her and toss them back. Now it's time to make our requests.

We take turns, as in the Gnostic Mass, getting up to stand before her altar, arms outspread like a cross, facing Josh. He holds a scythe in one hand and a large chalice of incense in the other, a leather strap studded with tiny bells wrapped around his wrist, and Jay, with a small chime, stands behind the supplicant. While you hold your ground, spread-eagled, the two work their way down your body, shrouding you in clouds of incense. I can see in his face, with each person's turn, that Josh is giving a lot: by the time I'm up, after so many others, he's nearly sapped. If, in his mind, he's offering us up to his patroness, he's also expediting *our* requests to the Skinny Lady: Josh is our hookup.

Each of us places on the altar a tiny scroll—pieces of paper on which we've written our appeals, tied with red string—along with an offering of candy. I choose gumdrops. (Paradoxically, Death has a thing for sweets.) Understanding her nature, her moral indifference, the ruthlessness of some of the requests she's entertained, I decide to get greedy—greedier than I felt free to be at the castle, reaching out to my family. I apply not to La Blanca, for whatever kind of purification, but to La Roja—because I *want*. And so must nearly everyone else in the room, because the booty on her side of the altar is already piled high. In the spirit of things, I ask for an injection of ruthlessness, just enough to lose my fears and hesitation and to feel less beholden to people: an antidote to the caution that prevents success.

Once the ritual is finally over, most of us linger in the kitchen, eating the extra candies and drinking the leftover rum and red wine. A handsome young Italian couple are visiting from the OTO branch in Milan, and they run down the list of bodies they'll be checking out around the country, wrapping up their Thelemic vacation in San Francisco and Los Angeles. The chatter is cut short, however, when Josh announces that we'll be walking the few blocks to the cemetery to leave offerings and ritual remnants at the gates in her name. And so we all search for our shoes and grab the stuff intended for Death.

We hit the streets, into the dense night, loud and slightly tipsy now, transformed into a traveling caravan bearing bottles of booze and cigars and cups of coffee and fruit. Everyone on a post-ritual high, we wind our way around the Bywater until we reach St. Vincent de Paul Cemetery. Josh is close to drunk—he's a real drinker, so it's remarkable when it starts to show like this—and maybe that's partly why, as soon as we arrive, he decides to up the ante.

"We should jump the gate."

The life of a witch or an occultist has these strange rhythms and rules that you have to settle into, and occasionally you find yourself involved in something that doesn't fit any previous idea of what your life should look like. I think back to the story Karina told me, of the first time she performed late-night magic in a cemetery, years ago. "I saw myself, walking through a cemetery under the full moon at one in the morning, carrying a shovel and a shopping bag," she said, "and I thought, 'This is it. I've crossed a line. Karina, you're fucking insane!'" She went home that night and called a close friend she knew would be up late. "I was in the cemetery at one in the morning *burying* shit!" "You're a witch," her friend replied. "Isn't that what witches do?"

But this crowd has its share of first-time visitors, a couple of college-age guys in black T-shirts just along to check things out, and people seem to be stalling.

"We should jump the gate!" Josh repeats, louder now. (Sometimes I think he deserves a bigger audience.)

Sophia, ever his counterbalance, says, "Well, maybe not everyone feels *comfortable* jumping the gate."

He rolls with this. "Okay, let's take a vote. Does anyone have a *problem* with going inside?" This is how to rig a vote with the renegade crowd: the loose collection of occultists naturally pauses, stands around, waits it out. Decision by default.

One after another, we take turns hopping the fence, the first guys on the other side giving special help to the women (myself included) who showed up for ritual in short dresses. As we drop down, Josh shoos us away from the gates, telling us to take the second pathway on the right to meet at the center of the cemetery, "at the crossroads."

At the crossroads is a small mausoleum for the Clarks, and I wonder if this family had any idea of how awkward their location would turn out to be. We place a lit candle there, and sweet tamarinds, and an apple. Then Josh swigs the bottle of red wine and sprays it through his teeth across the tomb's frontispiece, a nameplate listing those interred within, the oldest relative born in the 1860s. Some of the others take their turns, with the coffee and the rum and the tequila, until the tomb has been anointed with a few kinds of beverages and the saliva of strangers—all in honor of Santa Muerte. Together we repeat the prayer yet again, pretty much yelling now: "Santísima Muerte! Beloved of my heart! Do not abandon me without your protection!"

By the tenth time, we're wiped out, and our voices reach an almost hysterical pitch. But I'm still thinking about the Clarks, whoever they were, wherever their descendants are today: is it fair to rope them into this? I doubt the family, especially back in the nineteenth century, were anything but Catholic—never mind sympathetic to the cult of a Mexican death saint—and they would not have appreciated this spitting on their resting place. Every now and then in my occult experience, I step outside of myself and I'm shocked. Had a Catholic priest been present, his face would have turned red at the blasphemy, breaking into cemeteries at night like a posse of teen vandals. He would have told us to quit the Skinny Lady while we still can—don't we see she's a gateway drug to the Devil?

What do we talk about when we talk about Satan? Even if you can be objective about him—that is, depending on your beliefs—he's far from an absolute. From where I stand, the Devil comes in at least three flavors.

First, there's the Devil of Christianity, the Antichrist—the dark angel who disrespected God, became an instant, venal enemy of mankind, and has been plotting a hostile takeover of the universe ever since. He's the Devil who bled into popular culture as the ultimate bogeyman, the prince of darkness. This is no one the witches have a relationship with. As Gardner quoted one British witch as saying, back in the fifties, "I don't believe in the Devil, so how could I worship him?"

Then there's the Satan who is Lucifer, angel of light, bringer of the dawn. Lucifer is the name by which early Christians referred to Satan before his fall. But the story of his fall has more than one version. There's the Christian story of sheer arrogance, on the one hand—Lucifer was an angel so cocky and rebellious that God cast him out of heaven—and there's an esoteric story on the other, a story of loyalty. In this alternative tale, Lucifer had sworn to hold no one above God, as Creator of the Universe, and so, when God asked him to bow down to man, Number One Angel could not believe his ears: it was one thing to worship the immeasurable, timeless power behind everything, but quite another to kneel to some newborn clay creature. Having taken that particular stance, Lucifer was asked to get the hell out of heaven.

A contingent within the Feris holds up Lucifer as a central god, born in this way: God Herself, the Star Goddess, was the first darkness, darkness complete, the darkness before creation, the black unformed universe, the beginning of everything. And maybe she was lonely, or maybe the darkness sort of turned her on, or maybe she turned *herself* on—they say she saw her reflection in the jet-black curve of the pre-universe and loved that image—but she orgasmed. And there was *light*! And that light, from the deepest part of her, still entangled with the dark, splintered off into two new beings, a pair of gods who are twins and lovers, sometimes simpatico, sometimes gripped in tension: the Divine Twins, whom Karina's coven calls "the Serpent of Earth and the Bird of Heaven." And some say that, when the Twins come together, the serpent and the bird, the Peacock God rises up; and some call this god Lucifer. He brings light into the universe, and tension. And his light is forever tangled up in the complex, bottomless darkness that predates everything.*

For the Feris who worship Lucifer, this is not Devil worship—nothing to do with any Christian idea of the Devil.

The same goes for the broader Pagan movement. Who is the Horned God that looms so large in the pantheon of many Wiccans? This isn't the Devil but Pan, the crudest and lowliest of the Greek gods—until the English Romantics resurrected him in the mid-nineteenth century, elevating him to a force of truth and primitive instinct against the cool economics and mass production of the industrial age. Natural man, unafraid of his animal self, versus upright Christian man; a freewheeling Pagan god who allows for a guilt-free, mystical connection to the world versus a pleasure-free Christ who is the only route to salvation. It's no wonder that the popular image of Pan is of a horned half man, half goat—not unlike the image predominantly Christian Western culture has of its public enemy number one.

Aleister Crowley, though infamous for dubbing himself "The Beast 666," did not believe in anything like the Christian Satan. "The Devil does not exist. It is a false name," he writes. "'The Devil' is, historically, the God of any people that one personally dislikes." In his Thelemic rituals and writings, he invoked the Beast and Babalon (i.e., the Whore of Babylon) *not* as defined by Christianity but as powers, equally creative and destructive, that could be found inside every man and woman. As Crowley put it, "This serpent, SATAN, is not the enemy of Man, but HE who made Gods of our race, knowing Good and Evil; He bade 'Know Thyself!'" And so Satan

---

* Whereas in Christianity God sees the darkness as an empty void and creates something separate from himself in order to fill it, in Feri the Star Goddess sees the darkness as *part* of herself, and sees herself as part of all things.

becomes our teacher and collaborator, showing us that the world is complex, not the domain of absolutes.

To take the whole range of stuff that makes us human and separate it out into stark, unbending categories of Good and Evil requires an unnatural strain—and perhaps this broader use of the name "Satan" is a way of acknowledging that, of embracing the whole human mess. As Josh puts it, interpreting Crowley: "All these ideas of the Devil have been misunderstandings of mystical visions by people who are so invested in the dichotomy between moral opposites—a war between opposites. Someone who understands the unity of the universe could never hold that." The Abrahamic religions, he says, divide man's intrinsic qualities against himself. "They believe in the damnation of man *as* man; that man in and of himself, as a fleshly creature, is sinful." In radical contrast, Thelema embraces the fleshly creature that each of us is, and the whole spectrum of darkness and light—our greed, our pride, our gross impatience and envy, our lust—as a reflection of the entirety of the universe.

"I am the flame that burns in every heart of man, and in the core of every star," Hadit, sometimes called Satan, announces in *The Book of the Law*. "I am the secret Serpent coiled about to spring: in my coiling there is joy. If I lift up my head, I and my Nuit are one. If I droop down mine head, and shoot forth venom, then is rapture of the earth, and I and the earth are one." Hadit represents the center of each creature, is always stretching outward in a desire to possess the infinite—the infinite, which is Nuit. Hadit + Nuit = everything that's carnal + everything that's transcendent. The serpent (Satan) is of the earth, sometimes dark and full of venom; but the serpent can also lift its head to commune with the infinite stars. Dark and light are part of a greater swirl, an Everything that is bigger and messier than Good and Evil.

Why not accept these tensions as essential to the fabric of things, part of who we are?

To be honest, my first crush was on the Devil.

I saw him for the first time at about eight years old, on a VHS tape I played over and over again at my friend Becky's house. For months, even years, afterward, this was how I saw Satan: a dark red man-beast, just tall enough to be superhuman, swaying backlit by a tremendous roaring fireplace that must double as a gateway deeper into hell. He's dancing with a girl—a grown woman, really, but young enough to be my babysitter, strapped into an intricate black gown. And though she's a Good Girl, literally some kind of woodland princess, Satan has swept her up without resistance, made her over into a hell-bound, ultra-gothic shadow-image of herself; and now she's spinning around in his enormous arms, in these slow, broad circles, the kind that make a person's neck go limp.

Forget the girl (merely my stand-in) and watch the Devil: hooves and shaggy haunches, red barrel chest, and, towering above that, his massive horned head. His horns, a high-sheen black, are three times those of a tremendous bull or water buffalo. His red fingers are veined and prehistoric, capped with fat black claws. He has all the heft of a beast, but he carries himself like a dark aristocrat. It is so easy to imagine being swept up by him.

The movie was *Legend*, a pretty terrible 1986 fantasy film by Ridley Scott, scored by . . . Tangerine Dream? But there was no such scene in the movie, of the girl dancing with the Devil in front of the fire: the details and the setting are right, but I'd fabricated the moment, created it myself. In the months and then years of remembering, I'd added my own action. At eight years old, I'd already begun to give the Devil life in my imagination.

Not that the filmmakers had any idea, but that movie was released at a moment of renewed life for the Devil in this country. Shortly after the seventies counterculture and women's movements derailed all kinds of assumptions about American family life and sexuality, a collective nightmare emerged from the deepest circle of hell: the notion that an invisible underground network of Satanists was lurking in the shadows, poisoning the water with sexual and moral depravity, waiting to turn out or torture our children. This period in the eighties and early nineties is now known as America's "Satanic Panic." As absurd as it sounds now, the Panic was a time of *thousands* of accusations of "Satanic" abuse of children—so many that authorities coined the term "Satanic ritual abuse," or SRA. Charges were brought against child-care workers and suburban parents around the country. In courtrooms, prosecutors relied entirely on the accusers' personal narratives; in no case was conclusive physical evidence found. It would have been a bizarro comedy of errors if the charges hadn't been so disgusting—and if some of those accused hadn't gone on to spend decades in prison.

The catalyst for the Panic—the case that set the pattern for those that followed—came in 1983, when the teachers at the mostly family-run McMartin Preschool in Manhattan Beach, California, were accused of extravagant abuse by one boy's mother. The initial accusations were so over-the-top—not only was there baby killing and blood drinking, but clown costumes were involved—that the DA dismissed them as utterly unsubstantiated. (A year later, the mother would be diagnosed as a paranoid schizophrenic—but this fact would have little relevance once the panic was fully under way.) At this point, the Manhattan Beach chief of police took it upon himself to send around a "confidential" letter to parents of two hundred present and former McMartin students outlining the charges in detail, and advising them to ask their kids if they, too, had been assaulted. When the children denied mistreatment, the authorities recommended that the parents take them to a new clinic specializing in child abuse, where they were interviewed with puppets and anatomically correct dolls and asked leading questions. Some caseworkers outlined very specific abuse scenarios for the kids before they were given a chance to answer on their own.

The families of forty-eight children eventually filed claims, charges that expanded to include sexual abuse in cemeteries and in secret underground tunnels painted with images of the Devil, as well as a Satanic ritual (they were made to drink rabbit's blood) in a nearby Episcopal church. Their testimony during an eighteen-month preliminary hearing was wildly inconsistent. The SRA charges were eventually dropped, and the McMartin defendants narrowed down to two. They were ultimately both acquitted on all counts—but only after a seven-year trial that, at $15 million total, remains one of the most expensive in American history.

Over the decade following the initial McMartin charges, more than twelve thousand recorded cases of organized Satanic child abuse were investigated—accusations ranging from group sex abuse to baby sacrifice and cannibalism—and in no instance was physical evidence uncovered. No traces of human blood or carnage were found; medical tests on the young victims were later discredited; there was never any proof.

Investigators working on new cases sought advice from those who had interviewed the McMartin Preschool kids. At the same time, on a national scale, law enforcement, prosecutors, and social workers began meeting at conferences around the country to hear from self-proclaimed experts on how to deal with the SRA plague. (One of the lead social workers in the McMartin case testified before a congressional committee in 1984, warning of SRA involving the ritualistic slaughter of animals in front of small children.)

Among the more high-profile SRA "experts" was the Canadian Michelle Smith, the first documented "survivor." Her bestselling 1980 memoir *Michelle Remembers* detailed her wildly graphic abuse by her mother and a group of "Satanists" when she was five years old, including her rape with crucifixes, forced participation in baby killing, and live burial (with snakes). Her abuse was uncovered during months of hypnosis by her therapist (and coauthor) Lawrence Pazder, who dubbed these memories "repressed," a concept the book popularized. Pazder's treatment of Smith included exorcism (both of them were Catholic). *Michelle Remembers* was later criticized as impossible to corroborate—but not before Smith had advised parents in the McMartin trial and been interviewed by Oprah Winfrey; and not before Pazder, who married Smith, had become a major SRA consultant himself. A procedural model was set: the many allegations made during the Panic were based either on adults' "repressed" memories (nearly all retrieved during psychotherapy sessions) or reports by children, often interviewed with suspect methods.

Throughout all this, the best-known, most official "Satanists" in the world did not even believe in the Devil.

The Church of Satan, founded in 1966, is easily the largest religious non-profit centered on Satan—they trademarked that goat's head (Baphomet inside an inverted pentagram)—and its members are, above all else, cynics and pragmatists, atheists and libertarians. *The Satanic Bible*, their bestselling central text (over one million copies sold to date), is founder Anton LaVey's unrelenting critique of institutionalized religion; and, given the violence that continues to take place in the name of God (or Allah, or Whoever), whether here or abroad, certain passages read like brutish common sense. LaVey slams religion as fueled by self-hatred, false feelings of guilt, and a denial of man's essential nature. Man is a self-interested animal, he writes, and there's no reason to go around apologizing for it. "Just as the Satanist does not pray to God for assistance, he does not pray for forgiveness for his wrong doings . . . Confessing to another human being, like himself, accomplishes even less—and is, furthermore, degrading." Each Satanist, members like to reiterate, is his *own* god. In keeping with its rampant egotism, Satanism's highest holiday is each member's own birthday.

Contrary to what most outsiders think, Satanists are repulsed by the notion of supernatural beings that hover above and play with us like puppets. "Man created God himself," writes LaVey—and that includes any conception of the Devil. They invoke the name of "Satan" for shock value. That said, LaVey became known as the "Black Pope," and with good reason: his church, from a Christian perspective, is extravagantly blasphemous (not unlike OTO), using the format of Catholic high mass to create its own brand of gothic theater. If the substance of religious ritual is guilt-inducing reactionary nonsense, Satanists believe, the *form* of ritual can still tap into some primal truths about man. And so they use high-mass drama to get the blood flowing (though, as far as I know, not in the literal, open-wound sense). "Hail Satan!" they chant, over and over: "Satan" and "evil" and "hell" are trigger words to encourage its members to embrace a freethinking, contrarian, wildly egocentric life outside the mainstream—a life-affirming mantra. "When we say 'Hail Satan,'" says Peter Gilmore, the church's current high priest, "what we really mean is 'Hail Ourselves.'"

But the stakes were ratcheted up higher for associating with the Devil during the Panic. Throughout the eighties, major media outlets fed the paranoia, from ABC's *20/20* and NBC News to *Oprah*. The material covered ranged from the ridiculous—*20/20* correspondent Tom Jarriel, after listening to "Stairway to Heaven" played backward, announced that Robert Plant was singing "My sweet Satan"—to the unverifiable. What these high-profile media reports all had in common was an insupportable logic: the "Satanic" networks are completely hidden, nearly impossible to discover, which only proves how wily they are. As Jarriel announced, in a bizarre call to action, "Nationwide, police are hearing strikingly similar horror stories—and *not one has ever been proved!*" Without proof, what exactly was anyone reporting?

NBC gave a hefty prime-time slot to Geraldo Rivera's special *Devil Worship: Exposing Satan's Underground*. Over the course of two hours, Geraldo roped the Church of Satan, heavy-metal fans, and a handful of serial killers into a bloodthirsty, "highly organized, secretive network" of Devil worshippers "over one million" strong. He trotted out an FBI veteran, remade into a "cult investigator," to back him up. Images of LaVey and his *Satanic Bible* were shown, while LaVey's daughter Zeena protested that the Church of Satan was a "legitimate religion" and Dr. Michael Aquino, founder of the Satanic splinter church the Temple of Set, explained, unsuccessfully, that Satanists didn't believe in Christianity's Antichrist. Geraldo showed interviews with former "breeders," women who claimed they'd been forced to give birth to babies for sacrifice by an unnamed Satanic cult. (A year later, *Oprah* would feature women who said they'd "recovered" memories of the family-wide Satanic sacrifice of infants.) These "survivors" claimed that their attackers were impossible to prosecute because of how thoroughly they cleaned up after their crimes: no blood, no bodies, you won't find a thing. Tangible evidence is not necessary for this, or perhaps any, panic—especially when the most depraved crimes can be blamed on a single book or metal album.

The guilty-by-occult-association line of prosecution culminated in one of the most recent, vivid, high-profile cases: that of the West Memphis Three. In 1993, three eight-year-old boys were murdered in the Robin Hood Hills of West Memphis, Arkansas. The friends were discovered naked, bound, and drowned, and, adding a horrific detail, one was found with his penis mutilated. Three local teenagers—Jessie Misskelley, Jr., Jason Baldwin, and Baldwin's best friend, Damien Echols—were convicted of the crime. The sentences—life for Misskelley and Baldwin, Death Row for Echols—were based largely on a confession coerced from Misskelley, who was mentally challenged, as well as depictions of the teenagers as outsiders and social misfits. Echols in particular was a perfect target: in a conservative small town, he was the kid in black who listened to Metallica, checked out all the library books about the Salem witchcraft trials, wore a pentagram necklace he'd bought at the mall, and scribbled Crowley quotations in his journal. He'd read Raymond Buckland's *Complete Book of Witchcraft* and copied out whatever spells he could find. In other words, he was a teenager dabbling in Paganism and the occult—back in the early nineties, before Wicca had been rebranded online as a friendly, earth-loving form of spirituality.

The case is famous now, but the courtroom transcripts still contain surprises: small moments of testimony that serve as snapshots of pretty standard adolescent pissiness, conflated here with occult extremism. As when the prosecutor cross-examines Echols, then eighteen, about his notebooks:

Q: *These books where you have handwritten things and certain symbols on the books and your reference that you made to Aleister Crowley . . . That is all just as a result of your interest in black magic, not that you practice it?*
A: *That, and being bored.*

Some of the Satanic Panic cases that received media attention have only been resolved in recent years. One of the men imprisoned in the Kern County trials, a wave of day-care-related cases in California that led to more than thirty convictions (nearly all were overturned on appeal), won $5.5 million in a lawsuit against the county in 2009. In 2013, Fran and Dan Keller were finally released after twenty years in prison, having been wrongfully convicted on charges of SRA at their Austin day-care center. And years after the supposed end of the Panic, in 2006, a Georgia teen, Alexandria Boring, was sentenced to life for killing her mother—based primarily on her goth looks and on writings that were argued to be "Satanic." After she'd spent five years in prison, her conviction was unanimously overturned.

As for the West Memphis Three, they were ultimately freed under strange, unsatisfying circumstances. In 2011, in a very rare legal move, the state of Arkansas offered Misskelley, Baldwin, and Echols an Alford plea, which allowed the men to walk and publicly maintain their innocence while officially remaining guilty in the eyes of the state. They had spent nearly eighteen years in prison and have yet to be exonerated. Arkansas remains unaccountable for a gross miscarriage of justice, and the killer of three small boys remains free.

Being associated with witchcraft and the occult is still a terrific risk in many parts of the world. In 2011 alone, seventy-nine Saudis were beheaded for alleged "witchcraft and sorcery," with Amnesty International calling for an end to the executions. And in 2014, the United Nations reported on "extreme violence against older women" related to witchcraft accusations in forty-one countries in Africa and Asia, including India, Kenya, and Nepal.

Anti-Pagan bias is also very real in far more liberal countries. In the

United Kingdom, where religious discrimination was outlawed only a little over a decade ago, a 2012 University of Derby–led study found "substantial" discrimination against Pagans and "new religious movements"— discrimination that one academic described as being of a "particular frequency and severity" and "more 'in-your-face', verging on hatred." A study in Australia in 2011 led to similar findings. In the United States, back in 2001, twelve-year-old Tempest Smith in Lincoln Park, Michigan, hanged herself at home, leaving behind a journal that detailed her bullying at school for being openly Wiccan. (The Tempest Smith Foundation, active until early 2014, advocated in Michigan against bullying and for greater tolerance.) Pagans in more staunchly conservative and Christian parts of America still often stay in the so-called broom closet for fear of losing government employment or any job that involves children.

Absurd as the Satanic Panic now seems, its underlying assumptions about occult practice continue to bleed into our culture: once superglued together in the public imagination, terms such as "child abuse" and "Devil worship" are hard to separate from all things "occult" or "Pagan." Of the 1.2 billion Catholics worldwide, those who closely follow the Vatican's pronouncements continue to be inundated with extremist ideas about what exactly is involved in witchcraft and the occult. As the requests rise, both here and in Western Europe, the church's number of official exorcists has nearly doubled, with some priests citing interest in Wicca and the occult as justification enough. As the parameters of exorcism-worthy Evil expand, religious intolerance is given more and more free rein. Even today, some witches are quick to quote what Doreen Valiente told Gerald Gardner as he considered exposing Wicca: "Witchcraft doesn't pay for broken windows."

"We have heard a very great deal about 'The Black International of Satanism,'" Gardner wrote in *The Meaning of Witchcraft*, back in 1959. "Between the covers of a thriller such things are no more sinister than the activities of Dr. Fu Manchu; but when they are presented as sober fact, . . . it is time to ask either for some of that awkward thing, evidence, or for a halt to be called until it can be produced."

Putting aside all things "Satanic," there remains the enigma of black magic. Is it nothing more than a specter? An excuse to smear Pagans? A term, like

"Satanic," thrown around to persecute those who don't subscribe to the culture's religious mainstream? Or, if there are truly black magicians out there, what does that mean? Are they on the darker, taboo side of the Craft, or misunderstood?

Across witchcraft traditions, it depends on whom you ask. Some priests and priestesses think it's ridiculous to try to categorize stripes of magic, seeing it as more of a continuum: spells have to do with effecting change in your environment, and the magic you engage in shifts according to what kind of change you want to induce. Often witches will work in sync with the general flow of things, using magic (in theory) to push events in the direction they had a chance of heading anyway—but further and faster. Many believe that any magic used to bend someone else's will in an unnatural direction has crossed over into the black—but that doesn't necessarily come with an ethical judgment; it's a label, a technical category. In a conversation I had with a Wiccan high priest in New York City, he told me he considered the distinction between "white" and "black" magic not only bogus but insulting: "We don't ask Catholics if their prayers are 'black.'"

"Magic is in itself neither black nor white, bad nor good," Gardner wrote; "it is how it is used, the intent or the knowledge behind it, that matters." Most Wiccans, when asked what kinds of spells they're willing to perform, will simply refer back to the Wiccan Rede ("An it harm none, do what thou wilt") and their Threefold Law (Don't mess with stuff you don't want thrown back in your face three times over) as child-simple guidelines.

There are Pagan traditions, however, that embrace the "black magic" tag in the same way they've reclaimed the word "witch"—Feris, for instance, who don't follow the Wiccan Rede. Victor Anderson said, "Poetry is white magic. Black magic is anything that works." One of his first initiates, Gwydion Pendderwen, said, "He who cannot blast cannot bless": every witch should have the full range of abilities and be prepared to act as called for.

Karina once wrote to me: "Antibiotics are medicine—they kill bacteria. Every medicine is also a poison. We work both edges of the knife. Either edge is equally sharp." It's a matter of intent. Some witches would say that when I considered performing that binding ritual, considered sewing up an enormous tongue, I was contemplating black magic—but I would have said I was out to protect someone. As Morpheus put it: "If you came upon an accident scene, and there was a person there who was unconscious and bleeding, a reasonable person wouldn't turn away from helping them just because they could not get the person's consent first."

If black magic is specifically defined as going against the will of another, then there are traditions that regularly cross over into the "black." The types of magic that might be classified that way by the Pagan mainstream split loosely between practices of the African diaspora religions, stuff from medieval Europe, and spells resurrected from way back in Greco-Roman Egypt. On the racially black side, there are Palo, Kimbanda, and, far more prominently, Vodou and Santería—all traditions that are alive and active today, to some degree, in parts of America. Then there's medieval Goetia, from the grimoire *The Lesser Key of Solomon* (which Josh experiments with), giving detailed instruction on the conjuring of demons in order to predict the future or fulfill your needs. And, going even further back, the Papyri Graecae Magicae (PGM), or Greek Magical Papyri, a fragmented collection of papyrus documents from Greco-Roman Egypt uncovered in the eighteenth century, contain spells that range from demon evocations to curses and love charms. These are all traditions or forms of folk magic that stand outside of the clear karmic guidelines of Wicca, but practices that some present-day witches and occultists dip into on their own, in a syncretic approach.

Still, there are limitations: an internal logic, a code of personal ethics, the need for approval from the magician's own community. Personally, in my travels, I never encountered anyone whose magical practice frightened me—a black magician without boundaries.

Then I met Jonathan.

17

Sympathy for the Necromancer

I had known Jonathan for more than a year before I learned the lengths to which he goes in the name of black magic.

Jonathan is a necromancer: someone who summons up the dead to gain information, or to use the power of that soul to manipulate or harm the living. In his case, this means—and there's no gentle way of putting it—he steals bodies from cemeteries and uses them to channel demons.

This will take a moment to explain, and many readers will not try to understand or forgive him.

Jonathan is not his real name, and I won't say much about the details of his life—because what he and his inner circle have done could land them in prison in the state of Louisiana for several years. I'll say this: he is sharp in conversation, intellectually agile, quick with his gestures and leaps of mood. He's magnetic, an attractive man. Maybe some of his charisma lines up with what you can expect from a sociopath, if you'd like to categorize him that way—he'd be the first to say that the ability to handle human remains requires at least a touch of the sociopathic. But to my mind, dismissing him with a label lets us off easy. Because Jonathan's practice is connected, in a deeply uncomfortable way, to why many of us turn to religion in the first place.

Religion is ultimately about death: our fear of it, our poor attempts to organize it, to wrap our minds around the inevitable end. We argue over the pieces that constitute ourselves: Are we a body plus a soul? Do we have one soul, three souls, no soul at all? Are we animated matter, meat puppets that fall limp and rot once past their sell-by date? Is everything important about us contained inside our skulls—our entire reality? And when, eventually, we do die, what is left behind? For Jonathan, the answer to that last question is this: *material.* You die and you leave him "raw material." Depending on the combination of circumstances surrounding your death and your burial, Jonathan may appear, unannounced, ready to repurpose you.

Here is the blackest magic that Jonathan practices, a technique that, over the last five years, he has taught to about twenty younger occultists in New Orleans, a half-policed city uniquely suited to this kind of renegade magical working. In the middle of the night, with a rotating band of collaborators—today whittled down to his strongest, most reliable three—Jonathan drives to the appointed cemetery and jumps the gate (much as I did with Josh, or as witches might do for graveyard work). With a bag of tools both practical and magical, they approach the chosen tomb and break inside. Since nearly everyone in New Orleans is buried aboveground, this is easy: You remove the stone frontispiece with a flathead screwdriver, or, in a more derelict place, you pull apart the bricks. Then comes the stroke that once gave Jonathan pause, the moment that used to repulse him (though not any longer). He removes an ax from the tool kit, climbs into the crypt, and, straddling the body, cuts off its head.

A person inhabited this body—let's say a man, who breathed and walked and ate too much and laughed and had a boring job and a couple of children and people in life who knew his name—and then he died. Maybe it was sudden, or maybe he was sick and everyone who cared about him saw it coming. Then what was left of him, whatever you believe remains behind, was "laid to rest" at this spot with some amount of ceremony. Jonathan's is the very secret, very rest-less postscript to this story, the afterlife no one has in mind when burying their dead.

While Jonathan harvests the head—that's what he calls it, "harvesting," as if he were a surgeon saving vital organs—the others make a salt circle on the walkway outside the tomb. Jonathan exits the crypt and, setting ax aside, lays the fresh head down on a pentacle in the circle's center, out in the open air. The work must happen quickly and without hesitation. Before the soul of the dead man can escape, they begin the conjurations to "bind" it to his skull: they use an incantation found in the Greek Magical Papyri, a spell that goes all the way back to Greco-Roman Egypt, the heaviest part of which is the speaking of the name of Typhon, Father of All Monsters, "at whom the Ground, the Depths of the Sea, Hades, Heaven, the Sun, the Moon, the Visible Chorus of Stars, the whole Universe all Tremble, the Name . . . that consists of 100 Letters."

Then it's done. And Jonathan has a new oracular skull, a direct line to the gods, a hotline for the most pressing questions—access other humans simply have not got.

He wraps the head in a cloth consecrated with god-names and magical symbols, binds it with chains, and places it inside a box painted with hexagrams. This traps the soul and prevents other forces from latching on. The crew hides their work, restacking bricks like Jenga pieces; no one ever seems to notice the disturbance. They jump back over the gate, carrying delicate cargo now. They find the car, load their take into the trunk, and drive off. Over the coming days, Jonathan will sanctify the head and make a home for his new collaborator on a fresh altar. And over the coming years, he will call gods and demons through the skull, and through the once-human soul bound to it, and he will ask for many things—for money, and revenge, and a clear message from the gods themselves, about their true nature.

Modern-day necromancy is extremely rare; encountering a band of young necromancers in America is equivalent to coming across a pack of black unicorns. By anyone's definition, Jonathan is an occult extremist: he has as much in common with other occultists and Pagans as, say, a jihadist has with the average Muslim. "Unless someone's done human sacrifice, they've got nothing on me," he says. "I have no doubt that there's an enormous gulf between me and a normal person."

But his practice has plenty of precedent: necromancy has been conducted throughout history, by people ranging from black-magic outsiders to generations of Catholic priests.

In antiquity, necromancy was carried out in Greece, Rome, Egypt, Mesopotamia, and Persia. People might consult oracles, sleep atop tombs, or try to reanimate a human skull or even an entire corpse, to gain influence or insight. The earliest description of necromancy is in Homer's *Odyssey*: Odysseus, following the priestess Circe's instructions, travels to the Underworld and uses spellwork to raise the dead in order to learn how to return home safely. Plutarch, Cicero, and Horace all allude to necromancy in their work, and a few Roman emperors (including Nero) were rumored practitioners. The Bible, which warns against magic, explicitly forbids divination through the use of the dead in the book of Deuteronomy; in the first book of Samuel, King Saul is depicted as enlisting the help of a witch to gain information from the spirit of the prophet Samuel. ("Why hast thou disquieted me?" Samuel cries out.) During the Middle Ages, necromancers made up an underground of well-educated clergy, and their methods showed the influence of Christian and Jewish exorcism, as well as Arabic magic. During the early fourteenth century, Pope John XXII was particularly paranoid about attacks from necromancers and other types of magicians, leveling accusations against suspects from a radical Franciscan friar to the ruler of Milan. A century later, little had changed: Pope Benedict XIII charged a band of clerics with necromancy—only to be accused himself, shortly afterward, of hiring black magicians on his own behalf.

At that point, the Western history of necromancy—beyond, say, the more ephemeral stuff of Spiritualist séances—falls off. But Jonathan draws a hereditary line from these black magicians of the past to his present-day practice. He sees himself in a long succession of great necromancers—in his thirties, he calls himself the "young grandfather" of this technique. Of the occultists he's trained, Jonathan estimates that about ten have continued to grow into serious practitioners, including one who moved to New Mexico and passed the method on to a small clique there.

The start of his trip down this path—the "left-hand" path, as they call it—was banal. The black magician in Jonathan was born out of heartache, when his first love broke up with him not long after high school graduation. The breakup crushed his belief that anyone could be truly loving and loyal. "I just covered myself in my shitty trench coat and cried for, like, a year," he says. "For three hundred and sixty-five days. I couldn't let it go."

Moving on to college didn't lift the depression. "I never stopped being sad." He skipped classes. Already curious about the occult—Ouija boards, candle spells, whatever—he found new friends who were into hallucinogenics and eager to experiment, and with them Jonathan turned to dark magic. He felt reckless, ready to abandon himself. "It was a way to kill the empathetic soul that felt loss, that felt sorrow," he says. "I thought, 'I don't have to be in love if I'm a monster, and I don't have to suffer this.' The kid that I was, who was in love like that, was dead—he was actually *food* for this other creature that I became. I was reborn—like evil baptism."

But these early experiments—teaching himself to scry, attempting to evoke demons—failed to set him free. "Instead, I found out there was a *deeper* hole. And you know what happened? I fell down that rabbit hole, and I found new things. I found there were powers that I didn't understand." As Jonathan became increasingly serious about his black-magic investigations, his depression and suicidal thoughts at last began to lift. Magic was something to live for.

Jonathan's first, in 2008, was a woman named Ethel. At least, that's the name he says her spirit revealed to him. He tells me about her as we drive through downtown New Orleans on an overcast afternoon.

They discovered what remained of Ethel in a derelict cemetery somewhere out in the parishes, a cemetery with an enormous dead oak at its center surrounded by some of the worst graves Jonathan has seen in this city (and he's spent time looking).

All that week, his small crew had been on the hunt for a cemetery in which to perform some black conjurations, nothing more specific than that. But as they drove around, tools stowed in the trunk of the car—incense, a wand, the Greek Magical Papyri, a few offerings, an ax—an implicit understanding built up, the understanding that a line would soon be crossed. Finally, late one night, slightly drunk, cruising farther and farther out, they realized this was the moment—this was the spot—to do something big. "We felt like we were being guided," Jonathan says. (They'd been working with a particular demon named in the *Ars Goetia*, and he believes they were under its influence.) That night they would take their first head and bind it, using an ancient Greek ritual, and it would become their first oracle through which to draw the gods.

For some reason, they were attracted to one tomb in particular, an unmarked cinder-block grave. Jonathan struck the brick with the butt of the ax, and it smashed right through. With the light of an iPhone, they peered inside: the corpse was laid out in a ditch a foot or two deep, the head on the far end, beyond reach. They knew what to do—"It was totally intuitive." Without a word, one of Jonathan's partners got down on his knees and crawled all the way in. He called out to the others, "It's a woman!" And with that, straddling the corpse, he cracked the head off its brittle spine. He exited the tomb in a daze and dropped the skull at Jonathan's feet.

This first harvesting, Jonathan says, was "really clunky, really awkward, like bad first sex." They had no idea what they were doing, and the patches of leathery skin and thick hair stuck to the skull (a black woman's weave) were unnerving, covered in spiders. Once the binding ceremony was done, how would they transport the severed head? What about the smell? And their neighbors? They were also completely unprepared, on a spirit level, for the amount of fight Ethel had in her. "She was violent and nasty," he says. "Everything about her energy was angry."

But in the weeks and months that followed, they developed a system. They learned how to care for the vessel. Once back at their private storehouse, they left the head "raw," not cleaned or tampered with. Instead, they burned incense and poured rainwater and olive oil and pig's blood and wine over it until the teeth bucked out, invoking one of the kings of hell—the demon who'd been guiding them—through the cranial vault. Jonathan completed Ethel's altar with a Palo-inspired *nganga*, or spirit pot: a clay vessel he filled with local cemetery dirt and a sickle and myrrh. All the while, they continued "drawing" the demon through the head, meditating over it, performing magical experiments, asking for insight. And Ethel was reborn as "the oracle."

At the same time, the group was being punished for what Jonathan calls their "beginners' sloppiness."

He runs down the list of illnesses he and the others experienced in their first two years of this work: "Constantly getting the flu, sore throats, bloody noses. Malnutrition-type symptoms. Trauma and anxiety. Sleeping sixteen hours a day. Alcohol and drug issues spiraling out of control." One collaborator, who for months stored Ethel at his home, began having seizures that remained unexplained after several medical exams and stopped only after an elaborate magical working designed to curb the demon. "It became clear that this shit really works, that there are consequences and power there," Jonathan says. "Then we stopped doing the nonsense version and took time to study and focus."

They now realize the importance of taking thorough precautions. This makes sense: going back to the ancient Greeks, necromancers believed that the dead, shaken awake in their graves, were traumatized, furious, resistant. The magician, by stepping into the tomb, had to be ready for a long-term struggle with the soul he sought to bind. Based on experience, Jonathan and his crew now prep for about a week in advance, performing invocations to protect themselves. And once on-site, armed with backpacks of ritual materials, they perform ablutions with "military" discipline, and a banishing ritual to clear the cemetery space of any interference from the other side. They address the dead "from a position of authority and power."

At home, they are far more thorough about keeping the heads "fed" and their altars maintained. Jonathan has "sealed" their storehouse with Solomonic talismans and Hoodoo charms and keeps each oracle atop a pentacle, trapped within a Goetic triangle. They regularly serve them pig's blood and fresh water and dandelions "to feed their life force—to keep them from needing to drain life from us" (which he believes was the cause of their illnesses). "Once we started doing that, we stopped having all those maladies."

I ask how many are kept in this storage space.

"How many *individuals*? I can't answer that."

I ask how many "individuals" he's worked with over the last five years.

Jonathan laughs curtly. Occasionally I feel him grow vulnerable, maybe even embarrassed, by how these details might sound to outsiders. In spite of his bravado, some part of him fears I might pass judgment. Considering my question, he hums quietly, as if to relax himself. He counts on his fingers while driving.

"Ten. Twelve."

Pause.

"But that's, like, fully worked individuals—their skulls. In terms of *bones*, maybe thirty. I think? I'm talking about hands and other random parts for different things." Another short laugh.

"Okay," I say. We're both quiet for a little while.

. . .

The most crucial early experiments with Ethel were driven by Jonathan's desire to prove that he could control a demon, and even send it off on personal assignments. "We wanted to know that if we needed to make someone sick, to obsess someone with certain dreams, to *kill* someone, we could essentially haunt them to death. We could send out a wandering specter to work on that person and do things we needed done." In his mind, Jonathan is a scientist testing the limits of knowledge and matter. "I was like someone working with a hadron collider: I just wanted to know what was possible."

With Ethel, Jonathan trained himself to wed Goetia (the evocation of demons) with necromancy (the evocation of the human dead). Either practice on its own is considered heavy magic, but in combination the stakes are ratcheted up still higher: you are evoking the dead, harnessing that person's soul, and then forcing that human soul to channel a demon. Working off the centuries-old Goetia, you make a pact with a demon, luring it out with an offering—in this case, the most irresistible offering of all, the chance to reconnect with at least a remnant of human physical existence. "They have no form, but they *seek* form. They seek the sensory experiences that we love. It needs you to gain a form, and you need it for its power, and you guys make a bargain. You are wedding the energy of a human body and soul to something that is ancient. Half the demons in the Goetia are from Sumeria—think about how long that spirit must have been around! And it becomes your patron, and it teaches you how to do these things." In this way, you gain a mentor in black magic—but if you're able to bind the demon, you also gain a force that "you can send out to do your bidding, like a dog."

One day Jonathan convinced an occultist he works with to let him send the demon to his doorstep that night. The man lived about a mile away. Jonathan told Ethel, "You need to go to his doorstep and leave a symbol where he will know it's you and it could be no one else." The next day Jonathan received a phone call from this occultist-friend: the neighbor's dog had dropped dead at his door. From then on, Jonathan became increasingly driven and precise. One ancient conjuration (for Hekate) required a python skin, a Capricorn girl's blood, and deer penises. "That shit's just not done often anymore. And *we* did it. And we really focused on making sure that it was right."

In order to direct Ethel and her demon, Jonathan had to learn to create a magical link between her altar and the targeted person. To perform this "sympathetic" type of magic—like the spell Morpheus sent me—he needs some of the victim's personal elements: hair, blood, fingernails, a photo, their signature. He can then use these to make an object to bury in the person's yard, or send to them by mail. Or Jonathan's crew might perform a ritual with candles from the local botanica: they scratch the person's name on the candles, arrange them in a circle around the chosen oracle, and direct the spirit in its action. Not long ago, they sent a demon to haunt and harrass some people who owed them money, "to force them to resolve the issue." In two days, Jonathan says, he received a call: after a year of dodging, the debtors wanted to start making payments. Most recently, Jonathan began considering a more serious spell, against a man who raped a woman he knows. The NOPD have not made an arrest, he says, so he's considering taking action himself, through "subtler means."

But these goals are narrow, strategic. What Jonathan sought first was "proof that there is some sort of power in death, that something survives it. Or there's some kind of energy, and we can *harness* it." Think of America's early Spiritualists, with their mediumship and séances and all the people who have consulted them. The necromancer seeks something similar—his methods are simply much, much more aggressive. "What we really want is to hear a more audible voice of the gods. And we need to hear it in a human voice, through a human soul—*literally*. So I'm trying to draw the powers down and force them to speak with me."

There is something else at play: the huge, frustrated love Jonathan once felt for a girl has been replaced by a growing fascination with a force that dwarfs *any* human female. "*Darkness*. I knew she was there, and I wanted to be with her, to experience darkness as a living thing. It's like being in love with a phantom. Being in love with her, and wanting to see her, and realizing that some dead person's sockets are the first mirror you can see her reflected in. To amplify that into an anthro form, to actually be able to look it in the face, empower it, give it a personality, and have it walk with you: it's addictive."

"Why?"

"Because I feel like it's the actual fundament of reality. I need to *touch* that fundament."

. . .

At one point, I ask Jonathan why, as with Ethel, he would covet the remains of someone he knows nothing about. He dismisses my focus on the individual. Jonathan believes, as Feris do, that we each contain multiple souls—but it is the least "special," the most primitive, soul that he works with. "You want to make it personal. It's *not* personal. Because the *nephesh*"—the animal soul, in Hebrew, or what Feris call Fetch—"is not personal." And even if the individual was weak or unintelligent or unexceptional in life, the *nephesh* remains strong.

That strength can take a toll on the black magician. "You open yourself up to the malevolent dead, to haunting," Jonathan says. "To this day, I can't even sleep in my own bedroom: every single night, I feel someone standing over my bed on my right-hand side. I don't know who it is, *which one* it is, but it's strong enough to be there again and again. I just have to deal with the fact that someone's looking at me all night." He considers this the price of necromancy.

Even more powerful, he claims, is using the remains of individuals who have been dead for fewer than forty days—though this is something Jonathan has only carried out a few times, considering the challenges involved. In this scenario, the process of corpse selection can start weeks or months before he walks onto the cemetery grounds. To find the right body for a particular spell—a body not only recently buried, but buried in the right place (maybe a crossroads, or a spot dedicated to a particular saint)—he scans the obituaries, reading closely. Waiting, waiting. "You're, like, 'Oh, this guy was a professor in 1963, and he had four children.' And you know you're going to chop his head off." Funeral flowers may still be at the grave when Jonathan makes his appearance.

But the ultimate prize remains this: the head of a devout person—a priest, a rabbi, a monk, a yogi. Jonathan is waiting, specifically, for the death of a local Catholic priest, a man who would have spent his life "magically fortifying" his body, repeatedly, through his own religion's rituals, making him that much more desirable as a tool in the necromancer's hands. After decades of meditation and taking the sacrament, in death a priest would become the ultimate oracle.

"He would have real knowledge," Jonathan says, "a lot of illumination. He could become the lord of our crypt."

We sit outside behind Jonathan's house, armed with rum and cigarettes, and I watch him smoke. The sun went down hours ago.

"Look at what a living thing is: it is dying cells and metabolism. *Putrefaction* is what life is. Death in motion! Think about your own digestion: it's draining energy from other sources, like a vampire, and redirecting it toward your own homeostasis. And the death magician is not doing anything different."

Jonathan views the body, in life, as "death in motion," always aging, its cells dying off and shedding; after death, this steady progress accelerates as if hurtling into space. The moment the heart stops beating, the cells are cut off from blood and begin to wither in waves. The brain cells are the first to go, often within minutes; the skin and bone cells within a few days. The blood drains from the capillaries and sinks, gravity-bound. Rigor mortis sets in after three hours; the body's own heat has cooled after the first day. Bacteria begin to consume the dead cells. The pancreas eats itself. Body tissue emits a greenish liquid and methane gas; the collapsing lungs push fluid out the nose and mouth. The body is ripe with rot: flies feed on the corpse, each laying hundreds of eggs, which in turn spout a veritable waterfall of maggots. From the surface of the body they burrow their way inward, eating as they travel. Eating without stop, growing to ten times their length, they consume more than half the body in their first week of residence. And this relentless decay happens even faster if the body remains aboveground.

Like the process of decomposition, necromancy, in Jonathan's experience, follows an unstoppable phasic progression. "Initially, you just have to learn to do that sort of thing: random corpse-robbing. You have to be capable of it. But once you *do that act*, you're reborn. You're reborn as a necromancer. You're different from other people."

This sets off the first phase: alienation. "You feel separated from society, monstrous." At the same time, that feeling is accompanied by "the sense that you have access to this special place, psychologically, that other people don't have access to. Because you were willing to *go* there, and you *did*, and now you can live in the midnight hour, in the cemetery—and you feel like the place is populous. You're with *them*."

Next comes the high. After his first time, the black magician returns to the "normal world" with the sense that everyday stresses are trivial. "You feel freed from everyday life! Not that you don't have goals—we wouldn't be doing black magic if we weren't ambitious. But you're completely fucking free. Free from the obsession of . . . being human?"

This sense of freedom, at least for a time, places the necromancer outside of the rules of society in a radical way. He has become warped, but powerfully unique. Untouchable. "One time, we had a whole body in the car, covered in a blanket, sitting in the passenger seat"—he laughs—"and we just pulled up in the French Quarter and went and got a drink." He twirls a finger at the side of his head: the universal sign language for "crazy." "We felt immortal, like, 'What could happen to us?' There's no way for me to explain that psychology. At that point, maybe you didn't *kill* that person, but you're like a serial killer."

And so this feeling of uniqueness, the sense of straddling the line between life and death, begins to consume you—regardless of what you were like before your first night in the cemetery. "I've seen this kind of magic become an addiction, a dangerous one. It spreads, even to the most normal people. We're not talking about goth kids—I've seen the ditzy girls, dudes, nerds, all of them. I used to think this was just for perverted people, and now I think it is a part of every human being. Almost anyone can get this thirst—you can catch it. That's why it's regarded in spiritual circles as a disease."

Five years ago, Jonathan says, he developed an appetite for this that was "really extreme." "There was a moment, in fact, where I did think I was going to go the bad route and fall fully into Bundy Alley, you know?" (He means the killer Ted Bundy. I notice that when he mentions serial killers, which he does often, it's with a certain familiarity. I doubt many people call Ed Gein "Eddie.") "The taste for this just got so overwhelming—"

"When you say 'the taste,' what do you mean?"

"Just wanting to dissemble and tear and be dark and awful."

"Wanting to touch—"

"Dead flesh. Shredding it. It wasn't wanting to make someone dead so much as make art out of death. I don't know"—he sounds embarrassed again, shaking it off with another half laugh—"I get kind of sensitive when I talk about it. It's a hard thing to express." Like many great loves, this love of Darkness twisted in on itself, became obsessive. "Now I recognize that you can't survive and have that orientation"—an orientation that leaves you propping a body up in your car outside a packed bar. "If you get so enmeshed in these desires, you breed more and more of them and become honestly twisted. Your desires will become insatiable. You'll become a blood drinker, a cannibal, anything—and you'll still be unsatisfied."

With this addictive phase comes the loss of repulsion: the natural, primal, gut-level fear of a rotting human corpse starts to recede, and a new intimacy takes its place. Once, while cradling a head, one of Jonathan's recruits told the story of how his parents died while he was in high school. The man broke down, inconsolable, and began to kiss the skull. "There's a stage in this work where you start to identify with the remains," Jonathan says. "You are getting over repulsion to the concept that everything you are will rot." He talks about his cohorts: though each is an outsider, in ways deliberate or not, "none of them are social rejects." One guy is a bartender. "People like him; he's good-looking; he goes home with girls if he wants to. But this drew him so far that he was more comfortable hanging out with those deceased than with other people."

The confrontation with death and rot can be both a source of power and a kind of psychological torture. "The trauma of this work is so heavy. We've all dealt with it differently. The more stoic of us just drink too much—it's internalized." For others, however, the toll has been greater. He says that one of his cohorts slipped into a schizophrenic state shortly after a cemetery ritual and was institutionalized. "I've seen some of my best friends lose it, go nuts. And at first, I was really excited to see that. Because that's how I knew it was *real*. Regardless of your psychology entering into it, if you do these things, you will not walk out the same way."

I want to be clear: I *like* Jonathan. It would be much easier to process everything he's sharing with me if I did not. Like the heavier-weight artists and writers I've known, he gives the impression of having seen the other side, of possessing a secret knowledge that draws others to him.

This quality naturally has me on guard—he is, after all, an epic storyteller, a collector of outsized personal dramas. But if he's embellishing his tales, I believe it's in scale, not content. For instance, what if, when he says he's stolen twelve heads, there were only three? If you've robbed a grave to perform black magic with a stranger's skull, does it truly matter whether it was once, twice, five times? You've already crossed into another category of human being.

I know Jonathan well enough to say this: he simply lacks the personal boundaries, and the fear of taboos, that would keep the vast majority of people the hell away from this guerrilla form of magic. So, if you eliminate ethics as an obstacle, his stories can be judged by their plausibility—and in New Orleans someone can certainly get away with the desecration of a grave. Then there are the occasional details that seem frank enough to throw me off-balance—as when he sounds genuinely comforted by the "quiet" of the cemetery. Or how, soon after stealing Ethel's head, they returned to the graveyard to retrieve the rest of her body: "We didn't want her to be in pieces. But I no longer think it works that way." And, not least of all, when he describes the eye sockets of one corpse as containing "no eyeball but the *meat* in the eye, and the lid was dried and shriveled like an apricot."

Still, I cannot help myself: I ask to see the storehouse. The writer in me wants proof, but there's also a darker, very human curiosity. To see a collection of human heads, consecrated for magical purposes and carefully stowed away, would be to look the bogeyman in the face, to encounter evidence of the blackest magical practice that I've heard talk of in this country.

The request doesn't unnerve Jonathan. He simply tells me his rule: "I will show anyone anything they want to see; I'll teach anyone anything they want to know. But they have to bring me a human head that they've dug up themselves."

That will not be possible.

He shrugs. "I would never break that rule. There's too much at stake. Someone's going to turn me in one of these days, and I'm going to be like Eddie Gein at thirty-three. Fuck that."

A thin but meaningful line separates Jonathan from the serial killers he talks about repeatedly: Jonathan is not harming the living, at least not physically. And his magic has deep roots: he and his crew may have gone rogue, but their practice is grounded in Palo Mayombe, Kimbanda, the Goetia, and the Greek Magical Papyri. Of course, Jonathan has put a very lawless spin on the work that the Paleros would not approve of—but the spells in the Goetia and the *PGM* never adhered to any law beyond the black magician's own interests.

When a person is able to look at the human body as mere raw material, he's evidence of humanity either at our basest (Bundy, Gein) or at our most evolved (a surgeon, on the one hand, or a Buddhist monk). It's a matter of how you've reached that perspective, and it's a matter of intention. Perhaps most important, it's a matter of consent: these bodies were once living people, and their permission, or the permission of their families, is necessary even after death. Otherwise, the doctor or holy person or magician transforms from specialist, genius, guru into thief.

I mention this to Jonathan: isn't he stealing not only from the dead, but from their descendants, too? He is ready with an answer.

"Well, here's the thing: most of the people that we have, there was no name on their grave, and whoever buried them didn't give a fuck. We reappropriated that stuff"—the bodies—"sort of as a 'spiritual recycling' project. Now those people sit on shrines in adoration. Now they live in a temple."

I can't tell whether he's selling this notion to me or to himself.

Again, I think about Jonathan in relation to a surgeon. Whatever weird predisposition the surgeon brings to his practice, we don't question the value of what he does. But what if the practice of necromancy has the outside possibility of revealing something about what's left of us when we die? About our own potential after death? I understand this will not be the popular interpretation of Jonathan's work, to put it mildly—but what if? How different is what he does, really, from the nineteenth-century British and American surgeons who, desperate for cadavers to dissect, paid grave robbers for their goods, or even broke into cemeteries themselves? How much do we know now about the way the human body works, information that has saved lives for over a century, because of their macabre midnight-hour collecting of corpses? If we believed there was something to gain from Jonathan's experiments, a kind of magical "technology," would it do anything to excuse his crimes?

The final phase of necromancy, according to Jonathan, is the rejection of black magic, and the embrace of what he calls "black Buddhism." A dedicated magician eventually stops pursuing his petty desires—for sex, money, revenge. That pursuit, Jonathan says, "becomes like anything else: *repetitive.* Where are you going to go from here? Do you have to become Caligula—is that what your project is about? And because the answer is clearly no, then you have to ask yourself what is essential and start letting the rest go."

When Jonathan speaks of what is "essential," he means the essential nature of all things, which is their brevity. He believes the only pleasure is in appreciating the brief flash of life contained in every experience. This appreciation first requires you to accept that your physical form will come to an end, to embrace that fact, to stare into its sockets, kiss it on the mouth. On the surface, this may sound impossible and gruesome—but isn't that what most religion is about? Searching for a way, however counterintuitive, of making peace with the fact of your grandparents' bones, your parents' bones, the bones of your boyfriend or wife or child? And, finally, your *own* bones—the remnants of a life which is, inevitably, death in motion. "So necromancy becomes a boon suddenly. Because the idea of mortality is now natural to you. You can be with a thing, and there can be a beauty to that thing, but you can only have it for a moment."

The desire to hear the voices of the gods and the desire to "touch darkness" are essentially the same drive, Jonathan says, "because each is about seeking the extremes of the human experience. It's saying yes to the universe, which anyone can see is filled with light and darkness. So we have to understand them both.

"There's a bittersweetness to existence—but only some people are participating in it. Bittersweet, bittersweet, bittersweet. Every moment."

18

And the Crows Will Eat My Eyes

Morpheus views her life as outsized, and her death will be, too. When she dies, she does not want her body taken to a funeral home; she wants instead to be left in the California desert, exposed to the elements, her eyes eaten by vultures and ravens, and her skull and bones stripped bare. Then her loved ones and covenmates and the members of her priesthood will gather up her sun-dried pieces and build an altar from them.

She did not get this idea herself—the practice of excarnation, or "sky burial," is centuries old. The Parsis in India, at the edge of Mumbai, place bodies atop structures they call the Towers of Silence to be eaten by vultures; in Tibet, some Buddhists, after death, are flayed and left on a mountaintop for the birds and animals to consume; and on this continent, some Native American tribes once mounted their dead on outdoor scaffolds. But Morpheus absorbed her funerary fantasy, like so much else in her life, from the Celts: they left their dead warriors on the battlefield, for the Battle Raven to consume.

The body is left exposed, food for the carrion birds. The huge black birds—vultures, ravens, crows—circle and eventually, when ready, they descend and begin the dissection, picking, picking. Again and again, the process repeats, until the body is not *laid to rest* but spread across the landscape, as wide as the span of the wake. And what was a man becomes a husk, the casing of skin deflated as its innards are consumed, shredded, digested. And when these foul-smelling carcass-eaters are once again airborne, so are the tiny pieces of the person, scattered to the winds, buried in the sky. That human matter feeds back into nature farther and faster, the bloody scraps dropped to the ground, fanned out by an army of thousands. This is how the human body is reduced to bone—sometimes in a matter of hours—until there it is, bleached by the sun, contorted, twisted: the skeleton.

This is what Morpheus wants for her remains.

While some Pagans believe in reincarnation, all take satisfaction in the fact that we are each part of a much larger cycle, and that, with our death, we are broken down and return as new biological life. The Pagans I've met may be as touchy-feely as the average American—they're hardly stoic Buddhists—but most witches in the States seem far less terrified of our inevitable rot than the average Westerner.

One West Coast priestess, now in her sixties, told me how she used to have initiates in her line confront their deaths immediately, in practical ways: she requested that they draw up two wills (one for their mundane life, one for their magical life) and make the actual shroud they'd someday be wrapped in. Her coven once buried an initiate in the ground naked, up to her neck in sand, and danced around her, singing, "Ding dong! The witch is dead!" (It's okay to laugh in the face of your mortality.) At Circle Sanctuary, Selena Fox's Wiccan church and nature preserve, near Barneveld, Wisconsin—about two hours from where they hold Pagan Spirit Gathering—Pagans can have green burials, in which the deceased is wrapped in a shroud, or placed in a biodegradable pine or wicker coffin, and buried at a spot in the woods with a simple marker or mere GPS coordinates. It's the job of the mourners, passing around shovels, to dig the hole, lower the body, and cover it with dirt.

Americans used to handle the bodies of their dead personally: it was intimate, and it was how things were done. The family would bathe and dress the deceased, hold the wake at home ("funeral parlor" came from placing the body in the parlor room), build the casket themselves, and often bury the body on their property. But shortly after embalming was introduced during the Civil War—to make the shipping of soldiers' bodies across long distances possible—chemical preparation, makeup, and formal "display" in a funeral home became our custom. Our dead, handed over to professionals, were absorbed into an industry—one that now does nearly $21 billion in business each year.

But sky burial is a real, if rarefied, American fantasy.

There are two major forensic anthropology research centers, or "body farms," in this country, where the bodies of the recently deceased are donated, laid outside, and observed during decomposition. The largest is connected to Texas State University in San Marcos. There, at any given time, in a cordoned-off section of a working ranch, about seventy bodies are lying exposed to the sun. Most are placed under chicken-wire cages for protection, but some are left out for the Central Texas vultures, documented by video camera as they're consumed. The intended result is that researchers learn more about how the body deteriorates, to help law enforcement determine time of death; the *unintended* result is that the facility doubles as an acres-wide sky-burial site. A third of the calls the facility receives from potential donors are inquiries about taking part in the vulture study. "I want to be eaten by vultures"—that's often how they phrase it.

I spoke with several Pagans, at least on the West Coast, who would have loved to be left out—say, in a stark, cinematic stretch of desert—to be picked apart by the birds. The idea of being returned to the earth, in a way that might strike some as brutal, seemed for them the most fitting. A Bay Area healer who trains people to work with the spirits of their ancestors said of American funerary traditions: "If I did a poll of people who would rather get eaten by birds on a tower outside of San Jose, twenty percent of my friends would raise their hands. If you did a poll of Pagans, I think at least a third would rather have their eyes eaten by crows. It's the ethos of the community." A twenty-something priest in upstate New York told me the story of how his Pagan mentor, in hospice for cancer, dreamt of being naturally mummified out in the Arizona desert (which would not be legal) but was instead cremated by the state. That same priest said that he'd spent huge amounts of time researching the logistics of his own excarnation and, out of frustration, resolved to go renegade: out in the desert, he'd build his own open-topped structure, "like the Towers of Silence," leave the location and instructions for the bones with a friend, and move into the tower whenever he was ready to die.

For Pagans—as with, say, Tibetan monks—the bones have a life after the individual's death. A number of Pagans I spoke with told me of family members and covenmates who wanted to inherit their bones for use in ritual, maybe make their skulls into chalices—or they told me of a coven elder whose remains they themselves wished to keep. An Alexandrian Wiccan in Maryland told me that his coven had recently ordered silver charms bearing the imprint of their high priestess's left index finger, as well as rings embedded with jewels created from her cremains. (A company in Illinois, not Pagan at all, can actually heat-blast and pressurize the carbon found in cremains to create "diamonds" on demand.) Circle Sanctuary says that people have asked about sky burials on their grounds, as well as the possibility of having their bones dug up later for ritual use—all of which the group is looking into. If you can hand down your bones, the belief goes, you continue a magical chain, a link, a relationship, even after death. The desire for that inheritance is there; the donors are willing. It seems wrong to cut people off from their religious inheritance—and, for a particularly theatrical community, from the right to mark their death with flair and precision.

"The manner of your death puts the capstone on your life," Morpheus says. Not being able to choose freely how her body is handled after death "is like a wound for me."

I have not found anyone who's managed to keep the bones of a loved one at home, legally or illegally—but Morpheus does have a piece of bone from her close friend Tara, who died of a brain tumor at thirty-five—the friend on whose behalf I'd long ago seen Morpheus make an offering to the Morrigan. After she was cremated, her husband pulled out the remaining shards of bone and passed them on to her inner circle.

I send Morpheus information about the body farm I visited, and, over e-mails, I can see her brain start to spin. "Wow! Thank you!!! :D," she writes— the most enthusiasm I've ever seen someone muster over decomposition. And why not embrace this return to the earth? Is it really less gruesome to be injected and tube-fed with chemicals, painted with makeup, tucked into starched clothes, and sealed in a slick titanium vessel? Maybe the rest of us could glean something from this Pagan fearlessness of human rot. As Morpheus puts it: "We don't share the dominant culture's terror of dead things."

But Morpheus's vision for her remains extends beyond excarnation: the funerary altar, where her larger bones will be kept, will be incredibly baroque, with stained glass inlaid with jewels made from her bone dust. The centerpiece, she says, will be her head: a small shrine for her skull. That way, "people could come and talk to me. I could communicate with my community after I die."

She takes inspiration for her shrine from the so-called Celtic Cult of the Head. It's an apocryphal piece of history, but some believe that the Celts collected the heads of their fallen enemies and of their own kin—they believed that the spirit lived on inside the skull—and preserved them in oils to use as oracles.

I immediately think of the other uses that have been made of the human skull in magical work, across cultures and time periods, from the time of the Greek Magical Papyri up through African diaspora religions like Palo. And, of course, I think of Jonathan. Both he and Morpheus have envisioned working, or have worked, with the skull—but a wall divides them, both ethical and magical: the matter of consent. Whereas Jonathan steals from both worlds, Morpheus, if she could, would choose to donate her body to the magical science practiced by those she loves. One is a thief, the other an altruist. And both are certain their magic sets them apart from the banal lives and deaths of so many others.

When I see Morpheus next—back at the San Jose DoubleTree for another round of PantheaCon—she has hardened just enough for me to notice. I can see her narrative of herself sharpening, locking into place, heat-blasted and pressurized in the increasing intensity of her relationship to the Morrigan. When we first met, I was the one observing and documenting a story that would otherwise be lost, and she seemed grateful for that—but now I get the sense that, beyond our friendship, I'm superfluous to her. She understands the character she's playing; she's grown into that larger person.

Five years ago, Morpheus's mundane identity was that of a khaki-clad employee of a federally funded environmental agency. She spent her days meeting with ranchers who could never know about her life as a witch, the rest of her time cooking for Shannon, and somehow managed to plan rituals for Stone City and lessons for her small group of Feri students. Now she's in

Berkeley, sharing a house with another respected Feri priestess (Thorn), free from the rigid obligations of her marriage and her job, and the gritty isolation of her former trailer life. Her mundane identity is growing thinner, spectral, increasingly absorbed into her priestess self. She's apprenticed to an established tattoo artist in the Mission who not only knows about Morpheus's other self but was the one to ink the Morrigan spear along the top of her spine. She would say it's the work with her goddess that has given her life its focus, forged it.

I take the hotel elevator to the second floor—I know the routine—straight to the Coru "hospitality suite," Room 271. This is where I'll be staying, where the priesthood will be entertaining and receiving guests. As I step inside, the first person I see is Moon—who has changed his name to "Brennos," for magical reasons I cannot keep up with—and he gives me a big hug. He's wearing jeans and a bright red tee printed with a stylized raven designed by Morpheus. Looking around, I now see that the other priesthood members are in black-and-red Coru tees or tank tops: Scott, Amelia, Rudy, all in the same goddess-team jersey.

Everyone's either here or milling around the hotel or (in the case of Cruach) tucked away in a painted wooden box, preparing for the long weekend ahead. Then there are the allies of the Coru, who dip in and out: a Thracian priest, in wavy hair and furs (he keeps a live raven of his own); and two friends picked up at a ritual in Canada—Grant, in leather and armor, possibly the most perfect Heathen I've ever met, and Idalia, a slender, goth-complexioned Morrigan devotee. And then I notice the spread: below the Coru banners and cotton tapestries, every free surface is covered in plates piled with dates and grapes and cheeses and almonds and chocolates, which people are quick to offer me. As a group, they want to be known both for the intensity of their convictions and for their generosity. Morpheus learned of hospitality as a power move, Middle Eastern–style, during the early days of Stone City: even when they were strapped for cash, she and Shannon would lay out the most decadent food possible. The message is twofold: *Welcome* and *Take notice*.

Since their formation, the Coru have launched into spreading the word of the Great Queen. They held a "battlefield devotional" at the SCA's Great Western War in Taft, California, where, early in the morning, they invoked the Battle Raven—in Gaulish, with English translation—to bless the fighters and dedicate the day's "battles" to her name. They led a Samhain rite in British Columbia, and another, complete with the re-creation of a legendary battle of pre-Christian Ireland, at the Humanist Hall in Oakland. They sank a fine broadsword into Lake Merritt—near where I'd sat with Morpheus in downtown Oakland—in honor of the Morrigan. And at the last Panthea-Con, they collaborated with Thorn, leading hundreds in a ceremony about "the kinship of blood." The ritual asked, "What do you love, that you will fight for?" This was accompanied, in literal fashion, by a Stanford Hospital blood drive on-site, for which donors received ribbons that read "I gave my blood to the Morrigan!"

The Coru will hold a ritual this year, and another, larger blood drive—but what will matter most is the temple in Room 269. After last year's convention, at which they drew more devotees to the Morrigan, they began holding small monthly group devotionals around the Bay Area. So this time, with a couple thousand Pagans traveling from all over the country to be here, the Coru decided to convert one of this Hilton chain's hotel rooms into a fully dedicated temple, to be consecrated tonight and carefully maintained throughout the long weekend, open to all. Because, although Pagans are characterized by their confident connection to their own gods—why go to a local priest when you can build your own altar to the Horned God?—the Great Queen is different. "She starts haunting people, and that can be quite scary," Morpheus says. "People are sometimes nervous about starting a devotional relationship with her, afraid of doing something wrong." The Coru regularly get e-mails asking for advice on how to work with the Morrigan, about half of which start by describing her appearances in their nightmares and end with the question "Can you help me?"

Morpheus enters the suite: the consecration of the temple next door is about to begin. Her translucent skin and thin frame hide nothing, and, depending on the rhythms of her life, her stresses can show: face a little blotchy, shoulders hunched. But tonight—in a clinging black dress with broad sleeves and a wide leather belt, her lush red hair brushed out to waist length—she's vibrant. She turns and gives me a broad smile, a flash of her most at-ease self, and clutches me to her. I'm reminded that, for a priestess who commands so much space, she has a frame as small as mine.

"You're here!" she says, as if it's the day's happiest announcement, in her voice reserved for friends. But we've barely had time to talk when everyone is ordered into the temple. I shove my suitcase into a closet, between Coru corsets and a period cape, and join the others in the hallway, all readying themselves for action.

We proceed slowly into the vestibule, and I remove my boots (no shoes in the temple). I pause for Rudy to "clean" me, sprinkling me with salt water from a small glass bowl; then I pull aside the curtain and step inside.

We file into the darkened room, cleared of mattresses and bed frames. As my eyes adjust, I see the altars up against the walls, ringing the room: broadswords and daggers and helmets and dark wall hangings, details coming into focus in the half dark. I'm reminded of Alombrados, and how an obsessive aesthetic can sway a ritual participant, get her to shrug off any doubt or disbelief and throw herself into the rite—like giving in to the urge to jump into a lake from on high. The more precise the combination of intricate objects and fetishes and colors and smells, the more inevitable, even predetermined, your participation feels.

Those of us gathered, about a dozen in total, Coru priests and allies, form an irregular circle, and soon Scott steps into the center. Now he holds the bowl of water. He walks the inner perimeter, dousing the air and the rug, flicking the water with his thick fingers; with gusto, he splashes some of it up to hit the low ceiling. This water, he says, is the blood spilt on the battlefield.

Scott swings a broadsword over our heads, turning slowly, and I feel the blade come close. And now each priest takes a turn consecrating the five altars: every one Celtic, to a pre-Christian god or hero known through stories transcribed by early medieval monks—the retelling of oral histories passed down from the Iron Age. And above every altar hangs a piece of fabric the size of a wall mirror, like Snow White's wicked stepmother's; these serve as gates between this world and the other, ways of letting the chosen god into the room.

The altars tell the story of the Four Treasures, the magical tools of Tuatha Dé Danann, the epic heroes (and, some believe, gods) of pre-Christian Ireland, allies of the Morrigan. Here's a spear, for Victory—the spear of Lugh, a leader of the Tuatha. And again, for Victory, a sword is laid out— the sword of Nuada, the first king of the Tuatha—alongside an impressive collection of blades and a twenty-pound helmet that looks like a museum piece. In the corner, a stone, for Sovereignty—the stone of Fal, the coronation stone of Ireland. And on the carpet is a heavy, rust-colored cauldron, for Plenty—the cauldron of the Dagda, another king. The cauldron in which the Coru priests were anointed on a hilltop of the Diablo Range.

Finally, we arrive at the altar to the Great Queen herself, the Morrigan: an entire wall, dominant and black, built atop a hotel-room bureau draped in layers of dark fabric. In the dim light, I make out a wooden staff with a raven carved into its head; a two-foot-tall goddess figure dripping with black paint and raven's feathers; the Morrigan statue from Morpheus's home altar, and her vulture wings. And to the left Cruach's box (I know he must be lying inside). To the right, leaning against the wall, stands Macha—a goddess of ancient Ireland and, for some, another of the Morrigan's incarnations— here represented as a horse's skull on a stripped wooden pole, the bone painted with intricate whorls and dots of red and yellow and orange, reams of fabric hanging heavy from the peak of her horse's head like hair. A nightmarish man-sized stick puppet; a ravishing piece of mystico-primitive art.

The Macha skull came into the Coru's possession in Vancouver last year, in what Morpheus now refers to as "the infamous horsemeat ritual." That spring, with members of the Coru scheduled to drive north to Vancouver to lead a Morrigan devotional, Rynn had a vision: the Queen appeared to her as Macha, bearing the message "You need to eat horsemeat." Since Macha has a horse aspect, through her ancient ties to the land, you could say she was asking Rynn to consume some part of *her*, just as Catholics take the sacrament because Jesus invited his disciples to drink his blood (wine) and eat his flesh (bread). At first Rynn resisted—she used to ride as a girl, and considers the horse her "spirit animal"—but the Morrigan was clear: the meat would make her stronger, and help her to heal from her recent struggles with PTSD. And so the Coru dreamt up a ritual for Vancouver. They and a few Canadian allies (some here tonight) stripped naked, the men painting themselves with ocher (bright red) and the women with woad (bright blue), and processed across the land, holding up a horse skull as an effigy of Macha. Once they reached the sacred fire they'd built for the ceremony, they used it to cook horsemeat and serve it up. (Between the nudity and the horse consumption, plenty of Pagans were uncomfortable.) Several of the priests involved ate the meat that day, and since then, Macha has appeared to them. And when their Canadian ally Grant, who'd painted himself with ocher, presented them with a new horse skull, the priesthood gathered and ritually painted and dedicated it, and now it stands guarding the altar to the Great Queen.

In front of Macha and the Morrigan altar, Morpheus drops to the carpeted floor, gripping in both hands a ceramic bowl: it's packed with dirt—from her favorite cemetery in Oakland, and from Ireland. She lets out a stream of inspired speech, about the earth, the land, sovereignty. Morrigu's giving her people the kick in the ass they need to fight for space in the world. She rises up on her knees, legs spread behind her, arms stretched before her, and smears the dirt into the carpet in swift, broad circles: the black-flecked tan carpeting looks smokier now. (Housekeeping will never suspect the cause.)

And soon we are joining her in a Gaulish chant, rhythmic and half singing, to invoke the Great Queen: "Battle Raven, we sing to you! Queen of the Battle! Queen of Warriors! Queen of the Slain! Bloody Storm!" It transforms into a round, between the visitors and the priests themselves, building in volume:

"Cathubodua, canu ni risu!
Cathurigan! Cingethrigan! Marethrigan! Taran Cruach!"

At the end of each of her goddess's names, Morpheus kicks her voice up in a high-pitched trill: "Cathurrreee-GAN! Cingethrrreee-GAN!" This has a surprising effect on me—the ancient-sounding-ness of the language, its sheer unfamiliarity. Is human nature so simple that foreign-sounding words seem far more likely to contain meaningful secrets than our own?

Morpheus, of course, had a deep, gut-level response to Gaulish, tied to what she believes is a past life in service of her goddess. Two years ago, after the oath-taking ritual and while in the throes of drastically changing her life, Morpheus decided to learn the long-dead language. This chant, now the official chant of the Coru, had come to her while she was in a frenetic state, leaving Stone City. She'd finally loaded her human-sized statue of the Morrigan, spear and all, into the back of her truck and was driving down the mountain when she felt the Morrigan "very strongly riding with me—her presence was really there," she says. "And these words just sort of landed on me. And I could hear that it was Gaulish, and the melody pattern was fully formed, and I tried to hold on to the sound of them until I could get home and look up what they might mean." She sang it all the way down the mountain, until she got to her new home.

And now, in Room 269, Morpheus sways in broad circles, arms outstretched. From where I'm standing right behind her, it's hypnotic—the movement she creates in the air; her hair as it dips and swings, nearly touching the balls of her bare feet as she leans back; the underwater sound of these overlapping words; and others dropping to their knees now, too, gathered before a dead raven and a painted horse skull, in the presence of a war goddess.

At some point, it wraps up; we all get up on our feet again and shake off the trance, and Morpheus announces, "Before we go, someone should cut a door so we can actually get out of here."

"Oh!" Scott says: that means him. He grabs a sword off Nuada's altar and "cuts" through the air just in front of the doorway curtain; the tip of the blade grazes the fabric just enough to make a zipping sound, like fabric being sliced. Now we are allowed to leave the temple.

Back in the hospitality suite, they've rigged up a bar at the sink: three coolers of ale and hard cider, a huge bottle of gin, fresh limes. Someone passes around a small horn of rum they say was "charged" throughout the temple ritual. Lots of casual SCA references dot the conversation, as if we'd all understand: who makes the best armor, jokes about getting hit by pikes, how Morpheus needs a better-fitting helmet. She's suffered a couple of small concussions, Brennos says, "and we can't have any more of that." Grant sees the woman herself, leaning in the doorway, looking a little beat.

"I can see you're not totally back with us yet."

She smiles. "Nope!" With each ritual comes the post-ritual recovery.

I leave the room for a few minutes, and when I return, Morpheus and Brennos are gone. Rudy tells me, arching her eyebrows, that they've gone into the temple "to do some more consecrating." Reading between the not-so-blurred lines, I understand this means one thing: sex magic. As a young girl, Morpheus used to imagine her orgasm could alter her surroundings; as a Feri student, she learned to channel her sexual energy into magic; and now she and Brennos, in their private devotionals to a frankly sexual battle goddess, offer her the act of sex and sometimes anoint her statue with bodily fluids. And so, now that everyone's retired to the suite, draped over beds and chairs, drinks in hand, the priestess and her consort are next door, sanctifying the temple all over again.

. . .

As the weekend progresses, Morpheus becomes more no-nonsense than usual. Her presence in the hospitality suite is friendly, sure, but strategically so: her intentions are to spread the word about her Queen, and that requires focus. If you distract her at the wrong moment, she may simply walk away. The Morrigan has ratcheted up expectations of her priestess, and the Coru have become Morpheus's sole fixation, her identity, inextricable from her romance with Brennos. She's not a patient witch; she doesn't suffer bullshit or softness gladly, or at all. Rudy says that when she arrived she told Morpheus, "I've really been looking forward to this vacation," and Morpheus replied, "*Vacation?* Is that what you think this is? This is *work*."

She also has the sense of being watched within her community: some people now refer to her as "famous," a "Big Name Pagan." More recently, Morpheus has realized that she needs to bring on other priests who can do possessory work—to make things easier on her, but also to prevent the public from confusing her and the Morrigan herself. "I've become so identified with my work with the Morrigan that occasionally people can see me as her avatar in some way," she says. "And that can be unhealthy. It can get a little bit weird. I don't want people to wander into territory where they're deifying me in some way."

Then there's the exhaustion that comes from not only consecrating and tending to the temple but also sleeping on its floor each night of the gathering, half smothered by the spirits we'd invited in. At least, this is how Morpheus experiences it—she tells me as much, while dressing for ritual. I find her around the corner, alone, in front of the closet mirror. She's adjusting her long, fitted red tunic, one of a couple she's made herself using historically accurate techniques: the diagonal cut of the sections of fabric, the trimmings on the edges of the long, flared sleeves, the way it hugs her figure. She's pulling tight the black leather laces that run up each side of her torso, leaving two slices of pale skin visible. Her look is almost blank—calm, serious, faraway.

"I'm really depleted today," she confesses to me, and to her reflection. "And now I have *two* rituals. It's not how I would have planned it. So I'm not really socializing; I'm conserving energy. That's why I seem a little . . . remote."

This spiritual fatigue, the first time I've seen it in her, is genuine—she's truly tapped out—and it renders her "work" with these Celtic gods more real to others. Whatever a person's opinions of witchcraft, Morpheus is *living* this, not playacting for attention in this world of outsiders; and her exhaustion is for me, to my surprise, the final proof of her sincerity.

She smiles for a half second, as if asking me not to take her distance personally. I'm more than a little relieved to know she hasn't been icing me out—*deeply* relieved. I care that she's shared with me; I care whether or not she shines her gothic Feri light my way (a truth that embarrasses me). At first I saw Morpheus as a subject; and then as a peer and a friend; but now I see that she's also served as my glimpse into that peculiar breed of person capable of creating believers, or even disciples. She has that uncommon depth of presence found in the most convincing spiritual leaders I've met. As with spotting genius in an artist, it's not empirical; you can't break it down. The best word ever thought up for this phenomenon is, simply, charisma—and who knows how that works? It's the one kind of magic that everyone acknowledges.

I will not be joining Morpheus in the Battle Raven's army anytime soon—but is there something I *want* from her? Is there perhaps a part of her that I see in myself, though still gray and unarticulated?

Something more took place at the castle in New Hampshire, on my last night with Karina's coven—something that gave me a small taste, I think, of what Morpheus experiences at the center of a witches' circle.

At nearly four hours long, that Saturday's ritual—Karina's "mash-up" of Feri, Sufism, and improv—involved plenty of ecstatic, free-form dance. Not long after the circle was cast, we went deep into what some call the "group mind" and threw ourselves into dancing. I'd had an experience like this, on a minor scale, during the "exorcism" in the DoubleTree's carpeted ballroom. But this night was far more excessive. From movement alone, I quickly reached the point of exhaustion, aware that I couldn't break the circle—at least not lightly or without attention and ceremony (someone would have to "cut" the circle open to let me out)—and, anyway, I was there to learn, and it would all be over if I walked away. And so I stayed—through the first hour, then the second hour, then the third. And this is what happened because there was nowhere else to go:

In spite of my doubts, I threw myself deeper into the moment. My dancing became more and more rhythmic, and I felt the coven part around me. I felt myself changing rhythm to expand, expand, and take up more space in the center of the circle—and then I went *further*, moved more freely, altered my rhythm to change the movements of the group and the tempo of what Karina was beating on her drum. A surprising, sudden desire rose up inside me: part of me wanted to snatch a piece of control from the head witch, to overpower the teacher. And I *was* in control, just a little bit: I was tapping into something that, if not mystical or full-on magical, had power to it. In some small way, at that moment, I could imagine taking control of the coven, if it was what I really wanted.

This dancing of mine went on for what felt like a long time. I thought I sensed Karina move in and watch me closely for a moment, in case I took flight into possession—but since that wasn't going to happen, I simply kept dancing, and then breathing heavier and making sounds. And the coven responded, and soon they were swept up in a heavy-breathing collective, arms waving, heads rolling on loose necks, some waddling and swaying low to the ground like spiders. And maybe I was wrong—maybe I had seen this happen too many times from the other side, and here I was fooling myself—but I felt that *I* was doing this to them. I was high, and *not* from being in unison with the group. I was high from a sustained moment of feeling I was *influencing* the group. Whether this was a hallucination, my own delusion, or whether it really happened—and I think it *did* happen—the rhythm of my dancing brought the coven into sync with me. And I forgot Karina and the initiates—the pecking order of witches—and I went with it and did not care. I felt us moving together on my terms. And whether or not any of this held true for the others, the fact that I was competing with my witch-teacher for the center of the circle says something about me.

Then I stepped aside.

Tonight, a dance party is happening. A Pagan deejay in black denim sends goth-industrial music from his laptop through huge speakers and out onto the crowded floor. The Coru and I have returned to the scene of the crime—the same double ballroom where, three years ago, four hundred people, many of us included, took an oath on a sword.

The crowd is what I've come to expect: people in black, in leather, in corsets or nearly topless, in latex platform boots or barefoot, dreaded or shaven-headed, tattooed or perfectly pale-skinned, in man-skirts, in wigs, you name it. Though all in black, Morpheus, per usual, stands out like nobody's business, slinking across the floor with feline grace. She dances with herself—slowly swinging her hips in her low-slung skirt, swaying her gauzy black sleeves back and forth—and she dances with the women who enter her orbit, flirting. The Coru may seek to be a democratic priesthood, but they are propelled by her personal magnetism.

Throughout the weekend, the priests took turns staffing the temple. Whenever Morpheus was on duty, she monitored the situation: she might walk a visitor from altar to altar, or sit along the wall in meditation to give the guest space. Sometimes it played out (yet again) like religion-as-primal-therapy, with some crying and shouting out. The Morrigan, Morpheus admits, "seems to attract people who have some trauma to process"—making the Coru, I guess, a kind of Morrigan self-help cult. They cure others through her as she cured them: Rynn, bullied so much as a child that she tried to kill herself; Amelia, abused by her mother's boyfriend; Ankhira, unable to extricate herself from a dark relationship; Brennos, presumed mentally ill, nearly killed by a blow to the head; Morpheus and Rudy, both exhausted by painful divorces. Each came to the Morrigan, or was "claimed" by her; each came to Morpheus, sometimes meeting the banshee-goddess *through* her. They were hollered at by an enormous, shrieking hag towering over rivers of blood; or they awoke in bed at night to find a darkness, a "night mare," straddling their chest; or their dreams were hijacked by a bloody superhuman messenger. Through the Morrigan, they learned that their struggles did not diminish them—these were battles writ large! They'd been *chosen* to suffer, and to overcome! They were marked as members of a clan, an army, complete with a special vocabulary, a resurrected language, banners and armbands, ceremonies private and super-private, visions both sleeping and waking, an effigy, a spirit companion. And this was, for each, the beginning of "processing" their personal horror and breaking through to the other side a greater witch, a stronger priest. The Great Queen enters like a banshee and gives you . . . a life!

Watching her now, I turn over in my head, yet again, the question of what Morpheus is really fighting for, whether all this talk of battle is *true-life* battle or simulated warfare, like a first-person shooter game. I can't dismiss her as someone deluded—she's too compelling for that. But if she's not a soldier, a cop, a medic, an activist, then what kind of warrior is she? And I realize that, on the simplest level, hers is a fight against expectations. The people she's encountered every day over the years, in mundane life, have seen only her surface self—driving from ranch to ranch in a half-busted truck, spending less at the dollar store, answering the phone at a Mission tattoo parlor—someone with a low-paying job, someone with little or no influence. What she's fighting for is the part of her that rises above that, that exceeds those assumptions, those limitations, and transforms her into the person inside her head, the person she's *willing* herself to be: a priestess with her own priesthood, the devotee of a war goddess, the product of her own perfect invention. This makes her essentially American, a fighter in the battle to reinvent herself.

In the center of the room, Morpheus and Thorn and Anaar seem to find each other at once. A space clears around them on the dance floor.

Rudy and I look at each other on the sidelines. "Oh boy," she says. "Three incredibly powerful priestesses all in one spot." We both watch with a look on our faces that says, "This is the good stuff," as the three women stalk each other, weave their arms through the air, each in some combination of black leather, shit-kicker boots, and tattooed skin.

"What a funny place to land," Rudy says to herself, thinking out loud—and I immediately know what she's talking about. Them, us, all of this: how strange that any of this exists, and that we're here taking part in it.

Morpheus continues weaving her arms around her fellow priestesses, crouching low, dipping her head back so that her red hair nearly brushes the floor. And when she raises her head back up, I imagine something: I picture it encased in glass. I see her white, white face made bony, blanched further still; I see jewels, made from her ashes, in place of her eyes; and a velvet band holds her hair to the skull, hair faded now, but so long it's woven at the ends into elaborate braids. And in this image, she's become a Catholic relic—like the Holy Head of Catherine of Siena in the Basilica San Domenico, wrapped in a nun's wimple, the skin stretched drum-tight over her skull, the case framed with gold latticework and flanked by stone angels—now reimagined as the relic of a neighbor, the holy skull of an *American*. Think of the clarity required to transform your remains into sacred objects. At what point in your life do you begin to picture, in vivid Technicolor, your head encased as the centerpiece of a shrine? *This is the Holy Head of Morpheus Ravenna, transported in a silver container from the fields of San Marcos, Texas, under protection of the Great Queen, in the year 20—, to the temple of the Coru Cathubodua in Berkeley, California . . .*

Morpheus has that clarity. And maybe one day witches and Feri priestesses, like centuries of pilgrims, will come from all over the state—all over the country—to read the future through her bones.

19

Enter the Swamp

I wake up on the floor of the temple.

The first sense I have is of color: crimson everywhere, and one wall looming over me, jet black. I see crushed Moroccan cushions, eye level across the floor, and discover that I'm lying on my back. The temple is empty. Daylight seeps through the dark drapes and across the polished wood floors and the church pews that line the space.

I sit up and nearly hit my head on a low-lying, brass-topped table covered with the crumbled remains of ground lamb and chicken on the bone and phyllo dough. Everything smells like cinnamon and red wine. My body is shaking a little, still exhausted from three mostly sleepless nights, and three days and nights of sweating through my clothes and the constant threat of having the blood sucked through my skin by thousands of insects. (My hands alone are covered in twenty-two mosquito bites, beginning to swell.) I have been captured, roughed up, and claimed. I made many promises, and in exchange was given a secret sign and a secret grip—and a word: only two letters, but the key to everything.

On the other side of it all now, to tell the truth, I am feeling very good.

. . .

It started three weeks earlier. I became consumed with the swamp.

I learned that in southern Louisiana, the swamp houses snakes—mud snakes, ribbon snakes, king snakes, milk snakes, Texas rat snakes, copperheads—and gators—almost two million in the state, luxuriating in the dank, filthy black waters, occasionally pulling their long, low bodies up onto the muddy banks, only to belly-slide right back into the water. It's also home to possums, armadillos, flying squirrels, muskrats, owls, coyotes, big-eared bats, and free-tailed bats. And then there are the nutrias: tremendous semiaquatic rodents with massive orange incisors. Their bodies alone are two feet long, and they can weigh in at twenty-two pounds. I imagine a twenty-two-pound swamp rat lurking under the silky dogwoods, hidden among the water willows and alligatorweed, like a monster in some Russian folktale.

Josh is well aware of the terrific tool of intimidation that nature has provided him with. After mass at Alombrados one night, he calls me and Lucas, two of the three Minerval candidates, to join him in the library to discuss how best to prepare for our upcoming initiation. Chris joins him, and soon others begin to gather around.

Josh starts off with recommendations for gear. "Knee-high boots, something good in water," he says. "Because you're going to be in the shit."

"You want something that breathes, though," Chris interjects, "so your feet don't rot. I've got three words for you: Altama. Jungle. Boots." (Altama, I find out, manufactured boots for American soldiers during the Vietnam War.)

"Long sleeves," Josh continues. "Really tough pants, like Carhartts. You'll want to sleep in your clothes—that's a good idea."

He goes on: "Bring food for four days. Because I'm running the show, I say you can bring whatever—trail mix, MREs." Lucas, seeing my confusion, explains that MREs are "meals ready to eat."

"I hate those," he says. "We had to live off those during Katrina."

Josh says to pack "spiritual reading, something from our tradition," and a small light for after dark. "You'll have a lot of time to read."

"Especially if it rains," David chimes in. "And the way things have been going, it's going to rain hard. Don't worry—we've had people get initiated out there during a *tropical storm*."

"No drugs, alcohol, or weapons!"

Lucas asks if we can bring something small, for hunting.

"Since I'm running the show, I say you can bring a Swiss Army knife. But nothing large enough that you'll get into trouble if a ranger stops you. They're always looking for poachers."

Dan smiles broadly at that one. "They get one look at Alex, they won't think y'all are any *poachers.*"

Though Mark is Minerval-level himself, he's very thoughtful, and senior in years to everyone here save Dan, and he takes the opportunity to offer his own advice. "I'd say, use that time to really take a look at what's around you. When I was out there, we were surrounded by armadillos. Just so many of them! And when we got back, I found out that for the Mayans it was the animal that walks the border between heaven and hell—which was so perfect for what we were out there to do. So keep an eye out. You may see something that you won't understand until later."

"Augury," says Josh.

At last the lecture turns to the inevitable: "As far as the mosquitoes, they are not within my control."

A chorus breaks out all around us:

"Oh my God, bring bug spray."

"*So much* bug spray!"

"You're going to reapply all the time, day and night."

"All over yourself and your gear and all your shit."

Coming in a close second to the mosquitoes are the spiders. At these, even Josh shivers. "Huge. Hairy. I was out there once and I was, like, 'What are these delicate branches covering my face?' And then I realized I was covered in spiders."

Don't forget the snakes, someone says.

Josh sighs. "Yeah, you'll want boots that will resist pretty much any snakebite. Hell, if you don't have a snakebite kit, you'll want to head to the store and pick one up."

After he's gone on for some time, Sophia approaches and says gently, "You're such a gabber, sweetie." She suggests we all get dinner. Josh wraps it up like a coach.

"This is going to be a great experience! No matter what comes next."

. . .

It rains throughout July. And rains and rains and rains. Four or five days a week are interrupted by thick peals of thunder, then a burst of tropical downpour that stops as suddenly as it began. The swamps are filling up.

Five days before the initiation, it's still raining, and now there are flash-flood warnings.

David texts me: "You wouldn't want the swamp to dry out now, would you?"

Then Andrew: "As you can see, I've arranged for more rain."

And Sophia: "Submarines will be provided."

They are taking pleasure in being assholes.

And it's not only the natural threats that concern me, but the company. I speak with Andrew about our dynamic, this trio being sent out into the wilderness: a New York woman in her thirties and two young Southern guys with barely-there facial hair and baseball caps. "We're like *The Odd Couple* with three people," I say.

"Yeah, we've had some strange pairings," he tells me—such as when he took *his* Minerval alongside Josh's then girlfriend, who proved to be "a little crazy" (she's a mortician now). "But *your* group—that's the oddest we've had yet."

The night before heading out, I'm nervous. I do things to prepare myself—if there is a way to prepare yourself for an experience about which you know both nothing and too much. I draw on my Feri training, taking a beer bath for cleansing (I'm hoping for some clarity) and protection (for these uncertain few days). When I climb out of the tub, I let my body air-dry, as the spell requires, and lie down on the bed. I ask to be watched over; I ask to be permeable, open to this initiation, open to a revelation—whatever form it might take. I am not sure whether I believe a revelation is still possible, or if at this point I'm conning myself. In light of my divorce from Karina, and my lingering doubts that I'll ever metamorphose into a believer—a believer of *anything*—I think I'm viewing this journey into the swamp as a Hail Mary pass. Please! Bully me! Shove me ahead! *Push me into belief!*

On the morning of, I burn dragon's-blood incense until my apartment smells like an Eastern Orthodox church. I pack little food for four days (avocados, a bag of almonds, some cereal bars): a strategy (I guess) for discipline, restraint, focus. I seal inside a Ziploc bag my notebook and pen, my phone, and a pamphlet-sized edition of *The Book of the Law.* I dress in my thickest jeans, cheap sneakers (those jungle boots were heavy), and a thick, long-sleeved hunter's shirt, inside of which I fasten my mother's evil eye for good measure. My layers are designed not to breathe in the heat, but to create a protective layer between myself and the wide-ranging world of insects and reptiles.

After driving an hour and a half from where he lives in rural Mississippi, Nick, the third Minerval candidate, picks me up in his truck, ready to go. He's wearing a black cap from Rouses (the supermarket chain where he works behind the seafood counter); his jeans are a few sizes too big for his lanky frame, with big cutouts that show his knobby knees (the bugs will love him for this). We cross the train tracks and arrive at Alombrados, and Lucas is already there. He sits at the library round table, watching Josh pace back and forth, thoroughly jazzed up.

Josh is in fine, high-energy form, spiffed up for the occasion in black pants and black cowboy boots, a dark buttoned-down shirt and vest, his hair slicked back. He has the air of an emcee ready to kick off the evening's program, and, as he's reminded us a few times already, this is his show.

He goes over the rules and guidelines. Our cell phones are only to be turned on after sundown, and we may not bring any other electronics.

"Of course," he adds, "if you get really injured, like if you break your finger . . . Actually, *don't* call me if you break your finger." He turns to Nick. "Nick can set it."

"I'll try," Nick says, with a good-natured shrug.

Sophia announces she's ready to go. It's time.

The three of us load up the trunk of their old four-door and pile into the backseat, Nick's massive pack stretched out across our laps. A sharp animal tooth hangs on a chain from the rearview mirror. Josh starts the car and heads toward the highway. We don't get more than a few blocks before it starts to pour slapstick buckets of rain.

"It'll clear up," Sophia says, and she pops in a CD of Ukrainian music.

After about an hour's ride, we turn off the main road and down a long drive. Thin black trees and tangles of green rise up on either side. Josh turns onto a narrower road, then over a blackwater canal, and finally pulls into an empty lot. We step out of the car and onto the last stretch of pavement at the edge of the swamp.

A dirt path ahead leads straight into the belly of it, and Josh tells us where we're allowed to camp, deep enough so that only our initiators can find us. He reminds us of what we're expected to do: walk. Walk all day. Wander the swamp from dawn until dusk, then pull our gear out of hiding, repitch our tent, and disappear inside. Each day, at first light, we're to strike camp and do it all over again. We are not to leave the swamp. It is unclear whether or not we will be followed or observed, and this feeling will stay with us throughout the weekend.

Then Josh and Sophia get back into their car and drive away. Our circumstance is now entirely our problem.

Some people have the capacity to throw themselves into a situation with self-awareness and, at the same time, without reservation: that's what I'm doing now. I am submitting to this moment in the hope of learning something radical and new, and in this way maybe, just maybe, become freer. On an instinctive level, I've always been conscious of this paradox, the tension between the desire to live without restraint and the submission necessary to gain that freedom—submission, perhaps, to your most frightening fascinations and impulses. In Thelema, they call this the First Paradox of Philosophy. As Crowley described it:

> Thou strivest ever; even in thy yielding thou strivest to yield—and lo! Thou yieldest not.
> Go thou unto the outermost places and subdue all things.
> Subdue thy fear and thy disgust. Then—yield!

Yield—finally, yield! Push yourself into the outermost places; immerse yourself there. Adjust the straps on your pack, turn, and march into the swamp.

We pick a camping spot in a clearing tucked behind a stand of trees, not too close to two encroaching bodies of swamp water. We've borrowed a six-person tent from Jay's brother, punctured in only a few places, and now we spread out the canvas, hammer in the stakes, feed the poles through the frame—until it starts to rain.

We slip inside before getting too wet and settle in, lying down with our packs under our heads. This is when we realize that we've pitched camp directly on top of a gnarly group of tree roots that protrude from the dirt with complete defiance. For lack of another clearing in the Alombrados-approved zone, we decide to make do. This will cost us plenty of sleep and several precisely located black-and-blues over the coming nights.

As it continues to rain and the light starts to die, there is nothing to do but talk a little, try to read, speculate about what's to come. I feel the sweat settling deep into my pores and the tree roots settling deep into my back, and I begin to realize what we're in for. Every hour, every *half* hour, will drag itself out painfully as we pace ourselves in the smothering wet heat, rationing out the five bottles of bug spray between us.

We mark the passing of time with Liber Resh vel Helios, a Thelemite ritual done four times a day to mark your relationship to the sun as it orbits the earth. We perform this first at sunset—it reminds me of Muslims' five daily prayers, at certain hours and facing a certain direction (toward Mecca). Facing west, we strike the prescribed Egyptian-style pose and repeat each line after Nick, who has it all memorized:

> "*Hail unto Thee who art Tum in Thy setting, even unto Thee who art Tum in Thy joy, who travellest over the Heavens in Thy bark at the Down-going of the Sun.*
>
> *Tahuti standeth in His splendour at the prow, and Ra-Hoor abideth at the helm.*
>
> *Hail unto Thee from the Abodes of Day!*"

Then we each give the "sign of silence"—one finger held to the lips—and we're done.

We gather cross-legged in the tent and eat what we've brought. I slice up my allotted half an avocado; Lucas is subsisting on beef jerky; and Nick chooses from a duffel stuffed with canned foods: tonight, creamy soup, whose unheated contents he shovels into his mouth with nachos. Then it's time to sleep—a tall order in the pitch-black night of the Louisiana swamp. We are wrapped in layers and layers of sound: the throbbing call-and-response of owls, the frogs that sound like bleating goats, the armies of insects whose voices swell in volume as the night deepens. Between the alien noises and the heat and the roots digging into my side, I can hardly rest. I am surprised that I do not scream when a creature, some unidentified four-legged animal, brushes against the side of the tent just inches from my face.

When my alarm goes off for one a.m. Resh, I shake Lucas awake. Nick is already up: outside; his headlamp flashes around in the dark, beaming light through the tent at weird angles. We unzip the flap and see he's been building a tiny fire with mulch and twigs. Thick gray clouds of smoke rise up from the dirt. It feels good to hear that familiar, human-made crackling.

"A fire builds morale," Nick announces. He's grinning like a Boy Scout.

Together, the three comrades do Resh in the smoky firelight.

Tomorrow the forced march begins.

Thelemites have a name for the reason we are here in the swamp—the same reason I set out, a few years ago now, for Stone City. It's the source of that feeling I had, as a young girl in Greek and Catholic churches, of proximity to mystery. This is all part of a pull toward the Magnum Opus, the Great Work: the work of removing whatever obstacles lie between each of us and the realization of our true Will, our purpose as part of the universal whole. In other words, Nick and Lucas and I are here, in the bug-infested heat, because we're desperate, each in our own way, to understand our role in the world. The Minerval initiation is the beginning of a trip into personal knowledge—called "Minerval" after Minerva, the goddess of wisdom.

You carry out the Great Work, as a Thelemite, following the OTO's magical techniques, as revealed steadily, in hard-earned increments, through years of rituals and initiations. All initiations, across traditions, involve endurance—of pain or discomfort, of silence and stillness. Sometimes a conquering of taboos. (In my case, belief itself may be the taboo.) The event is meant to mark, through some kind of trauma, the initiate's passage into the group: the initiate has to decide to push through to the other side, the place where she will be transformed, reborn, and set on her path. The place where knowledge is kept that others are barred from access to. A price must be paid for this information, for this transformation, so the initiate will understand its value. On my Catholic side, I think of Jesus out in the desert for forty days and nights, forced to confront his doubts and temptations; and, on the Greek side, in ancient times, the Eleusinian Mysteries, in which the initiate played out Persephone's descent into Hades. I try to think of this time in the swamp as a time of endurance destined to culminate in a revelation—it *has* to. That is how this *works*. If I can just push through to the other side, a troop of occultists will be waiting there with an answer, a sign, a solution—my epiphany!

In other words, I'm hoping that, as a reward for sheer determination, a revelation will be foisted on me from the outside. But if I've learned anything from someone like Morpheus, it's that conviction is the root of magic. The current head of OTO in America, Sabazius X°, writes, "The ceremonial magician knows that the power of the wand is, to a great degree, determined by his own attitude toward it." The same, he says, applies to the order's mysteries. "Approach them as silly formalities which do nothing but get you into an interesting club, and they will, indeed, be nothing more to you." But approach them as a key to be turned in the world's most substantial lock, and that much more will be revealed to you in return.

No one who knows me—who *really* knows me—is here in the swamp. I am alone. There is nothing to lose. Yield! If I can just submit, give myself over to belief, will the universe give me something back? I am the candidate for initiation, and this is the moment when the candidate starts down her path. That is the plan, and I am here to stick to it.

We wake at six a.m., strike camp, and hide our things in black garbage bags under a shelter of palm fronds. It's time to set out.

We have a strategy of marching in line, each of us with an improvised walking stick: the person in the front sweeps the low-hanging branches for spiders' webs, the second scours the ground for snakes, and the third gets to breathe just a bit more easily. Of all the routes we could take, we decide to trace a tree line that winds its way around a body of water. This quickly proves to be the wrong choice. The trees are packed together closely at the water's edge, inducing a kind of swamp claustrophobia, and the air here is thick with bugs—horrific. As predicted, this will be a great theme of the weekend: the swarms of mosquitoes. Even more than my companions, I'm a magnet for the bloodsuckers, with my combination Mediterranean-

Caribbean blood. Though I'm covered in denim from neck to toe, socks over my jeans and sleeves buttoned close around my wrists, the insects find a way to reach me. And the mosquitoes hovering around us in clouds are joined by yellow flies, whose bites sting like hell. Lucas, second in our explorers' line, demonstrates his camaraderie by regularly smacking the back of my neck, calling out, *"Yellow fly!"* He surprises me every time.

We really are a motley crew: me waving a big stick in front of my face like a flag as Peter Pan's Lost Boys shuffle after me. The vast differences between us only underscore the loneliness of my predicament. Even if OTO has an answer for me—an answer that comes through this trial in the swamp—is it a community I could become a part of?

That said, Nick, despite his rangy appearance and complete lack of guile, impresses me. He's already established himself as the most advanced of our trio, the most lucid and straight-ahead in his beliefs. He's a proud, self-proclaimed Thelemite of two years, and, as suits Jay's mentee, he's taken to the program systematically, like a good Christian soldier. (Though Nick was not raised with religion, he did briefly catch Mormonism from Jay's large Mormon family.) In his pack, Nick's brought a purple spiral notebook, creased along the center from being crammed into his bag or back pocket: his magical journal, in which he writes during breaks from work at Rouses. He also manages to do Resh during work hours by ducking into the bathroom.*

I envy that level of focus, that certainty. I worry that I may be as much of a foggy-headed seeker as I was when I first pulled up at Morpheus's trailer home five years ago. I've joined in sabbats at Stone City; I've taken an oath on a sword in front of hundreds of Pagans; I've eaten and drunk the sacrament of Aleister Crowley's church; I've helped Morpheus give offerings to the Morrigan (whiskey, and my own breath); I've trained with Karina, circled with her coven, only to decide that hers were not my people. And now, with Alombrados, not only am I unsure what lies at the other side of these three days and nights, but it's unclear to me whether or not there is something to uncover there at all.

Meanwhile, the bloodsuckers continue their reign of terror. And what a

---

* Several Feris have also told me that they sneak into the bathroom at work to keep up their daily practice. I can't help wondering how many witches and occultists are practicing magic in corporate bathroom stalls across the country.

relief for them each time they touch down on our skin! *Blood, blood, blood*—so single-minded, so simple. That desire shapes their days. Their drive is singular, survivalist, without questions. Alive only to consume life, over and over again.

The bloodsuckers are not the only expression of nature's darker aspect out here. There's the banana spider, with its ambitious web (easily ten feet across). Its body is as large as a man's palm, in the purest shades of yellow or red, and its back is embossed with a death's head: a white skull. Then there are the devil's horses, fat black hissing grasshoppers that excrete a toxic foam if you step too close. Up to four inches long, with a thin red stripe down their backs, they make the animals that eat them sick with poison. They are always in our path, often riding one astride another, copulating in their armor in the heat. Pagans may worship nature and celebrate her cycles, but this is nature's bubbling spit, her lowest creatures, the life that resents our place in the ecosystem. The feeling of the sublime that I had, sitting under the pine trees by that lake in New Hampshire, is gone, replaced by the relentless low-level panic of this landscape.

Beyond the anxiety induced by the nature all around us, a great part of the endurance of this trial is the painful ticking of time. The three of us anticipated plenty of discomfort—but in the context of *drama* and *active struggle*. Not this deadness; not this deadly slow marching through the swamp. "I didn't expect all the *boredom*," Nick says in a moment of particular honesty. This is less a near-Biblical trial and more a form of slow, agonizing Chinese water torture, without a glimpse of transcendence in the distance— me, out in the wild with two kids, continuing to put one foot in front of the other as I duck the death's-head spiders, breathe through the itching, wipe the sweat from my face, and try hard to ignore Lucas's nonstop chattering. Is this the moment when I step up and in some way, with a laser-beam focus, convert the situation into a "transformative" experience? How would I even do that? Or is the big reveal simply this: how my skepticism has finally deposited me at a dead end?

But just as I'm at my lowest, the landscape suddenly opens up—to a tropical-paradise vista! Everywhere are green clusters of huge, fanned-out palm fronds. Stripped gothic bald cypresses rise up, slim, salty gray, and majestic, their highest branches hung with Spanish moss like tufts of hair; around our feet, bundles of bright white mushrooms flash the color of their slender cantilevered caps against the dark swamp floor. Overhead, black vultures circling in groups of five! But with nothing dead or rotten in sight—as if these huge dark birds have taken flight for the sheer pleasure of it. And straight ahead of us, swooning with sunlight, towering over all, the grandest of the bald cypresses stands ten stories high, two hundred years old and silver against the green-gold landscape, surrounded in the black water by the worn and pointed stumps of the trees that came before it. A prehistoric tree goddess. I think of what Mark said to us before we left: to look closely, to read the signs, to hold on to what we see. Some things, by their nature, only reveal their meaning much later—like the discovery of a dead raven, or the dream of a clearing of trees atop Mount Diablo. The trick is to remember, to hold the image in your brain long enough to crack it open.

We cross a bridge over the marsh beds, with their gatherings of green lily pads. They run without an end in sight in either direction. Just beyond, we reach a dock overlooking a vast golden field of tall grasses. We are giddy with the chance to lie on a flat surface, and immediately sink down onto our backs across the wooden boards, sliding our bodies into the sliver of shade at the dock's edge.

We are in no rush to leave this easy spot, light-headed from the late-July heat. The guys start to talk, and their conversation—at first about Nick's experiments with acid, and how the singer of that nineties band Tool is totally a Thelemite—eventually turns to their ambitions within the order. Lucas is in a rush, using the order as a way to measure his worth: an experiment, a personal dare. He's at the opposite end of the Thelemic spectrum from Nick, our steady, dedicated soldier who teaches himself through painstaking repetition.

Both of them, however, are concerned with impressing the hell out of Josh: the magician looms large for these boys. Over the course of the trip, they will talk about Josh as if he were legend, sage, and wild-man antihero rolled into one. "Even if nothing ever comes of me joining OTO," Lucas says, "at least I can say I met him." Lucas has been researching the A∴A∴—today the innermost, highly secretive body of OTO, the occultists' Vatican, into which Josh may soon be initiated—and repeatedly wonders aloud whether he'd be able to hack it. Beyond the hefty esoteric reading list and the intimidating magical requirements, applicants are made to fly to a last-minute location in Europe, where they endure a sadistic initiation rite (supposedly involving a whip lined with ball bearings) conducted by men in black hoods whose faces they will never see. This is what it means to climb the ranks in the occult underground.

If a person accepts Josh as a powerful priest and this Minerval initiation as a process that is real and effective, connected to Big Magic, then our time in the swamp makes sense. Then this is a process you can endure, give yourself over to, completely assured that it has meaning. If, however, you have serious doubts or skepticism, then Josh's running this show—Josh, a scrappy thirty-something guy, a death-metal aficionado and former hacker kid with a decadent past—seems an act of tremendous hubris, and we're simply responding to his personal charisma. In the former scenario, Josh is performing a duty, submitting himself to some higher force, acting as its servant. In the latter, he's simply indulging his ego, with the backing of an international society of outsiders. Our initiation is framed by which version of events the initiate believes. Nick's convictions are already clear; Lucas and I are up for grabs.

Our orders are to walk, and our job is to submit, so we strap on our packs and move on. Just then, we receive a beautiful, life-affirming stroke of luck: it starts to rain. Hard. With the sudden downpour, the air temperature drops a few degrees, and the three of us look at each other as if we might cry. I have never been so ecstatic about getting soaked. I instantly feel less dirty and sweaty and chemical-smothered (that's the illusion). And the sight is cinematic: on the horizon, miles away on the right, lightning touches down to the ground, connecting the sky and the earth. A sleek lizard appears and disappears at our feet, and pairs of blue dragonflies come out in the rain and trace loops around us. The skies are full of drama; the earth is huge! There is something out there much bigger than us—*of course* there is!

With this boost, we return to marching.

As it nears dusk, we reassemble our campsite. Lucas dips into his stash of beef jerky; Nick shovels through another can of cold soup; I eat my last slices of avocado. As it grows dark, the frogs drone on and on and on, until they start to sound like a chorus of warped human voices. I sleep a half sleep, tree roots settled into my ribs.

I wake to the sound of my alarm, calling us to Resh. The boys have a look of purpose about them. Here begin the final twenty-four hours before the ceremony.

The three of us, standing in a staggered triangle, assume the position. "Hail unto Thee who art Khephra in Thy hiding . . ."

The next morning, our last in the swamp, we assess where we stand. I'm down to two almonds and a cereal bar, a few face wipes, and half a bottle of bug spray to share among the three of us. Our cell phones are still charged, since we only turned them on at night, as requested. The boys seem capable of sleeping through anything, but I've probably slept only four real hours since our arrival. And then there's the itching, itching, itching . . . relentless itching that will continue to test our sanity long after we leave the swamp. I count over a dozen bites already on my hands alone; another dozen on my back and thighs have swelled up like big red blossoms. I grit my teeth and take deep breaths. In a state of semi-shock, Lucas says, "I'm starting to think of the mosquito bites as a blood sacrifice for our initiation."

We set out together, but soon part ways to walk apart, trying to deal with the source of the new strain now visible on our faces. Each of us, in our own way, has a lot invested in whatever takes place tonight.

The silence of walking alone gives me the privacy I've missed, and a sense of the Minerval ritual ahead at last starts to take shape in my mind. I picture the members of Alombrados and the Gnostic Mass inside that temple, the multiple times I've knelt with the others until my knees ached, my arms raised to form a pyramid shape above my head. My dead-stubborn curiosity alone has given these several months purpose—I know it. But now what? Is proximity to mystery just that: a closing in on it, never reaching its center or even touching its periphery? As with Zeno's paradox, will a well-aimed arrow somehow never reach its target? Are my questions worth much if an answer never comes?

The moment daylight begins to wane, we reunite at our secret campground in anticipation of the night's event. The initiation ceremony will happen sometime after dark, but who knows at what hour? Time dribbles on, and we wait. It rains lightly, and then it stops. The sky turns dark. We hang our battery-powered lantern from the top of the tent, pull out copies of *The Book of the Law*, and read it aloud to one another. I read Nuit's chapter: "I am the blue-lidded daughter of Sunset; I am the naked brilliance of the voluptuous night-sky . . ."

Crowley's prose is so purple and super-heroic, it feels good to pronounce the words. Whether you are a believer or not, his brand of occult sounds and imagery triggers something, sets you traveling in the mind, taps into a fantasy of the world as packed with secrets. (A devout Thelemite, of course, would say that's not merely a *fantasy*.) Tonight, more than ever, I feel the lines of this book sharing hints with me. The encoded messages, the stories of the ancient Egyptian gods, the Thelemic order of the universe, the references to secret words and the levels of initiation—they're all laid out here, built into this text that Crowley wrote down at a fever pace in that Cairo apartment over a century ago.

I try to imagine Nuit is near as I read the words aloud, the sound of my voice firm and deliberate against the creeping layers of swamp noise. I imagine I'm in close proximity to this ancient Egyptian goddess of the black-and-blue night, and that she has something to give me. I try to conjure her up, and the sense of her. She is the nighttime silhouette of the bald cypresses, and of the tallest and oldest among them, the tree goddess rising up from the black water. She is the deep black against which the vultures rest now and the owls keep watch. She is the stuff that holds in place the layers of stars, impossible to measure, that hang over us in this thick, wet summer heat. It is Nuit who sends the rain down when she's ready—or when we deserve it, like a cool reward. I sense her presence in all these things, enclosing us, palpable for a moment.

Then again, here in the dark confines of the swamp, I've lost perspective. How can I tell the difference between a transcendent experience and the *desire* for transcendence? Between magic and the *hope* of magic? Morpheus warned me that these distinctions can be subtle, that your training helps you to trust yourself—but she's someone who's had faith in her otherworldly connection since she was a teenager.

Nick has that faith, too. Before he reads aloud, I wonder if he will struggle with the performance (if that's what this is), because he's the least articulate of the three of us, the one with the slimmest book education. But when he recites the verses of the god Hadit—Hadit, who is the center of all things, the "core of every star"—Nick gains confidence and volume and feeling as he goes, working his way through the pages, the declamations, until this young guy who works the seafood counter is, in his own way, in the throes of magic, and the owls in the trees above us begin hooting wildly and do not stop for several seconds. Nick is so much younger than me, and unschooled and unpolished and barely getting by, but in this arena, apart from the rest of the world and the mundane, mainstream measurements of what makes a life, he has a clarity that I do not have. In this arena, he knows with perfect certainty what he wants—and I envy him.

Once we've put away our books, Nick says, "Let's not talk for a little bit—let's chill out." He's grown serious, ready: you can see it in his face.

The moonlight has been strong every night, and tonight is no different: it throws the palms and cypresses into silhouettes that stir lightly through the tent's black mesh screen. I lie on top of my sleeping bag with my cell phone on, as requested. We're waiting to hear from them . . . or be fetched by them . . . or be ambushed.

It's impossible to relax, waiting for a sign. I keep thinking I hear people gathering in the distance, or waiting behind the trees near our tent to surprise us. We have no idea where they will come from, or when, or what we will be expected to do. We are, all three of us, mad with anticipation now, waiting for the sound of Josh's voice.

I don't remember the first time I watched *Blue Velvet*, but I carry memories of that movie around in my head, in slivers: the waxy human ear in the grass; the fluorescent red of Isabella Rossellini's lips; the young couple slow-dancing at a suburban basement party; Laura Dern under the dreamy light of a streetlamp on a dark night walk; the high nasal pitch of Dennis Hopper's voice after he sucks on gas; the slow, slow torch ballads sung as if on a distant planet where it is permanently the 1950s. David Lynch's films have that effect, shredding in your mind like fabric pulled apart, the strands embedding themselves more deeply than any sense of a rational whole.

Ritual memory is like that, too: Lynchian memory, working on your brain through clusters of sounds and images, along a time line that pushes and pulls, alternately hyper-clear and seen at a foggy remove.

I remember the initiation unfolding like this:

My phone rings in the tent. A voice that sounds like Delia's says, in a well-paced, serious tone, *"Alex. Give the phone to Lucas."*

I pass it to Lucas, who holds it to his ear as Nick and I watch closely. He listens, says "Okay," returns the phone to me, and leaves the tent without a word.

I turn to Nick. "Well, it's started."

Down to two, we continue to wait. We lose track of how much time has gone by.

My phone rings again; this time the message is for me. *"Alex. Put down the phone and walk toward the place we left you at."*

I unzip the tent flap and step out into the swamp night (throughout our time here, we've never ventured from the camp in the dark) with only my plastic flashlight, the moon, and my sense memory to guide me. I push aside branches and slog through the undergrowth and onto the path, trying to avoid low-hanging banana spiders and any snakes that might be out at night. But mostly I walk in a daze, my heart beating hard in my chest, completely on edge.

I am out in the southern Louisiana swamp in the dead of night, and a band of occultists is waiting for me.

I am just getting my bearings, steadier now as I walk, the soft crunch of twigs underfoot, when, maybe twenty feet ahead of me, I see a woman step out from the trees, dressed in a white robe. Maybe she's carrying a lantern, maybe there is a dagger slung around her waist. I'm not sure, because, the moment I see her clearly, two large figures leap out of the woods—I *scream*—and before I can make them out, I'm tackled to the ground. *Hard.* My cheek slams against the gravel.

Men—whom I cannot see—pull at me roughly, shining a light in my eyes until they're done blindfolding me, and binding my ankles and my hands behind me with manacles (I can feel the sharp metal of the cuffs, and the tight length of chain between them). Facedown in the dirt, I submit—completely. I'm not sure why I do. Because this is what I'm here for, what I've endured the last three days in the swamp to get to? Because I keep waiting for these experiments of mine to climax, to fulfill a deep-rooted wish even I don't fully understand?

Now I know, though it's barely begun: This is it. This is that fantasy, that head trip, what I've always known would one day happen to me.

Someone checks that my hands cannot come free from the manacles, rattles them. Someone lifts me off the ground and sets me upright. One man's arm slips around my waist to steady me. And now feminine hands, smaller, are placed on my back, and gently push me forward into the nighttime woods, blindfolded, stuttering in my steps with the short chain between my ankles. As I'm gently routed through the damp woods, my face extra-hot from the thick black cloth tied tight around it, I feel as if I'm walking in the pitch black of another planet. I have so thoroughly left my life.

I'm steered along the path, hearing only the dirt-shuffling sound of my footsteps and the clink of my chains, until I am brought to a stop. I am presented to someone—I already know who it is. In an enormous, theatrical voice, Josh speaks: he asks who I am, where I'm coming from, what I'm seeking. Calling him "Mighty Saladin," the woman who's guided me here— it must be Delia—announces my name, and that I am traveling to "the City of the Sun, in search of Light and Truth, of Wisdom and of Peace." Josh asks me, still blindfolded and bound, to restate my identity and purpose: I am traveling to the City of the Sun, the seat of wisdom. This is code—this is to say that I am at the start of my journey into OTO.

I swear to study and protect the Mysteries of the order. Josh tells me the punishment for breaking this oath: I'll be mutilated and my "carcass devoured by dogs." To drive the point home, someone draws what feels like the dull side of a sword across my stomach.

Now I can feel Josh—Saladin—step closer. He says quietly, firmly, "Chew this and swallow it." I open up, and he slips what tastes like heavily salted bread into my mouth. (Few things are as submissive as an adult allowing herself to be fed.) As I chew and chew and chew, he speaks to me—a warning to "not betray the bread and the salt." Later, I will understand: I've just accepted the hospitality of the order, vowed never to cross it, prepared myself for the first dose of its magical knowledge. The combination of the bread and the salt is also an alchemical mixture representing creation, a creation that takes place inside the body of the initiate, a kind of immaculate conception. I will soon give birth to my own true Will, and to the part of myself that is godlike.

Now that I am pregnant with the tiny new Thelemite growing inside me, my chains and my blindfold are removed, and I finally see where I am: in a scene out of *Lawrence of Arabia*. Inside a narrow tent, striped black and white, I stand across from Josh, who is seated on a makeshift throne. He wears a turban, thick black eye makeup, and a long white belted robe. He has rings on his fingers, and on an altar before him are placed a lit candle, a parchment scroll, and a sword. Just beyond the parted curtains of the tent is the dark swamp night, broken by standing torches, and Delia, awaiting instruction. I know there are many, many more people present, just beyond what my eyes can make out. After three days in the slow, thick boredom of the swamp, to be at the center of this spectacle is dizzying.

In my bottomless exhaustion, I almost miss it happening: the secrets. Here they are: Josh hands them over, the secrets of my degree. There is the sign (on the forehead), and another (across the stomach), and the grip. And, now the most loaded: the word. "The word is—" He pronounces it in full, and then, separately, each of the two letters it is built from. The word has a special meaning and I am intended to seek it out. This single syllable contains pieces of all the Order's mysteries. These will be revealed gradually, through the many initiations for the many degrees—should I last that long. I repeat the word in my head, roll it around inside.

Josh welcomes me into the camp. He calls me a "Minerval," and gives me the scroll: "the Charter of Universal Freedom." Delia steps forward and replaces the scroll with my own deep red, gold-embossed copy of *The Book of the Law*, inscribed with my name. It's a small object, maybe two inches by four inches, but it has the weight of a historical object in my hands, a cuneiform tablet, a fossil. Tangible proof of the pact I have made.

Delia leads me, walking freely now, into another clearing. We step between two torches, and I can hardly believe what I see: an Orientalist fantasy that's appeared out of whole cloth in the swamp at night. About fifteen of the members of Alombrados are in staged positions of repose: some seated around a small tabletop covered with dates and nuts; some keeping watch at the rear; some fanning themselves with long green palm fronds, gathered around a fire that Sophia is tending. All are surrounded by tall torches; and everyone, no matter how they are posed, is reading their own red, gold-embossed copy of *The Book of the Law*.

I take a seat on the bench next to Lucas, who, like the rest, has his book open in his hand; he stares down at it with a dazed look, every bit as drained as me. David stands behind us in the dark djellaba worn by many of the others. Andrew and Jay stand guard at the spot where I entered, Andrew in a white toga, and Jay dressed like a Roman sentry. Kneeling on a rug laid across the swamp-forest floor, Sophia boils coffee over the fire in a brass

Turkish pot, and offers me some. I accept; the thick melted sugar makes it sweet. I take a date and roll it around in my mouth as I try to decipher what to do, how to behave.

We're in the middle of a scenario that has to play itself out, clearly: the others will not make real eye contact with me. They continue reading their books as if to make the rules of the game very plain. So, as tired as I am, and as little as I have the patience and focus to read an elaborate occult text, I, too, open the book, stare at the pages, try to make out the words—

Now, beyond this clearing, the last prisoner is announced. I glance up— the others barely lift their heads—just in time to see Nick, hooded and skinny in his "Mardi Gras: Fat Tuesday" T-shirt and torn jeans, shuffle forward in his manacles and disappear from sight.

We continue to sit and read and pretend to read. When Nick finally joins us, this has been going on for a long time, and part of me is scared that it's yet another test of endurance, an even more surreal one, and that we'll be expected to prove our seriousness by reading and meditating with the group until the sun comes up. And at this point, such a thing could possibly break me—

Fortunately, that's not what's in store. Because once more we're called before Josh, our Saladin, in front of his tent—the entire company this time, gathering in rows like a small army, flanked by torchbearers, the three initiates in the front line. We declare the Law of Thelema—"Do what thou wilt shall be the whole of the Law. Love is the law, love under will"—and swear to defend it with our lives. We promise to fight for freedom while following the magical regimens of our new order.

Things move quickly from here. A feast is announced; Josh gives the order to "break down the camp!" The sentries follow us back to our campsite and, in military double time, haul everything out to the cars. By penlights and lanterns, a swarm of people gather up tentpoles, roll up rugs and reams of fabric, and collect bundles of torches and duffel bags of equipment and holy books and daggers. We snatch it all up, moving as one body now, and rush out of the swamp.

Riding away in the back of Josh and Sophia's car, I see the clock on the dashboard: 4 a.m. We are leaving as we arrived—but now the priest and priestess are in full costume, and I stare at the back of Josh's turban as we travel. Josh flips on some old-world Middle Eastern trance singing and, emerging from the swamp, I feel giddier and more exhausted than I can remember feeling in a long time.

We arrive at Alombrados and drag our sorry bodies through the backyard and into the house to find the place lit with candles. We're asked to take one of three seats that have been lined up in the library and wait. We're silent, pretty much beyond words. More Middle Eastern music radiates from the temple.

Delia appears and finally leads us through the doorway.

The temple is a *scene*—triumphant!

The room is cool and candlelit, and rugs and cushions have been laid out all across the floor, with a low brass table covered in dishes of food that smell thick with Moroccan spices. The altar is open, and in front of it another spread has been laid out: Cornish hens and leg of lamb and couscous and a sweet pie made of chicken and sugar and phyllo dough. And everywhere are members of the order, ready to welcome us home. Lucas and Nick and I stand stunned—until we understand that we're meant to join them. In half disbelief, I sit on a floor cushion (it feels impossibly soft), and someone pours me a glass of red wine.

There is a toast, and we eat—my body trembles as it finally understands that it's lived for four days on a few avocados and a couple of cereal bars. I taste seasonings I'd forgotten existed. My defenses are very, very low, worn into the ground; I am relieved and suggestible. But I am positively *giddy*, and grateful to be sitting on a comfortable pillow in a cool place, surrounded by people who are plying me with food and booze and so much laid-back company.

I ask Andrew, next to me, who my captors were.

"*I* was. And Jay." He gives me a soft smile. "I was the one who picked you up off the ground."

Every dish is delicious. Lounging is delicious. Sophia, laid out on her belly, smokes a hookah: jasmine. They offer it to me, and I take a drag, and Andrew does, too, and soon a small group has gathered around us. People start sharing stories of their Minervals—whether here in the swamp (Andrew) or out west in the desert (Sophia and Chris) or in a stranger's Victorian house in Seattle (Josh).

Talking for hours in a temple full of magicians, all swapping tales of magical mayhem—I feel *happy*. I've always wanted to know what was on the other side of the looking glass, and here I am. Everyone seems just a little friendlier now, more open—including some, like Jay, who were a bit reticent with me before. I mention that I'd gotten a faceful of gravel tonight, and he says, with a big grin, "A good face-plant was requested of us this time around."

More drinking and smoking and talking—until eventually I look around and see that everyone has left and gone to sleep. Everyone except for Josh: he and I are the last men standing. We sit, facing each other, on one of the old church pews pushed against the wall, him—my Saladin, just hours earlier—now without his turban, in only black boxer briefs, his Rosy Cross on full display.

We argue for a long time about "meaning," and his belief that everything we do is in the context of "a meaningless universe," and that everything we make—our art, our work—has nothing more than relative value. "But, at the same time," he says, "there are so many little things that keep me from killing myself. All the little things that I would miss—like, *I like coffee.*"

I want to say something—this devoted occultist, this man with his fifth degree tattooed across his chest, has found meaning in more than *coffee*, believes in far more than that. As I start to wonder if he is testing me, a thought cracks open in my mind, an important thought—I should say it out loud! But I'm nearing delirium from sleep deprivation, and instead a question comes out of my mouth: I ask his first impression of me, the night we met after the Gnostic Mass.

"I don't know," Josh says. He pauses for a moment. "I think I wondered why you were here."

At that, I slink off the pew and onto the floor. I lean back, just for a second. It is the last thing I remember.

Until I wake up, that is, and it's afternoon. I lie still on the floor, under the tabletop, and think to myself: It is Sunday, I am in the temple, I am a "sister" now. And though I am not yet *bound* to the order—that will be my next initiation, should I choose to take it—something has happened.

And what more do I remember, as my brain fog clears? I remember what I'd meant to say to Josh, with his talk of meaning or the lack of it. I'd been tired, sure, and I'd lost the thread—but the thought had *seemed* like a revelation. I'd meant to say this: that we don't *need* a consensus on what does or does not have meaning. Instead, these are all—what I write here, or what he chooses to have carved into his chest—strategies for staying alive. Some are simply more elaborate and inexplicable than others. And maybe I will take my next initiation, and maybe I will not. And in the days and weeks that follow the ceremony in the swamp, after I'm no longer drunk on it, I will realize that I am just as much a priest as Josh is, or Karina or Morpheus, and I have just as much ritual in my life, because I have *built* that ritual, built it around the thing I live for—which is *this*, the collecting and scrubbing and remixing and chiseling out of other people's stories. And this collecting and connecting with others, sometimes as a kind of trick, as a way of getting what I need, necessarily draws me out of myself and mixes Me up with Them, and we all become part of a new beast in the writing of it.

When you have that feeling, of an encounter with something greater than yourself—however subtle, whatever form it takes—trust it. It is evidence enough. Any other line of thinking is a trap.

Acknowledgments

First, a few brief notes on the writing and researching of the book.

Though my focus was on the experience of being a practicing Pagan, witch, or occultist in present-day America, I interviewed many people and read extensively to better understand the history of those overlapping communities. Three books stand apart from the rest in their deeply reported contribution to the history of modern Paganism, its European roots, and its journey into American culture, and I'd like to acknowledge them here: Margot Adler's *Drawing Down the Moon* (1979, revised and updated in 2006); Ronald Hutton's *The Triumph of the Moon* (1999), and Chas S. Clifton's *Her Hidden Children* (2006). At Pagan Spirit Gathering (an experience I describe in chapter 6) I had the rare pleasure of wandering around with Margot, who was also a longtime NPR correspondent and an all-around excellent lady. Sadly, she died in 2014 and is mourned by the Pagan community.

Large chunks of the Pagan experience are not represented in this book—this is, after all, only a single volume. My hope is that some readers out there will see themes in these pages that I've only touched on and will be moved to do their own research. Different traditions, lines, and covens have differing views on subtleties of practice. My summary of Feri, for instance, comes through multiple sources—and through my own personal experience—but individual Feri covens may have their own styles in circle.

I'd also like to note that in a few instances, I condensed the time between events in favor of greater clarity and smoother reading as I moved between story lines in different locations. I did not alter descriptions of the events themselves, and I changed very few names—in those cases, because the subjects were underage or still in the broom closet.

I may eventually publish an essay updating readers on what is happening in the lives of this book's subjects. Until then, keep in mind that a lot has likely changed for each of them since I finished the book.

And now some very important thanks:

Effusive thanks and respect to all who chose to speak to me for this book. And to those who do not actively appear in these pages but who contributed their insight along the way, including Margot Adler, Flora Green, Jonathan Korman, the onetime residents of Annwfn, and the extended Stone City community. To Jason Pitzl-Waters, in particular, for his friendship, smarts, and sense of humor (even about the witchy stuff).

To Yaddo, MacDowell, and Millay artist colonies, where pieces of this book were written. There is incalculable value in creating spaces in this country where the arts are treated like deadly important, magical business.

To three very formidable women who taught me everything about living as an artist: Christine Schutt, Joan Jonas, and Marlene Dumas.

To my dear friend Jonathan Ames, for his support.

To Roger Hodge, the first editor to give me total freedom.

To my friend Nicholas Shumaker, without whom my documentary, *American Mystic*, would not have been made.

To Nicole Cota, David Siegel, Alistair Banks Griffin, Anastacia Junqueira, Mark Binelli, Jessica Lamb-Shapiro, Rebecca Wolff, and Tom Bissell for their friendship and their confidence in me.

To Morpheus, for her guts and integrity. Ours is a unique relationship that now spans several years, from the making of *American Mystic* to the writing of this book.

To Farrar, Straus and Giroux and Sarah Crichton Books. Special thanks to my editor, Sarah Crichton, and her excellent assistant, Marsha Sasmor. And, of course, great thanks to my agent, Sarah Burnes.

To my brother and co-conspirator, Stefan.

To my people on the other side: Stephanos, Eduardo ("Tuto"), Josefina, Norma, and Ana.

And finally, thanks most of all to my parents, Mercedes and Paul—for EVERYTHING.

A Note About the Author

Alex Mar is a nonfiction writer born and based in New York City. Her work has most recently appeared in the *Oxford American, The Believer, The New York Times Book Review,* and *Elle.* Formerly an editor at *Rolling Stone,* she has been a guest correspondent for CBS, ABC, National Public Radio, and the BBC, as well as a fellow at the MacDowell Colony and Yaddo. Mar is also the director of the feature-length documentary *American Mystic,* currently streaming on Netflix. *Witches of America* is her first book.